The New Account Manager

by

Don Dickinson

The New Account Manager

Redefining the Crucial Role of Account Service in the Changing Business of Advertising

by
Don Dickinson

The New Account Manager:
Redefining the Crucial Role of Account Service
in the Changing Business of Advertising

©2003 Don L. Dickinson
Director of Advertising Management
Portland State University School of Business
ISBN# 1-887229-14-0

For further information, contact:
The Copy Workshop
2144 N. Hudson • Chicago, IL 60614
(773) 871-1179 FX: (773) 281-4643
www.adbuzz.com or thecopyworkshop@aol.com

To Anna

Table of Contents:

"Now that we have _the book_,
does that mean we're supposed
to know what we're doing?"

FAST FORWARD TO OPERATOR'S GUIDE:

THE ADVERTISING BUSINESS is very special. For the right people, there's nothing like it.

It's fast paced, ever changing, and allows you to put creativity to profitable use. Few other businesses allow so many people's work to be so visible. The thing that makes this possible is the working relationship between the advertising agency and its clients. A strong agency-client relationship is one of the most important assets an agency has.

This unique relationship is rooted in partnership, trust, profound consumer insights, a passion for creativity, strategic thinking, and an unwavering dedication to the client's success.

Hard Job. Soft Skills.

The agency account manager is the steward, the caretaker of this crucial asset – this relationship. It's a hard job requiring the mastery of soft skills. Not only is it one of the most fun and stimulating jobs ever, account management is an incredibly important part of the agency business. It's just too important a job to be any longer neglected in terms of formal training.

When it comes to the creation of great advertising and the delivery of effectively integrated communications programs, there is no function more important than good account management. If you don't believe that, just ask any client.

Account management is one of the first jobs of the Information Age. It involves managing information, relationships, and resources, including one of the most important resources of all... critical creative thinking.

As such, account management is as challenging as it is stimulating. If anything, it is getting even more challenging.

1

There was a time when smart young people and the agencies that hire them could afford traditionally informal and predictably inconsistent training methods.

Even with the new efforts of some universities, agencies, and professional organizations, most young and aspiring account managers are still left pretty much to their own devices.

A Growing Need for Training.

But the changes in the agency business and the growing needs of the client have punctuated the necessity for much better training for account managers.

As the new Director of Advertising Management at the largest business school in the Pacific Northwest, I find myself in a unique position to help. In 2000 I introduced a new course in Account Management at Portland State University.

Finding no comprehensive textbook on the subject, I devoted two years to writing one. The result is this book – covering a big and useful set of skills for a role that is growing in its importance.

Best Practices and Traditional Skills.

Here in Portland, the proximity to nationally respected agencies allows us to spend up-close-and-personal time with the CEOs and directors of account service for Wieden + Kennedy, Borders Perrin & Norander, and other agencies like Moffat-Rosenthal which, in spite of their small size, have distinguished themselves nationally.

As a result, we've been able to combine current best practices with the traditional fundamental skills you'll need.

This book is intended to give you a realistic look at what agency account management is all about, the good and the bad. You'll see what it's like day in and day out.

You'll understand the functions and nuances, the processes and outcomes, the facts and fiction, the tools and tricks. They're all here for you to absorb and use.

Advertising is the business for the self-motivated, creative thinkers, people who march to a different drum. This book will help you prepare yourself and help you make your own opportunities.

What's in a Name?

The New Account Manager is written for the college senior and for the college graduate who recently signed on for an initial venture into ad agency account service. For students, the book is intended to give valuable context and tips on what to expect. Now that academia has a viable textbook, the number of account management courses offered around the country will hopefully increase.

For people new to the business, this book is packed with tips on how to succeed in the earlier years in the business. While agency training has suffered at the hands of the recent economic downturn, this book will hopefully foster a resurgence in that badly needed area. To that end, there are agency training suggestions at the conclusion of each chapter.

Even seasoned account managers will find the book helpful as they evolve to fit a "new" definition of their job due to competitive pressures and rapid changes in the industry. See Chapter 1.1, "Evolution of the Advertising Agency and the Emergence of the New Account Manager," for a detailed and, hopefully, enlightening explanation of how and why the role of account management can legitimately be called new.

Managing Expectations, Always Managing Expectations.

In an attempt not to duplicate other work of a more general nature, this book assumes that you have at least taken an introductory course in advertising. The more advanced advertising courses you take (media strategy, creative strategy, campaign planning, etc.), the more you will understand the issues addressed in this book.

So, in an attempt to manage expectations, I need to add that there are a few things this book is not. First, it is not specifically a basic text on advertising, though you'll learn things in this book you'll never see in a basic text. As far as basic introductory texts go, my publisher suggests *Advertising & the Business of Brands* (20% off at www.adbuzz.com).

This is not a book on account planning, though I'm especially proud of "Straight Talk about Account Planning." I also suggest you read *Hitting the Sweet Spot* by Lisa Fortini-Campbell and *Truth, Lies and Advertising* by Jon Steel (AdWeek Books).

Nor is this a book on integrated marketing communications (IMC). For that, I suggest a rather heavy text by that name written by Tom Duncan, currently at the University of Denver.

This is not a book of creative strategy and creativity in advertising. For that I suggest *The Copy Workshop Workbook,* which does an excellent job of explaining contemporary advertising creativity as expressed in current campaigns.

This is not a book on media planning and strategy. Unfortunately, I know of no good book on the subject.

This is not a book on how to run an advertising agency and pitch new clients. To my knowledge there really is no such book, but the closest to it would be *Advertising Realities* by Wes Perrin.

Finally, there are lots of other good books on advertising listed at the end of 8.5, "Other Resources."

This Is Dedicated...

At the same time, this book is dedicated to many thousands and to a very few. "The many" are the thousands of account managers across the country who work tirelessly on behalf of their clients.

Most account managers work in agencies with fewer than 100 employees. These agencies work without many of the benefits of the big national and international firms, thus making the account manager's job even more important. It's demanding work, and they deserve great credit for the contributions they make to the success of the brands they serve and the agency bottom lines they enhance.

"The few" must begin with my longtime friend and partner for many years, Tom Hougan. For the last quarter of the twentieth century, Tom was one of the most liked and respected men in the Pacific Northwest advertising community. Tom played leadership roles in both the American Advertising Federation, where he was national president, and the American Association of Advertising Agencies (4As).

During the years I was being courted by Cole & Weber/Seattle and Foote, Cone & Belding/San Francisco, Tom was the reason I stayed in Portland. Any student who finds (as I did) a mentor the likes of Tom Hougan is a lucky person indeed. Any agency owner who finds (as I did) a partner the likes of Tom Hougan is even luckier.

I also need to attribute a great deal of this book's development to the late Roger Ahlbrandt, Dean of the School of Business at Portland State from 1994 to 1998, who offered me the directorship of the program.

He gave me the opportunity to apply my knowledge and love of the business in a scholarly way. We lost Roger to cancer in 1998 and miss him a lot.

As I was busy learning the lessons shared in this book and building a career, I'm sure my two grown sons, Eric and Evan, did not get from me everything they needed.

Thanks, guys, for putting up with (and without) me.

I should also mention the students who spent their summers taking the initial account management classes. Had it not been for their willingness to take on a new class with no formal textbook, most of this material would have never been committed to paper.

These students were instrumental in telling me, during and since, what the course (and this book) should contain. Their input has been complemented by my advisory committee of agency principals. Each had an opinion on what the book and course should be. As a result of all of this input, I'm happy to say this book is road-tested and market-driven.

Finally, the most important acknowledgment. Anna Dickinson, supportive wife, saw the passion I had for my new job as educator and program director. So she gave up her hopes that I'd retire early and unselfishly acknowledged that I "really needed to do this…" filling a need that had not been filled. Thanks, Honey!

You Can Blame Them.

Among the students who used this book in manuscript form were seniors ready to graduate and people who were a year or two into the business. These students, especially the "young professionals," showed me with their comments and a look in their eyes that this book was the real deal.

My review committee also consisted of:

> John Michelet, longtime friend and small agency owner with a Stanford MBA and big-time LA agency experience with Grey Advertising.

> Pamela Hamlin, Managing Partner, Arnold Worldwide, Boston.

> Ed Herinckx, President & CEO of HMH, an integrated marketing communications firm in Portland, Oregon (HMH is the kind of agency I'd build if I were to do it all again.)

> Bruce Bendinger, Publisher at The Copy Workshop. Without any prospect of gain, he made a huge contribution to this book because he also knows the industry needs it.

A handful of academics also made a contribution by reviewing and critiquing the book:

> Robert Gustafson, Associate Professor, Ball State University School of Journalism in Muncie, Indiana.

> Roger Lavery, Dean of the School of Communications at Northern Arizona University in Flagstaff, Arizona.

> Bourne Morris, Professor in the School of Journalism at University of Nevada/Reno. Before finding her second calling in teaching, Bourne spent 25 years with Ogilvy & Mather and was ultimately President of Ogilvy's Los Angeles office. Professor Morris was especially helpful in my efforts to fashion meaningful exercises at the end of each chapter.

More Thanks...

I also need to thank the following publishers for allowing me to reprint articles that helped me make a point:

Primedia Business Magazines and Media Inc. for articles reprinted from *Promo* magazine.

Crain Publications for articles reprinted from *Advertising Age*.

SPI Communications/VNU Media for articles reprinted from *AdWeek*.

I'd also like to thank Richard Cline for the cartoons in the book. Richard has an uncanny way of finding the humor in this business. His work appears weekly in *AdWeek*.

Hope Springs Eternal.

My hopes in writing this book are:

1. That it persuasively presents the new definition, the new relevance, and the new importance of the agency account manager.

2. That it projects and confirms a new level of professionalism for the position and becomes the bible for a new generation of account managers.

3. That it be a textbook first, but still a book that a VP of Account Service would find interesting and timely reading for themselves and their account managers and supervisors.

4. That it be structured around a highly successful course which has been field-tested.

5. That it act as a long overdue catalyst, spurring academia and industry to get serious about account management training.

Hopefully, I've succeeded. After you've been in account service for a couple of years, I'd love to hear what this book has meant to you.

You can reach me at: Don Dickinson
Portland State University
School of Business Administration
P. O. Box 751
Portland OR 97207-0751
(503) 725-8533
e-mail: <dond@sba.pdx.edu>
Web site: AdBiz.sba.pdx.edu

Operator's Guide:

This book is meant to be a textbook for seniors and MBAs and a handbook for those on the job. It's a "soft skills" book in a high-touch business, designed to show the environment in which account managers provide their valuable professional service, the demands placed on them, and the skills needed.

Bruce Bendinger, my mentor on this project and himself a seasoned agency person, implored me with stern voice and strong hand to deliver this information with "big, clear architecture." Here it is:

1.0 THE VIEW FROM 20,000 FEET

Every job is executed within an organization, and every organization operates within an industry. Two sections provide a context and contemporary overview in which the agency and the account manager do their work:

1.1 Evolution of the Advertising Business and the Emergence of the New Account Manager describes driving forces that have brought account management to a new level of importance.

1.2 Contemporary Advertising Agencies describes what agencies do and how they do it. This chapter includes an organizational chart showing how the typical large agency is structured and an operational chart showing how things get done. Since there are many variations on the agency theme, specialty agencies are also discussed.

2.0 THE VIEW FROM 200 FEET

Before we hit the ground running, there is another level of overview that will help new account managers understand the context and the practices that define the agency business and the job.

2.1 Account Management Overview provides a broad-stroke view of the account management position. The lessons in soft skills and multitasking begin here.

2.2 Master of the Mixes discusses the ever-growing array of communications mediums and how the account manager has an important role – and sometimes full responsibility – for the selection and orchestration of the client's communications mix.

2.3 **Shop Talk** is the language of account management. Every industry has its own lingo and lexicon. This section explains terms you may have used many times before, but now they take on a new meaning.

2.4 **The Money Side of the Business** shows how agencies of every kind make money and the changing nature of agency compensation.

3.0 TOOLS OF THE CRAFT

The account manager position in an advertising agency is like no other. While there is a lot of science and methodology in advertising, management of the agency process is an artful craft requiring equal parts of energy, knowledge, discipline, flexibility, creativity, insight, integrity, and intuition.

There are many tools that account managers need to perform their job effectively. While these tools allow for flexibility and adaptation, there are some basics to be aware of and platforms from which to start.

3.1 **The Information Management System** presents a structure for capturing and retrieving the wide variety of information dealt with on a day-to-day basis.

3.2 **The Conference Report** is a basic communications document which helps keep the account team and client "plugged in." This chapter includes a transcript of a typical meeting between client and account manager. This transcript provides the basis for you to write your own report.

3.3 **The Campaign and Creative Briefs** describes these crucial creative input documents. An award-winning print campaign from the creative heavyweights at Wieden+Kennedy serves as a practical demonstration of what campaign and creative briefs look like and how they are developed.

3.4 **Evaluating and Presenting Creative Work** sheds light on two sensitive issues: critiquing the conceptual work of the creative team and then presenting the final creative product to the client.

3.5 **The Status Report** is a key project management document that helps account managers and clients track the progress of multiple projects through the agency.

6.0 EVERYDAY SUPERHUMAN

The "What a Ride!" chapter looked at account management from the standpoint of function and time. This chapter looks at roles and personality characteristics that define success.

6.1 **Two Dozen Hats** discusses two dozen different roles, with examples, that will be played in the execution of account management duties.

6.2 **The Eight Traits of a Successful Account Manager** is the result of a mini-survey among senior agency people who supervise and hire young account people.

7.0 THE BUSINESS OF NEW BUSINESS

Growing existing clients and landing new clients is the lifeblood of an agency. Account managers who are good at these activities are destined for stardom in the agency business.

7.1 **Evolution of the Agency-Client Relationship** exposes the gritty side of the agency-client relationship, how to tell if it's good, and what to do if it isn't.

7.2 **In Search of the Ideal Client** provides a tall order for account managers in their never-ending effort to evolve existing clients to the ideal and to find new clients like them.

7.3 **In the Hunt: New Business 101** describes how an agency's new-business development process works, what clients are thinking during agency reviews, and common mistakes made by agencies in the hunt for new clients.

7.4 **A Short Course in New Business** provides a short but proven road map in organizing a new business presentation.

8.0 MANAGING YOUR CAREER

This comprehensive chapter deals with the best ways to prepare for and enter the business. It also introduces career issues to keep in mind in the early years.

8.1 **Educational Preparation** describes all the things that can be done to learn about and interface with the advertising business before graduation, including national standard templates for internships and mentorships.

9.0 HOUSEKEEPING
A few things we had to put in somewhere.

Other Features:

Sprinkled strategically throughout the book, at the end of most chapters, are one or more of the following features:

BUZZ:
Selected articles that add validity to the thesis of this book.

If you comb the trade publications for the last few years, you will find many articles that focus on the future of account management – a reflection of clients needing and insisting on tighter integration of all marketing communications activities.

JUICY CASES:
These are provocative, real-life situations that at least prove that an account manager's life is never dull. They provide stimulating thought on how to solve problems, or better yet, avoid them.

AD-ROBIC EXERCISES:
Problems to solve and short projects to do.

BURNING QUESTIONS:
Provocative questions to help you "think inside the business."

1.0 THE VIEW FROM 20,000 FEET

EVERY JOB HAS A CONTEXT within an organization, and every company has a context within its industry. It is important for a young account manager to understand how their important position has evolved, how the agency is organized to deliver service, how an agency is compensated, and, in broad strokes, what an account manager does.

This chapter's purpose is to provide an historical perspective and contemporary overview. First, we'll cover the evolution of the advertising agency and the emergence of the new account manager, then, the changes that have affected contemporary ad agencies.

1.1 Evolution of the Advertising Agency & the Emergence of the New Account Manager.

Advertising agencies have been around since the late 1800s. They are organized, staffed, and managed to serve the marketing communications (MarCom) needs of clients with whom they have an ongoing working relationship.

Operative terms here are "clients" and "ongoing relationship." Agencies don't have customers walk in the door, want an ad done while they wait, and then are never seen again. The work done by agencies is part of a long-term, coordinated effort to build brand awareness, change a client's image, stimulate sales, or accomplish a myriad of other marketing communications objectives.

As explained in the following paragraphs, the agency business came roughly full circle in the 30 years from 1970 to 2000, but it did not end up in exactly the same place it started.

Evolution is funny that way. Follow this story to its conclusion and you'll see why I'm so excited about the future of the account manager.

The Agency's Mission.

The mission of the agency is to serve the MarCom needs of its client, to make money doing so, and to grow as a result of its success. This entails being able to provide expert advice and deliver customized solutions in a wide variety of communications categories.

Traditional creative services in measured media still account for the majority of agency billings, but this is changing. Now, successful agencies are eager to provide, or at least manage, other MarCom services such as sales promotion, interactive, PR, graphic design, direct response, events, and multimedia sales presentations.

The broadening of MarCom services has spawned a number of new, or relatively new, specialty agency categories now used to provide a wide range of MarCom expertise to clients.

This broadening of the agency service portfolio has direct impact on the importance of the account manager.

"Must have been a tough day.
That's your third Pellegrino and lime."

First, a Little Relevant History.

For many years, advertising agencies called themselves "full-service." That meant the agencies believed they were offering all the MarCom services their clients needed.

In other words, the agency was offering creative, production, and media-buying services.

If a client needed a high quality direct mail program, a sales promotion, brochure work, or public relations, they would often have to do it themselves or employ firms other than their "full-service" agency to get those jobs done.

In-House Ad Departments.

Many advertisers still maintain large in-house staffs for work they do not want to send to an agency. There are a number of reasons for this.

First was the decentralization of authority on the client side.

While brand or ad managers had responsibility for branding ad campaigns, the sales promotions and public relations programs, for example, were often the responsibility of someone else in the client organization. That someone else normally fought with the brand/ad managers for budgets.

Second, certain kinds of businesses, particularly retailers, have a lot of "tonnage," such as price/item sales circulars for supermarkets. It's simply more cost-effective to have an ongoing department dedicated to pumping out these materials plus other related collateral such as in-house signage.

Finally, some sales managers and PR directors did not always agree with the direction of the branding campaigns.

Since it would have been impossible for an agency to keep all these factions happy, the agencies went where the money and the excitement was – in the big budget, big media branding campaigns.

At the same time, the agencies looked down their noses on "peripheral communications disciplines" as being inferior or even detrimental to the work of the branding campaigns.

The Boutique Explosion.

Then in the '70s and '80s there was an explosion of "boutique" agencies. These shops were almost always populated by at least one owner who had a strong creative flair – one that often matched their aversion to media planning and collateral work (brochures, catalogs, and other sales literature).

The success of the creative boutiques of the '70s and '80s coincided with the advent of media-buying services which are now the global power houses of media buying.

Sales promotion and direct response tools then followed, gaining respect and popularity as mainstream advertising tools.

Big-time branding agencies, however, wanted nothing to do with these minutiae-ladened disciplines. (Sales promotions, direct response, events, and other peripheral ad tactics were seen as unsexy, labor intensive, heavy on detail, and too accountable.)

For the big-time agencies who wanted to do multimillion dollar television image campaigns, sales promotions required too much time, too much work, not enough profit, and not enough opportunity to do "showcase creative" work.

In addition, sales promotions were often controlled by another decision-maker inside the client organization. This person did not deal regularly with the agency and was much more concerned with immediate sales results rather than long-term image building.

The success of the creative boutiques, media-buying services, and sales promotion agencies was followed by the emergence of large national public relations agencies and then the interactive shops. Get the drift?

A Wake-up Call for Agencies.

The availability of specialty shops gave brand managers even more choices over the so-called full-service agency of the day. As a result, many agencies lost accounts when the brand mangers decided to hire a group of specialty shops and coordinate the MarCom program themselves; not a good thing for the mainstream agency business.

While the agency business was getting carved up and program coordination became more difficult, the concept of integrated market-

16

ing communications (IMC) was being born in the minds of forward thinkers in academia and the private sector. The recognized father of IMC, at least as a formalized concept, was Don Schultz of Northwestern University.

IMC is a simple concept... so simple and logical, in fact, that it is hard to believe IMC is not the norm. But the real marketing world is sometimes a strange place.

Basically, IMC says that all messaging for a brand (advertising, direct mail, brochures, sales promotion, publicity, events, trade shows, customer service, employee communications, whatever) should be tightly integrated and coordinated for maximum effectiveness. Duh!

The newest name for IMC is brand contact management, in which a "contact" includes exposure to any brand message through any medium. IMC, brand contact management, or whatever it is called in its next incarnation will similarly state that marketing communications programs are most effective when a single person or entity is responsible for all activities that result in a customer coming in contact with the brand. Double duh!

Actually, Don Schultz noted that IMC had been practiced for many years by smaller business-to-business marketers and their agencies where all these functions could be coordinated by a few individuals – as opposed to larger groups with conflicting agendas. However, for big marketers and agencies it was often a big problem.

By 1990 the big agencies saw they could no longer survive by cherry picking the glamorous parts of the advertising business and leaving the rest to others. Integration and consolidation started to become the mantra for agencies. The timing was none too soon.

The Impact of Client Consolidation.

A decade of mergers and acquisitions on the brand side meant that more brands were under the control of fewer parent companies. While mergers and acquisitions sometimes actually mean increased revenue and profits, they also mean more central control of marketing. Central control means more advertising dollars controlled by fewer companies who are – no surprise – driven to cut costs and increase market share.

Finally the big agencies saw the light. They changed their tune, their pricing, and the way they serviced clients.

Two Fundamental Changes.

To regain the clout, prestige, and profit they once enjoyed, advertising agencies had to make two fundamental changes. Neither was easy. Both were painful.

First, Broader MarCom Services.

First, they had to broaden their service portfolio so clients could get everything they wanted in one stop. This new agency model made it easier for clients to manage message consistency across multiple mediums in the promotional mix. This is a growing challenge.

The explosion of media alternatives, for example, means that almost all target audiences are more fragmented. An audience that once could be reached effectively through mainstream, measured media now requires a more sophisticated mix of message vehicles.

Sales promotion, direct response, PR, graphic design, and other specialty MarCom services are called a variety of different things, such as "below the line," marketing services, or specialty services. Large agency groups, like WPP and IPG are finding more and more of their income coming from what they call "below-the-line" services. Whatever they're called, they prove the new agency model is more full-service and integrated than ever before.

In addition, the number of specialty agencies is at an all-time high (we'll talk about them in the next chapter). Many of these specialty agencies act as subcontractors to full-service agencies or clients' in-house marketing operations.

Second, a Change in Compensation.

The second big change in the agency business was the way agencies charged for services. Pricing strategy is a competitive tactic used by many business categories, but it was a new and not-so-welcome concept in advertising.

Almost since the industry's beginning, ad agencies generated most of their income through the media commission system.

If you are a serious ad student, you know the commission system gave the agency 15% of every dollar placed for clients in traditional measured media.

Under such a system, an agency placing a $3 million Super Bowl "buy" would earn a $450,000 media commission for this one ad buy. Not bad. But not all of the effects were good.

For years, this system had an unfortunate effect. It motivated agencies to find commissionable media solutions to client problems rather than possibly recommending other media and tools (like direct mail or sales promotions) which would not generate media commissions.

Clients, however, did not consider the agency's work worth $450,000 in the case of a single Super Bowl buy, especially when the agency was also making production commissions and service fees on a spot that might cost $15,000 a second to create.

Growth of the Fee System.

So, as a competitive new business tactic, some agencies started offering to bill prospective clients on a fee-for-service basis rather than a 15% media commission.

Becoming unshackled from the media commission system and being compensated for good communications solutions, in whatever form they took, was liberating for some agencies and threatening to others. Now they had to be professional service providers and become experts in the entire promotional mix of communications mediums, not just the big commisionable mass media.

The move to fee-for-service has caused a major change in the way that agencies look at themselves. Acting more like a consultant is now the paradigm in the business. This new consultancy paradigm has a direct impact on the client relationship and the role of the account manager.

When your revenue depends on your professionalism and how many services you provide to a client, you are much more interested in offering, or at least managing, everything a client could need.

An agency that is good at many things, and good at integrating them, is hard to beat. And clients know it. But wait, there's more.

The evolution in agency compensation continues – with more performance-based compensation proposals being reported.

Agencies which, in the '80s, were happy to take commissions on big media buys and let others worry about results and the little stuff are now singing a different tune.

Now some agency compensation includes a bonus for achieving or exceeding results having to do with increases in brand awareness, the success of a repositioning effort, or sales increases.

With agency compensation hanging on measurable results, you can bet agency management wants total control of every aspect of the communications program as well as tight integration of all elements.

Squeezing every bit of effectiveness out of the campaign assumes two conditions: that the agency can provide a wide variety of communications services under one roof and that the campaign will be managed by someone with a big-picture view and leadership skills to match.

IMC Becomes Reality.

Selfish motivation has pushed IMC closer to reality. But, who is going to guide the integration of all components being recommended by the agency (with big bucks riding on success)? That would be the account manager of the new millennium.

In more cases, the account manager is responsible for integrating and coordinating all advertising-related activities, even those services not provided by the agency. In these cases, clients realize the importance of integration and have confidence in account managers performing this important duty.

The client pays the agency a professional fee for this management service. Message consistency and efficiency across multiple media is the name of the game.

The role of the ad agency as a communications management service will continue to grow. As time goes on and advertising continues to get more complicated, the account manager position will be more important and more demanding.

This will be even more true with smaller clients, where the level of client marketing and communications expertise is likely to be less than the big brand accounts.

Agency accountability will continue to increase, and clients will expect that their marketing communications programs are more effectively integrated and orchestrated.

Many clients do not want to hire a bunch of specialty organizations and do the integration and coordination themselves. They want to hire the expertise of a truly full-service agency to do it.

Some critics say that the job of the full-service agency has been marginalized by specialty firms and marketing consulting firms. Though when you look at what is actually happening in the market-place, the opposite seems true.

The majority of client moves nowadays are toward consolidation in the "new full-service" agencies. The agencies that are thriving and growing are those which provide more (not fewer) services under one roof and do a more effective and efficient job of program integration.

While media-buying firms are a permanent and growing part of the advertising landscape, the full-service agency is usually still involved in a big way.

Media-buying services can get really good prices on media because of their clout, but the client still relies on their full-service agency for overall strategic guidance and coordination – including elements of the media mix that are not mainstream media.

This bodes well for the future of the account manager as the key player in the development of the advertising strategy as well as the coordination of all the parts of the client's marketing communications.

A chapter has been devoted to the concept and application of account planning. But as an overview, account planners are hybrid researchers whose job it is to provide the creative people with insightful and inspirational input on what makes the customer tick.

Some say that the job of the account manager has been marginalized by the account planning movement. Again the opposite seems true. The account planner, where used effectively, has added credibility to the whole creative process.

Account planners have allowed the account manager to spend more time thinking about overall brand strategy and campaign integration and less time dealing with subjective creative issues.

When done correctly, account planning has actually added another facet of sophistication to the role of the account manager as consultant and integrator extraordinaire.

In this new environment, account management is challenging, exhilarating, and sometimes stressful work. But guiding a client's program, knowing more about it than anyone else, and being the consultant and implementor in a creative, competitive business is what a rewarding career is made of. Are you ready? Let's start with a chart.

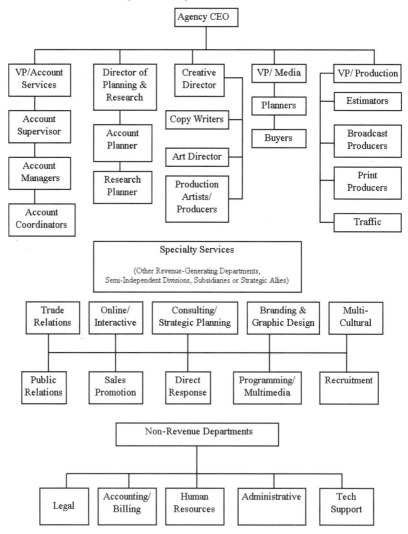

1.2 Contemporary Advertising Agencies: What They Do and How They Do It

Like any business category, there are numerous business models for advertising agencies. But if we were to draw an organizational chart for an agency with 100 employees, it would probably look pretty much like the chart on the opposite page.

Actually, many smaller agencies would look similar, minus a few layers of account management and a few of the specialty departments. Compare this organizational chart with the operational chart (on page 50), which shows how the agency actually works.

Organizations need to communicate to a variety of audiences, though communication might not be a core skill. For this reason, advertising agencies have a permanent place in the landscape of business and the public sector. Their basic function is communication.

This communication process continues to become more complicated and more expensive. Companies, government agencies, and other organizations could employ a large captive staff to create these important communications programs, and, in fact, many organizations do have large in-house staffs for this reason.

But the advertising agency is the recognized source for critical communication strategies and programs. Why? Because agencies are where clients can find that unique blend of creative insights, talent, objectivity, campaign management skills, and a hunger to succeed.

The chances for client success and high impact communication are simply higher when the right agency is on the team.

As a business category, advertising agencies are unique. They often feature unconventional work styles, wild surroundings, people arguing openly in the halls, glamour and grit, passion and professionalism, chaos and focus so hot it burns holes in the impossible – at least on a good day.

The advertising agency, as an organization living in a changing environment, is constantly evolving. The trend is toward a more full-service marketing communications package which can provide and coordinate all the services needed by clients. By expanding service offerings and expertise, agencies are also developing a wider range of revenue sources.

This section will explain how the contemporary advertising agency is organized and what each department does, helping to put the job of account manager into a physical context. The positions discussed and the comments made are meant to add depth to the young account manager's understanding of how things operate, who does what, and who has the most impact on the account manager.

This explanation is built around a composite organizational chart. Granted, this composite agency is probably a larger shop. In-house, it has all of the departments or divisions to deliver a full list of services to its clients.

While you will find many agencies which look similar to this organizational chart, you will find many which are different in some way.

Media planning and buying, for instance, is something many agencies and clients are now farming out to media specialist firms.

Sales promotion would be another type of department not found in many agencies, except the very large ones.

But if they don't have a sales promotion specialist "in the shop," they probably have an outside subsidiary or independent firm – some sort of strategic ally – who will provide this service on an as-needed basis.

This method of providing basic services and relying on specialty agencies has given rise to a group of agencies who provide expertise in direct response advertising, sales promotion, event planning, ethnic marketing, interactive, and other narrow disciplines.

While there are many talented account managers working for smaller agencies (under 50 people), it is important to understand what a full-service agency looks like and how it operates.

The main point is this: whether the services are provided in-house or by a strategic ally, the account manager is still responsible for the integration and coordination of all services provided to the client.

Actually, the account manager's job in a smaller agency is often a bigger job. Because fewer service capabilities are provided in-house, access to specialists is less. When access to specialists is less, the account manager has to know more about all the communication disciplines the client needs.

Other than the size of the agency and the type of clients it serves, the other variable in agency organization is its creative orientation.

Sure, all agencies are in the creative business, some more than others. Shops that were founded by creative folks may not have as large a media, account service, or research department as agencies which want to provide both mainstream and specialty services such as sales promotions, interactive, direct response, and PR.

Here is what our contemporary and evolving agency looks like and what it does department by department.

Account Service.

Account managers are responsible for managing the agency process of serving the client's needs, including strategic leadership and the building of an excellent client-agency working relationship. Sometimes called client services, this group of account managers is headed by a VP-level director of client services or director of account management. This person is normally a senior partner in the firm and is also often involved in soliciting new accounts.

In large agencies, the next step down from the director is the group account director or the management supervisor.

These are senior management people responsible for overseeing the delivery of account services for a group of clients. They are ultimately responsible for total agency performance on an account in all areas.

This includes the quality of media planning and creative work.

Management supervisors see all major campaign work before it's presented to the client. This ensures that they know about it and they think it meets agency standards on strategy, creative quality, and integration.

Account Supervisors, Account Managers, and Assistants.

In smaller agencies, account supervisors provide this oversight. These are seasoned account service people who may oversee the activities of two or three account managers. Account supervisors are there to provide input on strategic issues.

Through the account manager and other members of the agency team, they stay close enough to know what is going on with each account.

Account supervisors will often attend the less frequent high-level meetings with the client and can pinch hit for the account managers as needed. As the people responsible for training, good account supervisors are a real blessing for young account managers.

The assistant account manager positions, where they exist, are a transition between entry-level and full-fledged account management. Assistant account managers get more responsibilities for client contact, more responsibility for working with the rest of the agency team on an account, and more responsibility for the account information management system described in Chapter 3.

Account Coordinators.

Account coordinators are the entry-level position. They do all the little stuff. If they're good, the account manager will quickly start giving them more responsibilities, including client contact.

Being an account coordinator is a fun job, and the learning opportunities under a good account manager are tremendous. The normal time for an account coordinator to advance to a full-fledged account manager on a small account is one to two years.

While most agencies of any size use the account coordinator or assistant account manager system, some agencies subscribe to the senior account manager model. Here, senior account managers do everything and rely only upon a central clerical pool for support.

Branch Offices and Field Offices.

In some large agencies with national retail, automotive, fast food chain, or beverage clients, there may also be small agency offices around the country to serve the needs of local franchises or dealer groups.

These offices are normally run by a senior account manager to take care of special needs that local client groups, like the Southern California McDonald's franchises, have for localized ad programs and to make sure national programs are implemented correctly at the local level.

Creative Department.

Here's where most of the ad ideas come from.

Creative Directors.

The department is overseen by the creative director (CD), who normally has vice-president or higher status. The creative director is a seasoned creative mind who is responsible for the creative output of the agency.

Most CDs were copywriters earlier in their careers and are normally excellent concept thinkers.

Depending on the culture of the agency, the CD can ultimately dictate the concepts to be presented to the client, even if the account manager does not totally support them.

CDs are the chief creative officers because they have a proven ability to inspire great creative work in others, they are good strategic thinkers, and they are excellent at presenting creative work. These are the things you should expect from your CD.

The working style of creative directors can vary from collaborative to dictatorial, and they will set the agency tone relative to the account manager's involvement in the creative process.

Besides playing a major role in the creating and selecting presented work, the CD does something else that directly impacts account managers – selecting the creative team. Just when you think you have a creative team "in sync" with your client, guess what? The CD may decide your team needs to work on a new account and you get to break in a new team, or that team's great work has attracted an offer they can't refuse from another agency.

This is one of the reasons that account managers don't like to let the client know who is doing the creative work. It may not be the same team tomorrow. This is seen as instability by the client and detracts from client confidence in the agency.

In defense of most creative directors, they understand the importance of creative team interaction with clients and the client comfort zone created by having the same creative team over time. Typically the larger the account, the more stable the creative staffing is.

However, some CDs are unrealistic in their assertion that since they (the CDs) are deeply involved in all creative work, it doesn't really matter who the copywriter and art director are. Wrong!

Creative Teams – Art Directors and Copywriters.

Art directors and copywriters are the folks who actually think up the ads. They work as a team to come up with striking headlines and visuals.

Often, the main value of copywriters is not writing copy, but coming up with the overall concept for a campaign embodied in a headline or tag line.

The art directors are the visual folks. They can bring an idea to life. But don't expect every art director to be able to draw, particularly in this computer-driven age. Some of the most talented art directors have a wonderful graphic sense and yet they can't even do an acceptable thumbnail sketch. I've never understood this.

Hand skills can still be vital. Having a "good wrist" is a talent that account managers treasure. It's as nice as it is rare to find an art director who can do a one-minute thumbnail layout and show you what the ad concept looks like. If you find it, treasure it.

The impact of technology is more evident in the art/creative department than anywhere else. Today, art directors are expected to be proficient in the latest software programs for layout, image creation, image modification, assembly, and production output.

With so much emphasis on technology-based creativity, it can be rare nowadays to find an art director who can draw.

A lot of conceptual art for layouts and storyboards is now done on a Mac platform. Nonetheless, there's still a fair amount of freehand illustration used in the development of layouts and storyboards. When the art director knows exactly the type of picture he wants, sometimes it's best to have an illustrator draw it instead of using a stock photo that does a poor job of representing the idea.

Some of the work done by layout and storyboard artists is beautiful and amazing in its ability to communicate exactly the emotions and meaning intended by the creative team.

Sometimes the layout illustration is more effective than the final photo. It is a real pleasure to present that kind of conceptual work. But it can be a problem later.

A beautiful storyboard or print layout, all matted and pretty, is hard to throw away... especially if it was for an ad you especially liked. I would often keep a great layout in my office just because it was a great example of the advertising craft. Many creative teams appreciate that you care enough to save and display their layouts.

Freelancers.

The use of freelancers to supplement creative staff is now a common practice. This is done for many reasons, but primarily so the creative department can maintain an affordable core staff for ongoing work and then use freelancers as project volume increases or specialists are needed.

The important thing for the account manager relative to creative freelancers is that the work should be "seamless." That means that the work looks like agency work and the client need not be concerned about whether someone inside or outside the agency actually did the work.

Planning and Research.

In the largest agencies, there is still usually a formal research department headed by a director of planning and research, or some title like that.

But more agencies are adopting the account planning model for research. We'll deal with both in general terms.

Five Categories of Research.
The type of research done or supervised by agencies generally falls into one of five categories:

1. **Exploratory and Qualitative Research:** Focus groups, product use observations, and in-depth interviews are exploratory techniques that probe opinions, feelings, and attitudes. These techniques are not meant to be projectable to a large population, but the information developed by exploratory research often ends up as input in the creative process.

2. **Quantitative Research:** Projecting quantitative research to a large population requires methods that measure more people on consistent criteria. Phone surveys and mall intercepts are two common methods used to study attitude, brand awareness, product usage, and consideration sets. Quantitative research also involves the analysis of data from Simmons, MRI, and other companies to help build a profile of the target customer.

3. **Concept Testing:** After preliminary creative work has been done, it can be helpful to get some feedback. Concept or copy-testing techniques like focus groups, perception analysis, account planner panels, and online polls help provide a reaction to campaign themes, headlines, layouts, copy, offers, etc.

4. **Audience Measurement:** The measurement of an audience is primarily a media department function. Determining who uses what media and what media delivers which audience is a key concern of the media planner. This research often involves the analysis of Simmons, MRI, Nielsen, and Arbitron media data cross-referenced with product usage information for the same sources.

5. **Performance:** The effectiveness of individual ads and entire campaigns is a chief concern of everyone involved. Advertising performance is broken into two main classifications: communications testing and measurement of overall results.

In communications testing, individual ads are tested for recall, message clarity, and persuasiveness. Campaigns are measured to see if they increased awareness and understanding, if they changed attitudes, or if they motivated a specific behavioral response such as a toll-free call, Web site visit, dealer visit, trial offer, etc.

Performance testing can be done in a variety of ways depending on what is being tested. Traditional and online focus groups, mall intercepts, perception analyzers, magazine readership studies, campaign awareness tracking studies, attitudinal studies, and response path monitoring (800 numbers, Web site activity, dealer polling, and sales increases) are the most common.

Advertising agencies often do some research themselves. However, any research that measures the success of the agency's work is performed by an outside research firm. The most common type of this outsourced research is attitude and awareness tracking studies plus pre- and post-campaign evaluations.

Research Departments – Before Account Planning.

Until the introduction of account planning as a formal agency discipline, the research department was the home of quantitative and secondary researchers. These people pored over Simmons tables, cluster analyses, and the research done by others in order to gain some new insight into the target audience.

These researchers loved numbers and tended to deal in general conclusions about target markets and audiences, conclusions they drew from masses of demographic and marketing data.

Account Planning – The Newest Discipline.

Account planners are the newest discipline in the effort of advertising agencies to find ways to make the advertising impactful and relevant to the consumer. Account planners are hybrids – part creative strategists and part qualitative researchers – and they normally live in a department now called Research and Planning or Planning and Research.

They have the ability to find a new customer insight or product insight that will help the creative team say something new or something old in a new way.

In some agencies, account planning is a billable service that clients agree to pay for or simply don't get. In other agencies, account planning is part of the package of services provided under a retainer agreement.

The application of account planning in American agencies has been a topic of great debate, disagreement, and interpretation.

Since account planning definitely impacts account management, it deserves its own place in this book: Chapter 4.4, "Straight Talk about Account Planning."

Media.

Talk about detail – these folks are buried in it. If you haven't taken a class in media planning, you should, so you'll know the "media basics" and can appreciate what it takes to develop a comprehensive media plan.

Media comprises up to 80% of some account budgets. So, in one respect, the media department is a financial consultant, advising clients on the best way to invest their money.

The advertising media industry is a lot more complicated and expensive than it used to be. As a result, there are now a number of approaches agencies take to provide media planning and buying services to their clients.

Smaller agencies tend to have a strategic alliance with a freelance media buyer. Medium-sized shops still tend to handle media internally and use a media-buying service for larger or more complicated media buys. Larger agencies also do both internal and outsourced media, depending on the complexity of the media involved and their ability to generate revenue from the media function.

A handful of media-buying services – like Carat, Initiative Media, and OMD – have grown to become industry giants and have had a huge impact on the cost of media and how it is purchased.

Eager to get rid of labor-intensive, noncreative functions and seeing new billing opportunities emerge as large marketers began to put their media businesses up for bid, some large full-service agencies dismantled or "unbundled" their media-buying departments and turned them into free-standing profit centers.

The emergence of these mega-media specialty agencies has been one of the most interesting ad industry trends in the early years of the new century.

First, the clout of media-buying services put downward pressure on the cost of media and tended to make traditional media a commodity item.

Second, and more important, the mega-media-buying services created a new spark of creativity within the advertising media industry.

Companies whose concern was selling space in their magazines or time on their television networks were now cooking up creative ideas on how to better serve the advertisers.

The result has been a string of new programming ideas, new publishing ideas, and new media promotion ideas that are being custom designed for specific advertisers. The whole concept is that media should be something more than just the channel for the ad message; the medium can be part of the creative message package. This new conept is called "integrated media."

Given that the creative message might now include what the media vehicle actually looks like, many full-service agencies who unbundled their media service are now bringing it back. The earlier involvement of media in the creative discussion and the potential to customize the media is an exciting new dimension to the advertising industry. This is the ultimate legacy of the recent evolution that the media side of the advertising business has undergone: again, full circle, but not exactly where it started.

Regardless of whether the media planning is done in-house or is outsourced, the account manager is normally responsible for providing the media planner with the campaign brief explaining the media needs and target audience. The account manager is also responsible for evaluating the media proposal before it goes to the client.

The media department in a medium- to large-sized agency is run by the media director, who is typically the VP-level contemporary of the creative director, director of account services, and VP of production.

Media directors oversee the work of media planners and buyers, approve all media plans before the plans go to the account manager, and are personally involved in the negotiation and placement of large media buys.

Media planners, as the title indicates, do most of the planning. They're the agency media people with whom account managers work most closely.

Based on input provided in the campaign brief, media planners develop the comprehensive media plan. The plan includes recommendations on target audiences, media selection, exposure level, timing, and budget.

The media planner is normally the one who will do the initial cost negotiating with the media. Tough negotiating saves clients money.

While the media department is supposed to be the source of wisdom on media, in reality, most media departments specialize in mainstream mass media. They know a lot less about some of the peripheral and new media.

This is particularly true at smaller agencies.

Ask a small agency about national in-store sampling programs, product placements, or spot market e-mails, and you may get blank stares or funny looks.

This is no criticism of the media department. They just don't spend much time working on peripheral and new media since the lion's share of the dollars they spend are in traditional measured media.

They're happy to get information about placing ads on the back of store receipts or in airports, but don't expect immediate expertise.

Production and Traffic.

After the copy and layout have been approved, someone has to move the project through the steps needed to get it produced on time and within budget. This is the production and traffic department. They are your friends.

The department set-up will vary. Bigger shops will have production departments which deal in both print and broadcast projects.

With the awesome capabilities of today's graphic computers, print production is commonly handled inside the agency from start (typesetting) to finish (print-ready images on CD).

Estimators may develop detailed costs for projects before the creative has even started. Doing so relies on a number of assumptions about the parameters of the project which may or may not be true when it comes out the other end. As a rule, the more parameters you can give the estimator, the more accurate the estimate.

The Video Production Process.

Effective video production is both a business and an art. Depending on the size of the agency, you may have an entire department dedicated to video production with full-time producers and coordinators specializing in things like traffic and talent payments, or you may have a few skilled creatives and a coordinator who helps out part-time.

Whichever is true for your agency, when it's time to produce a TV spot, there's a lot at stake. The media budget will usually be sizeable, the cost of the production itself will be significant – often well over $100,000 – and the reputations of the client, the agency, and the creative team are all at stake.

We won't even begin to deal with all of the business and technical complexities here, except to say that if video production is part of the task, your job just became even more interesting.

Broadcast producers take television storyboard concepts and coordinate the process of getting a spot produced. This often includes working with an outside director. It is the job of the agency broadcast producer to bring the spot in on time and within budget.

Account managers can avoid major amounts of angst and anguish if they deal with broadcast budget issues ahead of time. For example, make sure the creative team, the creative director, and the broadcast producer know what the budget is for a commercial.

They may not like the budget (it's way too small, you know), but at least they won't spend a lot of time dreaming up concepts only to find the budget can't support them.

The Print Preproduction Process – Electronic Prepress.
Once the ad concept and layout have been approved, preproduction specialists often take care of production details such as the final typography and the cropping and electronic preparation of the photos – whatever is needed to get the project ready to send to the publication or to the printer.

Sometimes the art director does this, but usually the electronic prepress specialist works with the art director and a production manager at the same time... the art director for the artistic elements and the production manager for technical preparation. Today, virtually all prepress work is done electronically.

Sometimes the account manager arbitrates in a disagreement between the way the art director wants a piece done and the way the production manager needs to produce it in order to stay within budget.

The need for such arbitration shows that information about budget and creative parameters were not adequately discussed up front.

Print producers do essentially the same thing as broadcast producers, only they deal with magazine and newspaper ads, outdoor boards, logo specialty items, direct mail pieces – anything that is printed. Printed projects tend to take longer to create and produce. The production and traffic people will ride herd on the creative people, who actually select typefaces, line up photo shoots, get illustrations created, and all the other things needed to get a print piece done.

Traffic Managers.
Traffic managers are the circulatory system of the agency. They are the agency's air traffic controllers. They often physically move the work from department to department, paying attention to all types of details.

On ads, they work closely with the media department to make sure each ad gets to the right medium in the right format with the right running instructions.

The traffic department normally runs weekly status meetings.

Traffic managers are responsible for knowing the status of every job in the shop. Every project has its own timeline, budget, approval process, specifications, and peculiarities.

Traffic managers do a tremendous amount of juggling and negotiating behind the scenes with producers, art directors, production artists, media buyers and even account managers so that the most time-sensitive jobs get immediate attention.

When they start getting worried about one of your jobs, pay attention. And if they suggest that you get a project started now instead of waiting, it's good advice. They probably know something about the agency workload you don't.

Traffic is a thankless job, and traffic managers are not known for their pleasant dispositions. But a good traffic manager is a lifesaver, deserving regular recognition and appreciation for riding a tough project through the agency production maze. Chocolates are always nice.

There is an old adage about the agency production department. It says that production managers will tell account managers the "facts of life about low price, speed, and quality. You can have any two. You pick." If I had any advice to account managers relative to the traffic and production function, it would be these five things:

1. Learn as much as you can about production so you can anticipate problems yourself.

2. Be relentless on proofing. If errors get through to a completed job, the agency will often have to pay for the redo. (And don't count on spell checker – it doesn't know the difference between "account manager" and "account manger." An account manger is a place full of hay and old memos that they send you to when you make mistakes.)

3. Make sure the production people see the creative concepts before they are presented to the client. The creative people will sometimes come up with an idea that cannot be done within the time constraints or budget.

4. Make sure your client delivers on their deadlines for approvals, information, and materials.

5. Don't deal directly with production vendors except when asked to by production and traffic managers.

Other Revenue-Generating Specialty Communications Services, Divisions, Subsidiaries, or Strategic Allies.

As the agency business has evolved to offer more services, what these new services are called has evolved. Originally they were called "below the line" services because they were in a different revenue class than media commissions. They have also been called marketing services and (the one I like the most) specialty services.

Even in agencies that do not have specialty-service departments as described below, the agency must take a leadership role in finding and managing the right resource to provide the specialty service to the client. This resource is often another agency that specializes in, for example, sales promotions or interactive media.

Full-service agencies often get to be full-service agencies by perfecting the art of managing in-house and outsourced services in a way that is totally seamless to the client.

Good account management is the key to this success.

As you read about these specialty services remember that they can be either inside the agency or provided by a specialty shop.

Sales Promotion.

Once frowned upon by mainstream agencies as beneath them and demeaning to the brand equity, sales promotion has gained in respect and importance.

Sales promotions (also known as brand promotions) are activities which involve contests, sweepstakes, incentives, on-pack coupons, in-store sampling... the stuff that drives mainstream agencies crazy because it is so detail oriented and labor intensive (and frankly, not that sexy).

The kind of promotions we see as private citizens are "consumer promotions," designed to stimulate retail sales. Co-promotions with other brands are also handled by the agency's sales promotion department or a specialty agency.

There is another type of promotion, called a "trade promotion," that we don't see because it is designed to stimulate support among the dealers and distributors who carry the product. These trade promotions involve contests, prizes, incentives, co-op ad deals, and special pricing, all designed to get the products more local ad support, better shelf space, and better pass-thru savings during the promotional period.

Because they are more measurable and tend to stimulate short-term sales, sales promotions are now almost an expected part of many consumer goods and trade campaigns.

If the agency does not have a sales promotion resource, then by default, guess who gets to be the sales promotion expert? Don't despair.

Sales promotion is becoming one of the most interesting and creative parts of the agency business and an important account management function. Just read a few issues of *Promo* magazine and see all the ideas you'll get.

Sales promotion has three things going for it:

1. It's measurable. Clients like that.

2. It can be every bit as creative as a pure branding campaign. (You may have a hard time convincing the creatives of this.)

3. It can be an agency money maker, generating service-fee revenue.

Part of the sales promotion department is "specialty items," also lovingly known in the biz as "trinkets and trash." (It's the wrong image today, but it still causes people to chuckle.)

Regularly, there is opportunity to tie in some specialty item that increases brand use or reinforces the brand's unique selling proposition. It may be an attractive incentive to entice first-time trial, or a logo'ed brand loyalty item or a souvenir item that ties in to the theme of the annual dealer sales meeting, just to name a few.

One of the best specialty items I ever saw was for a brand of nasal decongestant that was mixed with hot water. The specialty item was a coffee cup with a handle on one side and a life-size nose on the other.

Clients are well served when their account managers at least think about the appropriateness of specialty items as they look for ways to heighten the visibility and longevity of the agency's work.

Graphic Design and Branding.

Graphic design firms (or "design shops" as they are sometimes called) are not agencies. Likewise, the art departments in many agencies are not design shops. Graphic design firms and graphic design departments specialize in the design of logos, packaging, annual reports, exhibits, signage, retail design, and all manner of other non-ad-like visual communications.

For years, advertising agencies have surrendered such design business to the design specialist. Advertising art directors are one breed, graphic designers are another.

For years, it was believed and practiced that to have two art functions under one roof was impossible.

Now, in their search for more diversified revenue sources, more agencies have a graphic design department or subsidiary which can be deployed and managed under one roof. Graphic design departments are happy to take on one-time projects and don't worry so much about a long-term relationship with a client.

Design shops have actually become a valuable new business tool for agencies seeking smaller accounts they can help grow.

Example: a company comes in and wants a logo and some packaging done. The client likes the way the design shop works and invites it to make a pitch for an ad program.

There are still some political problems about who supervises the graphic design work for existing advertising clients. Should it be the creative director or the head of graphic design? The other political issue that comes up is what jobs for existing clients are handled by the graphic design department and who makes the decision whether the agency art director or the graphic design department gets the assignment.

These are interesting questions that might impact how an account manager works with the two departments.

Sometimes the assignment criteria are set and there is no question on where an assignment should go. Other times it may be the decision of the account manager or the creative director.

Some graphic design shops and departments have morphed into another hot specialty: branding. Concerned with much more than what the logo looks like, branding agencies get involved with corporate and product projects that include naming, audio and video signatures, defining the brand experience, licensing issues, brand extension strategies, and such.

Interactive.

Some of the biggest complaints clients have about independent Web site builders are:

1. They don't always pay attention to the communications strategy developed by the ad agency.

2. They are often more interested in the latest tech gimmicks than in meaningful content.

3. They don't embrace the importance of the user-friendly "brand experience."

The big argument for having a captive interactive department in an agency is to ensure that the people who build the Web sites won't make the same mistakes as the independent Web site builders.

They focus on branding, user interface issues, architecture, hosting, and other issues that make the complete package.

In my experience, even a happy Web site building experience can soon go sour if the issue of maintenance is not handled up front. It's amazing how quickly even the simplest site becomes outdated.

Who does the Web mastering and how that process happens will be a big issue in how happy your client stays with the agency's interactive services. Be ready.

If the client decides to act as Web master, it's important that the account manager stay involved to ensure that agency-created off-line communications are properly adapted online. Good Web mastering does not happen by itself.

The interactive department, when it works well, is one of the best examples of the "fully integrated agency" concept in agency practice. With the Internet being such a factor in marketing communications, the account manager is well served and well advised to consult frequently with the interactive department.

Two Big Questions.

Today, in almost every communications plan, clients will want two big questions answered:

1. What is our interactive strategy?

2. What does our Internet presence look like?

These questions also address the second part of what an interactive department does – preparing and placing Internet advertising.

On this issue especially, the account manager should make sure the interactive department, the sales promotion department, the media department, and the creative department all know what the other is thinking on a campaign.

There are bound to be differences of opinion on strategy and tactics that the account manager will have to resolve.

Whether the agency has an interactive department or a close working relationship with an outside firm, the role of the account manager is not to be the "techie." The subject is much too complicated. The important role of the account manager is to guide the formation of the "brand experience"; to answer the questions "what exactly are the components of the Web site that will enhance the customer's relationship with the brand and how do those components work?"

A good account manager, relative to interactive, is the steward of the brand, overseer of integration, and guarantor of good Web mastering.

"Scope Creep."

When handling a Web site development assignment, be particularly aware of tech-driven features and "scope creep." Tech-driven features are those "cool new apps" that the technical people get all excited about even though they're distracting.

Scope creep occurs when the goals, functionality, or components of the Web site grow beyond the original assignment. What seems to be a simple enough tweak may end up diverting time and money away from the main focus of the brand experience.

Direct Response, Fulfillment, and CRM.

Like sales promotion, direct response has increased its credibility as a legitimate MarCom tool. Direct response (DR) used to be considered junk mail and infomercials. The use of information-rich databases has changed that reputation.

Highly predictable direct mail and e-mail campaigns can be aimed at the highest potential prospects, and infomercials have become so polished they are sometimes mistaken for content programming.

In some DR departments the third part of the direct response program is the commercial Web site development.

While nonselling content sites are almost always designed by the interactive department, the DR department is called on to provide advice on design of sites selling consumer goods and impulse items.

Fulfillment services mostly handle the assembly and mailing of response materials and products. When people respond to advertising and request literature, someone has to field the phone call or mail request, send the correct information, and enter the name into the right database. This is what fulfillment houses do.

Customer relationship management (CRM) is a new specialty that combines direct response, interactive, and telemarketing. CRM is a way to stay in regular contact with prospects and customers by using Web site accounts, opt-in e-mails, direct mail, phone, and Web-based customer service and telemarketing to sell products, deliver services, and provide information that customers find helpful.

While a new agency specialty, CRM programs themselves are normally housed at and maintained by the client. Part of CRM is to make sure that the follow-up programs are properly integrated into the ad campaigns.

A formal CRM program increases the possibility of a seamless transition between advertising and the ongoing relationship that brands try to establish with customers and prospects.

Multicultural/Niche Marketing.

Minority populations, especially Hispanic, continue to grow in the U.S., and they are maintaining more of their ethnic culture than previous generations. As a result, some agencies have developed expertise in marketing to these groups.

Sometimes called "urban" marketing agencies, these firms can also have expertise in marketing to Asian, black, gay, and youth audiences. Niche agencies can also define themselves by an industry specialty such as health care, technology, sports, or business-to-business.

Public Relations.

The public relations (PR) department provides communications services generally characterized as nonadvertising in nature.

Most large PR departments provide PR counsel on marketing issues, corporate issues, and public-policy issues.

Examples of marketing PR (MPR) services include product releases, feature article placement, and publicity events.

Corporate PR (CPR) includes advocacy advertising, investor relations, employee communications, government relations, and crisis management.

Public-policy PR can include government and regulation-related issues. These services normally rely on presenting newsworthy material to the news media, which then broadcast the message.

A creative marketing PR idea that is in sync with the advertising strategy can dramatically increase the impact of an ad campaign.

The operating question for an account manager on every campaign is "What's the PR component?"

The contact people in PR departments and outside firms are also called account managers or account executives.

Many PR departments bring in "PR-only" clients who might one day become advertising clients. PR people are strong believers in their craft and will fight to not sacrifice the PR budget for an ad campaign. Can't blame them.

Multimedia and Programming.

This department produces sales meeting presentations and marketing videos, along with a growing amount of sponsor-produced cable television programming.

An example of sponsor-produced television programming is a 30-minute program appealing to teens produced by Coke for cable networks and channels.

The programming looks like any other cable network programming except there's Coke branding throughout, not just in the commercials.

When you see this kind of programming, you'll know it was produced by the multimedia and programming (MM&P) department of an ad agency.

These are also the folks who usually handle placements of client products on the sets of popular TV drama programs, sitcoms, and game shows. As television and cable networks look to replace ad dollars lost to other media, product placement has become big business.

In the media department section of this chapter, the evolution of "creative media opportunities" was discussed. The popular BMW high-energy mini-films of 2002 and 2003 are examples.

Content-driven mediums like the BMW films and products written into major roles in TV programs are often the work of the MM&P division working closely with the media department.

Event Planning.

Sales meetings, touring shows, trade-show exhibits, and other such events are the domain of this department.

Logistics are their specialty. Many of the nonmedia deadlines for items produced elsewhere in the agency (like literature, a campaign roll-out presentation, or new package design) will be driven by an important event.

Close coordination of such agency projects with the events team will ensure that the right stuff gets to the right place at the right time.

Trade Relations.

The greatest ad campaign in the world can fall short of its potential if the "ground game" is not in place. (What the heck does that mean?)

"The Ground Game."

Here's what it means. The ground game is how an ad campaign is executed at the local level.

- Are dealers adequately informed about the campaign?

- Do they have the correct literature?

- Have point of sale (POS) displays arrived and been erected in time?

- Are the factory customer-service people trained and ready to assist dealer-sales people?

- Are the dealers and distributors aware of and involved in the trade promotion and sales contest?

That's the ground game.

"Trade relations" is the term applied to those services that make sure the ground game is in place and well executed.

Clients whose products are sold through wholesale distributors and dealers often need some sort of trade relations function.

This function can include:

- Planning and executing trade promotions, dealer sales contests, and the like

- Dealer liaison and coordination

- Running of the client's co-op advertising program
- Coordination of Yellow Pages trademark advertising with dealers
- Distribution of dealer POS and literature
- Local promotion and PR assistance
- Spot market campaign planning

Service Offices.

The term "service office" is often used to refer to a branch office of a national agency. The service office is staffed by an account manager and support staff whose primary job is to take care of the trade relations requirements of their region.

Automotive dealer groups and fast food chains are famous for needing a high level of trade relations support. The agencies that service these groups are extremely important in the success of ad campaigns and other promotions.

Consulting and Strategic Planning.

Some agencies are now into marketing consulting and strategic planning, which involves them at the highest levels of the client organization. Clients have found that research done by the agency for the purposes of crafting better advertising includes valuable projections about changes in markets five years from now.

These projections can have ramifications for product design, distribution, and pricing strategy. Young & Rubicam's Intelligence Factory and McCann-Erickson's Future Brand are examples of this kind of consulting and strategic planning division.

One of the research techniques that feeds the strategic planning process is called futurism. A futurist like Faith Popcorn examines the "porous edge" of human culture to predict what trends will shape society in five or ten years. Futurists try to predict what issues currently on the fringe of society will become mainstream and what impact they will have on the client's business.

Many of the people who now populate agency consulting and strategic planning departments have come from the large consulting firms like Accenture and Ernst & Young.

Recruitment.

Recruitment advertising has long been a specialty of a few agencies who work closely with the human resource departments of large companies and with large recruitment firms.

It's not very exciting, but it can be profitable. There's not much interaction between the rest of the agency and the recruitment division except when a creative radio spot, brochure, or job fair booth design is needed.

As an account manager, the most important thing to keep in mind about the recruitment division is to keep them informed about new product and corporate ad campaigns for their accounts.

The recruitment agency must make sure to keep ad copy consistent with new themes or tag lines. The client MarCom director will most likely not think to advise his own HR department of a new campaign. So the agency must cover that communications gap.

Directory Advertising.

Not very sexy... which is why many accounts are happy to pay someone else to manage their telephone and shopping directory ad program.

When an account has a large national trademark Yellow Pages program in support of dealers, directory advertising can be very important.

Nonrev Support Departments.

Larger agencies may have other departments to keep things running:

Legal.

If an agency is large enough to have a legal department, this department is consulted on questions of advertising legality. Health, safety, and performance claims are the types of issues reviewed by legal. However, in most cases the client bears the responsibility for the final approval of all claims with legal import.

Accounting.

This department prepares billing and pays the bills. (See Chapter 3.7, "Billings, Budgets, and Financial Management" for more details.)

The accounting department is very important to client relations and therefore is your friend.

With the wide variety of services now provided by agencies and the numerous ways agencies are compensated, producing a totally accurate client billing each month is difficult.

Account by account, commission rates can vary, mark-ups can vary, hourly rates can vary. The accounting department has to get it all right.

Human Resources and Administration.
This department formally handles hiring, although the functional department heads will also make hiring decisions.

Administration and HR also handle employee benefits, policy, and other key procedural issues.

Operations and Technical Services.
These people develop information systems to improve efficiency and capabilities, and then they hang around to keep the computers running.

The Operational Chart: (The Real Organizational Chart)

The Hub of the System.

While the organizational chart shown earlier in this chapter is useful for understanding what agencies do, the operational chart is much more useful for explaining how things get done. As the coordinator of all agency services provided to each client, the account manager is functionally the hub of the system.

The account manager matches up with every department in the agency as the client representative.

Likewise the account manager matches up with the client contact (sometimes multiple client contacts) as the agency representative.

Virtually all communications between agency and client go through – or at least include – the account manager. As indicated by the two short dashed lines between the client and the media and creative departments, some account relationships do have multiple channels of contact with the client.

Still, the account manager is responsible for knowing everything that is going on and managing the agency services as well as the client relationship.

This practice is represented by the large conduit that goes between the account manager and the client.

Client

Media
Creative
Production & Traffic
Planning & Research
Public Relations
Interactive
Account Manager
Multi-Cultural
Sales Promotion
Other Specialty Services
Direct Response
Legal & Accounting
Branding & Graphic Design

Within the agency, various departments and specialists talk with each other (for instance, media and production) in order to complete projects and get the correct materials to the media.

Keep this operational chart in mind as you read Chapter 5.1, "Journey of the Job," and 5.2, "Fifty Hours on a Roller Coaster."

One agency business claim to fame is that it pioneered account management and the consultative selling concepts used today by a host of other professional service specialties, including public relations firms, media-buying services, sales promotion, interactive agencies, and CRM consultants.

The Third Org Chart.

How agencies physically organize themselves is also an issue that impacts how account managers do their job.

Two Basic Logistical Systems.

There are two basic logistical systems: the "discipline" approach and the "account module" approach.

In the discipline approach, each department in the agency has its own space. If you want to talk to the media buy on your account, you go over to the media department and pay them a visit.

Ideally, each department has a conference room where meetings can be held and team work can be done.

In the account module system, everyone who works on an account works in the same area – with few walls and little privacy.

Obviously, we are talking about a large account that everyone in the module works on full time. If you want to talk to the media planner, you shout across the room. If you want to sneak a peak at what the copywriter is up to, you walk over and look at his computer screen. The whole module space operates as a giant, nonstop conference room.

As you might expect, there is great debate about which is the better system. I guess it's all a matter of what you're comfortable with.

R-E-S-P-E-C-T.

by Noreen O'Leary, AdWeek, *May 29, 2000*

Interpublic Group (IPG) announced an overhaul of its nonmedia marketing-services unit, which signaled the importance of those businesses in the company's future. While IPG derived just 20% of its revenue from that area five years ago, it expects to increase that level to 50% by year's end.

Larry Weber was named the new chief executive of Allied Communications Group, the IPG subsidiary that contains these specialized marketing companies. Nontraditional marketing services are finally getting the credit they deserve.

"It's not the information economy we're in; it's the communication economy," says Weber. *"We're in an era of integrated branding. Everything is about conducting a dialogue with the customer, whether it's through traditional advertising, the Web, PR or a big event."*

The Internet is speeding up industry change already in motion.

Driven by media and consumer fragmentation, the rise of relationship marketing, and the decline of media-based compensation, the communications industry is being transformed by marketers seeking integrated solutions.

"In London in the early '80s, I tried to sell one-stop shopping and kept hitting a brick wall. We got nowhere," recalls Saatchi & Saatchi North America's chief executive, Jennifer Laing. *"Now the pressure is coming from clients who want us to forge one strategy, one brand equity, one voice, using whatever weapons are most effective. It doesn't matter, it shouldn't matter, where the spending goes."*

Nonmedia marketing communications is comprised of a wide-ranging group of disciplines, including direct, promotions, digital, public relations, branding/identity, sponsorships, event marketing, contract publishing, recruitment, merchandising, medical, ethnic, and sports marketing and entertainment.

By some estimates, 70 percent of all marketing dollars is now spent on nonmedia communications, a reverse proportion to a decade ago, when media advertising dominated the mix.

The Saatchi's, like their English peer at WPP, were early advocates of recommending their "below the line" services to clients at their agency holdings. U.S. companies were packaging their own multidisciplinary resources as well. Young & Rubicam called its offerings "Whole Egg," Ogilvy referred its approach as "Orchestration."

"Below-the-line marketing has been growing faster than traditional advertising for the past decade and has higher margins," says Omnicom CEO John Wren. *"More and more concentration of money is going into those nonmedia disciplines because that's where the audience is."*

JUICY CASES:

1.1: A Sensitivity Threshold.

You're the senior account manager on a major import car brand. Minorities are a big target audience for your client's products. Three years ago you approved, for presentation to your client, an ad that was destined to run in *Jet*, a magazine for African Americans.

The headline on the ad read "Unlike your last boyfriend, it goes to work every morning." The ad created a lot of controversy and bad press among the black community and was pulled after one appearance.

Now the creative team has come up with a postcard to be mailed to a list of 500,000 persons who have indicated an interest in the brand. The ethnicity of the list is a cross section of the U.S. population.

The proposed card shows a close-up of a smiling black man with a gold tooth jewel in the shape of the car.

What should your reaction be to this creative concept?

1.2: The Jealous Client.

You are an account manager for a client who just hired a new advertising manager. While it looks like you are going to be able to work with this person, there is one issue that will probably hamper the relationship if not dealt with correctly.

The new client contact is jealous of advertising people in general and you specifically. He thinks that the advertising business is glamorous, that all advertising people have inflated egos, and is envious of the big salary he thinks you make.

What to do?

AD-ROBIC EXERCISES:

1.1: Scoping out the Big Shops.

Visit the Web sites for some large agencies and see how they present themselves and their services. Suggested agencies and their Web sites:

Foote, Cone & Belding   fcb.com

Grey Worldwide   grey.com

Leo Burnett   leoburnett.com

McCann-Erickson   mccann.com

NOTE: On this site you'll also find Robert Coen's industrywide ad spending tracking and projections.

Ogilvy & Mather   ogilvy.com

You'll find other links on the University of Texas Advertising World site (utexas.edu/world) and on adbuzz.com (Look in the Ad Museum. In the *Advertising & the Business of Brands* Study Hall, look up Hot Links).

How do the agencies differ in the services they provide and how they differentiate themselves?

1.2: Variations on a Theme.

Contact the largest ad agency you can find in your town and interview the person in charge of account service.

Determine how the agency's organizational chart differs from the one provided in this book.

Focus on how their client list has influenced the services offered by the agency and how the agency is organized to deliver those services.

BURNING QUESTIONS:

1.1:

Two trends have had a profound impact on the importance of account management. Identify these two trends and explain how they changed the practice of account management.

1.2:

What are the primary differences between the two organizational charts presented in Chapter 1 as they relate to the agency function of account management?

2.0 THE VIEW FROM 200 FEET

BEFORE WE HIT THE GROUND RUNNING, there is another level of overview that will help new account managers understand the context and practices that define the agency business and the account manager's role.

Account Management Overview is a broad-stroke view of the account management position.

Master of the Mixes introduces you to how the account manager helps shape the whole communications program for a client.

Shop Talk contains a list of words that have special meaning to account managers. It's the language of the craft.

The Money Side of the Business describes how agencies generate revenue and how the changing nature of agency compensation has raised the importance of account managers.

"Think they're trying to tell us something?"

2.1 Account Management Overview

In the old days, the job of the account manager was seen in a much narrower context. The title "account executive" was much more prevalent, indicating more of a sales orientation. Keeping the client happy was high in the job description. Being a proactive steward of the client's business was a relatively new notion of the account manager's reason for being.

As the short history in the last chapter explains, the days of the glad-handing, reactive account executive are pretty much gone. Today, being an account manager in an advertising agency is one of the most stimulating and challenging jobs anywhere. How is this so?

I'll let the eloquent words of one of my reviewers explain it for me. Arnold Worldwide, headquartered in Boston, is the agency that does such great work for Volkswagen, McDonald's, Royal Caribbean Cruise Lines, and many other lucky clients. Pamela Hamlin is a 19-year veteran of the ad business and the managing partner in charge of all account service at Arnold. Here's how she puts it:

"In what other job can you be exposed to so many interesting categories of clients, media, and marketing challenges?

"Where else do you have the opportunity to work with so many creative, intelligent, and high-energy people developing programs that stimulate business, build brands, and become part of our culture??

"And where else can you do all of this while having so much fun and getting paid for it??? Only in advertising.

"Much of the account manager's work is invisible and has to do with creating an environment in which inspired work can be done. The account manager's strategic insights, understanding of the client's business, and the respect-based relationship the account manager has with the client all contribute to great work that gets results.

"The trend (as mentioned elsewhere) of more clients looking to their agency for total integration only makes the account manager's role even more important, fulfilling, and interesting."

The purpose of this book is to describe what account work is really like. This isn't always easy because a lot of the best work done by account managers is subtle and intuitive... "soft skills" at their finest.

It could be a last-minute change in a presentation, the rephrasing of a point that only you know the client "didn't get," or an insightful conversation you had in a store with a user of your client's product.

This book is about relationships in general and most importantly the agency-client relationship. That relationship is one of the most important assets possessed by the agency, and the account manager is the steward of that relationship.

It may sound odd to call a relationship an asset, but without a good relationship there will be no client.

The account manager is the day-to-day contact with his working counterpart on the client side. The account manager directs the process of serving the client, constantly interacting with both the client and the agency team. The atmosphere is often chaotic, respect is earned, and soft skills plus intellect, energy, and integrity form the basis for long-term success.

Phone calls, meetings, reports, phone calls, lunches, presentations, more phone calls... these are the mediums through which the work gets done and the relationship gets built – it's not the golf games that everyone jokes about nor the expense-account lunches.

The account manager has full responsibility for what happens on the account but in many cases has no hard authority to order anyone in the agency to do anything. Success in account management takes finesse, intelligence, intuition, focus, and a passion for the business.

Good account managers are well organized, thorough, and perhaps most of all, possess an infectious desire to create and be a part of great advertising. They are leaders by nature and good communicators. They combine creative problem-solving with sensible decision-making. They thrive on chaos and can adjust to rapid changes in direction and environment.

Much of what an effective account manager does is invisible and unplanned.

It may be a long-term, behind-the-scenes effort to build client trust, or the ability to read situations and people.

Bringing order out of chaos, making the most of a disaster, instinctively making good judgment calls, being quick afoot and passionately articulate – this is account management.

The Roles of an Account Manager.

There are many ways to define the role of the account manager. This book presents a variety of perspectives on the subject, each dealing with a different perspective, level of detail, or subtlety.

For starters, and in very general terms, here is what the account manager does in the agency process of serving a client.

Is the Conduit for **All** the Information That Flows between Client and Agency.

There is an incredible flow of information and material between the client and the agency. The account manager is the gatekeeper, the external traffic cop. It is inefficient to have numerous agency people calling one client contact, or even worse, numerous people at the client company.

The account manager is the "go to" person at the agency. If the media department has a question and the account manager does not know the answer, then guess whose responsibility it is to call the client and get the answer? Hint: in the large majority of cases, it's not the media department.

Likewise, when the client has to report that the latest round of ad copy needs some additional changes, the client does not call the copywriter, he calls the account manager.

There may occasionally be a conversation between the client and someone at the agency other than the account manager, but the need for the conversation was discussed with the account manager.

After the independent contact with the client, the first order of business for the other agency person is to provide the details of the conversation to the account manager. To not do so puts the agency at risk of making a mistake or wasting time.

It is extremely important that these independent client contacts be reported to the account manager. Creative people and others in the agency are not responsible for the "big picture" client relationship. They are specialists.

The account manager is the only generalist in the agency who can see that some new input may have larger consequences for a project or the agency-client relationship.

This may sound paranoid. To some degree it is. But when you read Chapter 5.1, "Journey of the Job," you will start to really appreciate the amount of detail that needs to be communicated, both within the agency and with the client.

Represents Collective Agency Expertise to the Client and Collective Client Expertise to the Agency.
Agency departments include creative, media, account planning, research, sales promotions, direct response, PR, interactive, production, legal, accounting, and others. The account manager is expected to know 80% of what all the agency specialists know.

For example, the account manager is expected to know 80% of what the media director knows about media research, planning, negotiating, etc. Why? Because the client looks to the account manager to explain and justify agency recommendations.

Similarly, the account manager is expected to speak for the agency, to know a whole lot about creativity and why the agency is recommending one creative strategy over another. The same for advertising research, online, sales promotion, and all the other services provided by the agency or purchased by the agency for the client.

Likewise, the agency team needs the account manager to be an expert on the client's marketing plans, their organization, product line, customers and markets, their industry and competitors, even their internal politics.

Account managers are expected to know the client's goals and how they measure success in advertising. This knowledge serves the client and the agency well. It makes the agency more efficient and it adds value to what the agency brings to the table.

It also earns the account manager the respect needed to be the hub of the action.

This notion of "becoming the client to the agency" is a delicate balancing act. Account managers who become too much like the client do everyone a disservice.

The account manager serves the agency by knowing a lot about the client's products, markets and organization. But in becoming averse to risk, as many clients are, the account manager can inhibit the agency's ability to do bold work for the account.

Initiates and Coordinates Agency Work.
No project is undertaken by any agency department unless the proper documents are prepared. The account manager does this.

Good input is the stuff good agency work is made of. If you can get account managers to speak candidly about assignments that weren't as successful or as smooth as they could have been, you can usually trace the root cause to substandard input at the start of a project.

When it is said that account managers initiate agency work, it means they have done everything possible to ensure that the project gets off to a good start. Research, product briefs, campaign briefs, creative briefs, objectives, reasonable budgets, and deadlines – these are the things that matter.

Oh, and don't forget the inspiration. The specialists in your agency need to know how and why each project is important. Take every opportunity to bring research to life, to enlighten, to be the inspirational leader as well as the effective project manager.

After you have successfully presented and secured client approval for agency proposals, your work is far from over. There are deadlines to meet, in-process approvals to be obtained, and budgets to stay within. These will not happen unless you make them happen.

While the creative, production, and media specialists take over the projects at this time to accomplish what you got approved, any account manager who sits back and thinks everything will run on schedule is asking for trouble.

Agency production people manage many projects at once. It's amazing they do as good a job as they do. The quantity and quality of information you provide, your management of expectations, the problems you have anticipated, and the degree to which you are on top of things will all determine how smoothly things go in the production phase.

"Expediting the client" is very much a part of the efficient flow of work through the agency. Getting client approvals on time, retrieving production materials, and helping clients make decisions that keep things moving – these are all examples of expediting the client.

Fosters a Creative Environment.

Clients hire agencies for ideas. Ideas are the products of inspiration, vision, insight, innovation, intuition, and risk taking – in short a creative environment. But this environment does not happen automatically or all the time, without some nurturing.

The account manager must be sensitive to all of the pressures and behaviors that can dampen the creative spirit.

Manages Expectations.

Understanding what advertising can and cannot do is key to successful client relations. Understanding people's limitations is equally critical. Whether it is setting the right objectives for a campaign or setting the right budget for a project, if you manage the expectations up front, you'll save yourself a lot of grief later.

Areas of expectation management can include such issues as what a project will look like, what it will accomplish, what it will cost, how long it will take, and how much client involvement will be needed.

When we focus on managing expectations, we're not talking lowered expectations, pessimism, or sandbagging. We're talking about reality – expectations based on knowledge and experience.

We're talking about never making a commitment you aren't 100% sure can be met. It's great to be caught up in the excitement of the day. But remember, you are the one who has to deliver.

Managing client expectations is only part of the deal.

You also have to manage the expectations of everyone in the agency relative to your performance. This includes senior management.

Communicating clearly and early about what is expected of everyone will serve you, the agency, and the client well.

If you're still not clear on what managing expectations looks like, here is a short list:

- Making sure that everyone knows what the end result of an activity is supposed to be. How is success going to be measured?
- Ensuring that everyone knows which specific actions and processes are needed and who is responsible for doing them.
- Making sure everyone knows deadlines, budgets, and check-points.

This is basic project management and communication, with an emphasis on making sure performance and expectations are realistic.

Participates in Many Ways.

The account manager's job isn't just about administration. In today's "collaborative model" for creating advertising, you do actually get to participate in the fun stuff, the stuff you will ultimately have to evaluate and present. Depending on the project and the agency culture, you may participate in creative strategy meetings as an advisor or as a player in the creative process.

Exactly what role the account manager plays in creative work depends on two things:

1. Whether the creative culture of the agency is inclusive or exclusive of account people
2. Whether the creative people respect you as being able to add something to the creative process without getting in their way

There is much more on working with creatives later. Suffice to say right now that the job of account manager is most fun when you are allowed to participate creatively.

To do so is a right that others give you because you can stimulate them and then walk away to let them do their work.

Advertising is an idea business.

The account manager, while primarily a manager, has tremendous opportunity to contribute to the end product. Giving people ideas, information, stimulation, and encouragement are important ways to participate on another level.

Chapter 5.1, "Journey of the Job," explains 43 (last time I counted) steps where an account manager touches a typical campaign. Almost every step provides some opportunity for the account manager to make a contribution to the substance and effectiveness of the work.

Normally, the smaller the agency, the more the account manager is involved in all aspects of the work. In specialty agencies such as public relations or sales promotion, account managers can have significant creative or media responsibilities.

Evaluates Agency Proposals before They Go to the Client. As the person ultimately responsible for everything that is done by the agency, the account manager plays the extremely important roles of sounding board, judge, and gatekeeper. Not an easy job sometimes.

Before ad concepts, media plans, production proofs, billings, or anything else goes to the client, the account manager has the responsibility to evaluate it and ultimately approve its final form.

Creative proposals are by far the "diciest" area. (See Chapter 4.2, "What Creatives Want," for details.)

This evaluation stage is one more area where the account manager really needs to earn the respect of coworkers who bring forth their proposals. It's important that you understand you are critiquing the sincere work of others.

This must be done with the utmost professionalism and objectivity. The work of copywriters and art directors is their art. It must be treated and respected as such.

Whether you like it is not the issue.

The real issue is whether you think the proposals meet the objectives set forth in the campaign and creative briefs.

It's important that creative teams know your evaluation will be based on objectives and strategies – not your personal tastes, fear of the client, or some other hidden agenda.

Leads the Client.

The contemporary advertising agency is a professional service provider. Agencies are hired for their expertise and their ability to lead the client in all areas of marketing communication.

How successful the agency is in leading (in a macro-sense) depends on how successful the account manager is in leading on a micro-sense. This definition of leading is unique to advertising.

It means to anticipate, to push, to challenge, to keep clients aware of their environments, to move clients outside their comfort zone and sometimes to be a royal pain in the rear with persistence and conviction for an unpopular view.

Some clients who have a lot of other responsibilities can easily get lazy. They're happy to just do what they did last year in the way of advertising. "New for the sake of new" is something the agency must avoid.

But if the account's advertising needs a major infusion of energy, the account manager must lead the charge.

Conversely, there are clients who get tired of their own ad campaign before it has had a chance to work in the marketplace. Due to an extremely long production schedule, I had a client actually get tired of a TV commercial and suggest we do a new one before the spot ever ran. He had totally lost track of his own campaign.

Stellar agency work comes through strong account leadership – message-wise, media-wise, budget-wise. You get the idea.

Some clients inherently distrust creative people and their work because they think all that creative people want to do is build a portfolio using someone else's money. But clients will trust the account manager on the same creative work if the account manager is a strong leader.

Minds the Money.

In this case, money has three meanings: the client budget, the monthly billing, and the profitability of the account. These three items are also known as "The Three Bs": budgets, billings, and bottom line.

As a trusted advisor and "knower of all things," the account manager is the major architect of the client's budget. Once the budget is set, responsibility shifts to minding the client's budget to make sure that the agency lives within it.

Though some may chafe at having to stay within the budget, good account managers know that exceeding a budget without client OK can wreak havoc on the relationship.

Billings is an industry term with two definitions:

1. In the macro-sense, "billings" refers to the total dollar value of business done with a client each year.

2. In the micro-sense, "billings" means the actual bill the agency sends a client every month. One of the quickest ways to have problems with an account is to deliver sloppy billings.

Squeaky clean billings every month are absolutely imperative.

An account manager's job is demanding enough without the client distrusting your agency's bills.

Ultimately an account and the account manager are going to be evaluated on the basis of the bottom line. What you want internally as an account manager is a reputation as someone who "runs profitable accounts."

Grows the Business.

A primary duty of an account manager is to constantly look for ways to increase the billings on the account.

This will often come from successfully pitching another agency service that heretofore has not been used.

For example, this could be a successful effort to move the client's Web site business from an interactive shop to the agency's interactive department.

This upselling has two positive results: increasing billings and increasing the client's dependence on the agency.

Accounts can also be grown by finding new ways for the client to increase sales through more marketing communications vehicles. Account managers with the ability to grow client billings are more quickly tapped for advancement and given "new business" responsibilities.

Nurtures the Client Relationship.
The relationship between the client contact and the account manager can become very close, transcending the day-to-day business relationship. Some become steadfast friends. It may sound trite, but advertising is still a people business.

A strong personal friendship can benefit both sides of the agency-client relationship. Two people can enjoy each other's company, confide in each other, and still be able to be frank on business matters. This is the ideal situation.

When a client knows and likes the account manager on a personal basis, the client is more likely to be forthcoming with concerns about some aspect of the agency-client relationship.

As an example, there was a year or so when my agency's creative work was judged as somewhat lackluster. I knew that one of my biggest and most prestigious clients (who is still a friend) wanted to put the agency through a review. But he didn't. Why? Because we were friends.

Overall, the agency performance was good in every other service area and he knew that I would do everything I could to fix the problem. And we did. Without a review.

The personal relationship between account manager and client is a matter of trust and mutual respect. When a client understands you are a true friend, they know that you will do everything you can to make them look good and to make their job easier.

Within their own organizations, client contacts may not always get the respect they deserve, but when they are dealing with the agency, they should always feel respected and appreciated.

Clients can feel a lot of pressure inside their own organization. At the risk of being melodramatic, some clients say that sometimes it seems as if it's them and their account manager against the rest of the world.

Makes a Better Client.

In addition to all of the functions and all of the hats worn, a key function of the account manager is to "make a better client."

Now what the heck does that mean?

In Chapter 7.2, "In Search of the Ideal Client," you will find the description of what agencies would like every account to be. It's your job to spot where your client is deficient, where there is opportunity for improvement, and where, given all the demands on your time and talents, you are likely to achieve the most improvement for your efforts.

No client is perfect. What you want is a reputation for being able to take any client and make them better.

You do this through a combination of insight, talent, persistence, and your growing ability to get the client to trust your leadership. Good clients value good account managers.

Sleeps Occasionally.

ZZZZZZZZZZZZZZZZZZZZZZZZZZZ... with one eye open.

2.2 Master of the Mixes

In the broadest marketing perspective there are actually three "mixes" where the account manager is expected to have expertise. The first, as every marketing student knows, is the marketing mix, also known as the 4Ps: Product, Price, Place (channels of distribution), and Promotion. Account managers are expected to know the details of every account's 4Ps. You can't serve the needs of your accounts without this knowledge.

With special reference to the fourth P, there is an ever-growing array of communication mediums from which a marketer can choose. The success of every marketing communications campaign depends on the insighful selection, intelligent use, and effective integration of these mediums.

The Promotional Mix.

The textbook definition of the promotional mix is the complete list of marketing communication mediums available.

The purpose of this chapter is to demonstrate and emphasize the breadth of the expertise that the account manager must possess. Simply put, the account manager must know more about more things than anyone else.

Here is a sample promotional mix. Because of the speed at which new advertising mediums are being developed, any published list would soon be incomplete and obsolete. And, of course, different mixes will be more effective for different clients and programs.

The main purpose of this list is to demonstrate the breadth of the working knowledge an account manager must have in the area of media and all other communications tools.

- Traditional measured media (radio, television, newspaper, magazine, outdoor/transit)
- Interactive media (Internet ads, Web sites, promotional e-mail, viral marketing)
- Collateral and multimedia (brochures, CDs, videos)
- Packaging
- Customer relations management
- Product placements on television, movies, and Internet
- Direct response (direct mail, DR TV)
- Trade-show exhibits
- Co-op ad programs
- Events
- Point of sale
- Signage, wallscapes, and vehicle graphics
- Publicity
- Multicultural marketing
- Sales promotions (contests, coupons, sweepstakes, sampling, etc.)

- Advertising specialties
- Telemarketing and customer service
- Cause-related campaigns
- Trade relations
- Peripheral media (restrooms, gas pump-toppers, etc.)

The inclusion of packaging, trade shows, publicity, sales promotions, collateral materials, promotional e-mails, point of sale displays, and a host of other mediums demonstrates that the agency must master mediums that go way beyond traditional measured mass media.

The Media Mix.

The mediums actually selected for a specific campaign are often called the "media mix" even though things like new packaging, truck signage, and in-store sampling are not media in the traditional sense.

The term "media" has taken on a broader definition to include anything and everything that delivers a message to an audience – from labels on bananas to blimps.

Clients expect the entire promotional mix to be considered when the agency is crafting their MarCom plan. In order to select the best possible mix of mediums from all those available, someone at the agency has to know something about everything in the promotional mix, especially new media.

Clients expect their agency to stay current about media developments, and they will ask their account managers about the latest new advertising medium.

In practice (especially in small- and medium-sized agency offices), the account manager is ultimately responsible for the selection of the media mix and for writing the integrated communications plan that explains how everything works together.

In this respect, the account manager is a lot like an architect, conceiving the overall design, selecting the materials, and drawing the construction plans.

Strengths and Weaknesses.

On the next page, we've built a "MarCom Matrix": a spreadsheet that indicates the strengths and weaknesses of the various types of marketing communications. Let's review them in that context.

Advertising.

With advertising, you have total control of your message. You can say exactly what you want in exactly the medium you want to say it.

On the other hand, it can be quite expensive, target selection in mass media can be imprecise, and there are a lot of other people out there adding to the noise level.

Advertising is particularly good for new products and growing categories, packaged goods brands with frequent purchase, and durable goods brands where you have a strong story to tell.

Advertising is good at reinforcing purchase decisions and usually works best when you can afford some frequency.

Public Relations (and Publicity).

"Third-party endorsement" can be powerful. When a newspaper or magazine has something good to say about your product, it can be very effective – just think of how many times you've been affected by a good restaurant or movie review.

More and more, smart marketers are looking to find some sort of PR leverage for their brands – whether it's promoting commercials in the Super Bowl or connecting their brands to local events and charitable efforts ("cause marketing" is one very effective example).

When it works, it can be quite effective. However, you often have very little control over getting your good news into the media.

For start-ups with tiny budgets, getting PR is a must. You need to keep up the pressure with press releases and other media efforts.

Event Marketing.

A relatively new and growing area of MarCom, event marketing offers unique opportunities for consumers to sample or otherwise "experience" your brand. It ranges from local events to international spectaculars like the Olympics.

The MarCom Matrix Strengths & Weaknesses: Six Forms of Marketing Communications

Factor	Advertising	Public Relations	Event Marketing	Direct Response	Sales Promotion	New Media/Internet
Timing	moderate/long	long	long	short	short	immediate
Control of Message Delivery	total	little	moderate	moderate	moderate	high
Control of Message Content	total	minimal	high	high	high	total
Ability to Target	high	low	moderate	very high	moderate	moderate
Type of Contact	nonpersonal	nonpersonal	nonpersonal/ personal	nonpersonal/ personal	nonpersonal/ personal	personal
Typical Appeals	emotional/ rational	image/news	experiential personal	rational	rational	rational/ emotional
Added Perceived Value	high	high	moderate	moderate	low	varies
Credibility	low	high	moderate	low	moderate	moderate
Closes Sale	low	low	low	moderate	high	moderate
Trade Acceptability	high	low	high	moderate	very high	problematic (w. trade)
Expense	high	low	high	high	moderate	moderate
Accountability	low	very low	low	very high	very high	high
Profit Contribution	moderate	low	low	moderate	high	small (currently)

Examples include cause marketing, where your brand can hook up with a worthy cause; sports marketing, where you team up with local teams or activities like a marathon; and on-campus events, where you connect with your target with a card table and free T-shirts. In some fields, trade shows are very important.

It can be expensive, but sometimes it's your best option.

Direct Response.

As they say in direct marketing, "you're as good as your list." If you have a good database, such as a list of current customers, direct response can be a smart way to spend some of your marketing dollars. Even though it's expensive on a per-person basis, it's very measurable and you can test with a smaller group before you send your message to everybody.

If you have e-mail addresses in your database, so much the better. With the right message and incentive, it can be a tremendously cost-effective way of maximizing the value of your customers.

Sales Promotion.

When sales promotion is done well, you see a spike in sales. It can be effective in getting the trade to feature your product and getting velocity with impulse purchases. To some extent, you have control of the message, but much of the message focus may have to be on the incentive rather than the brand.

On the other hand, it can be quite expensive – remember, those incentives can be costly. And in competitive categories you may be competing with another great deal right across the aisle.

Sales promotions tend to be used in mature product categories as an incentive for the trade, as well as for consumers.

New Media/Internet.

This exciting field changes everytime you log in. In ten years, it has become a part of virtually every marketer's promotional mix, whether merely an information Web site or a full-blown e-commerce effort.

On the short-term, don't be overoptimistic, but smart marketing can show solid results. And for virtually every form of MarCom, there's a new media variation.

In advertising, marketers like BMW and Nike have found exciting ways to drive traffic to their Web sites with movies and interactive commercial messages.

All sorts of PR programs can benefit with an Internet platform for online press conferences. Informational Web sites can support events.

Direct programs using an e-mail database can be very effective if done well. And the Internet can do everything from delivering promotional incentives, to online contests, to linking up with promotional partners.

It's not a perfect world, though. Sometimes online e-commerce efforts can anger your traditional marketing partners (Levi's had to pull back when their retail Web site angered stores selling Levi's), and with all the options online, volumes can often be quite low.

But, when you have a "hit," you know right away because you can measure your "hits."

Mastering the Mix.

You will often have more opportunities than budget. Every ad program wants more frequency. Every promotional and direct program wants bigger incentives and trade discounts. The event opportunities are almost infinite and, if you have good PR people, they'll always be in there pitching.

In each case, you'll be comparing apples with oranges with avocados and, trust me, you'll never have a big enough budget to do it all.

Still, smart decision making can be the difference between a program that's only okay and one that knocks everyone's socks off. Every marketing situation is different, so I can't give you any hard and fast rules or recipes for cooking up the best promotional mix – except one.

Those who do it well have successful careers. Good luck.

2.3 Shop Talk: Learning the Language of Account Management

Like most industries, advertising has its own language.

There are hundreds of key terms listed in any advertising textbook. The account manager is the only person in the agency who is expected to know all the terms used throughout the industry and across all disciplines.

Remember, the same term may mean something else outside the business. For example, when you're talking about a CD, it's usually your creative director, not some of your favorite music.

Within the industry lexicon, account management has its own lingo. These are terms you might have used many times before, but now they take on a new meaning. In an effort to give a true flavor of the business, I have attempted to put as much revealing "shop talk" as possible into the book. (Note: suggestions for this working list are welcome.)

Account coordinator: The entry level job for future account managers.

Account executive: The old term referring to the primary agency contact person.

Account planning: The hybrid research/creative function that is intended to represent the voice of the customer.

Accountability: Popular term among direct response and business-to-business agencies. Refers to the ability to quantify the results of advertising in terms sales or other hard metrics beyond changes in target audience attitude and awareness.

Advertising objective: Advertising does three things: changes knowledge, changes attitude, and changes behavior. Ad objectives should focus on these.

Agency network: Holding companies like Interpublic Group (IPG) that own most of the large agencies in the world.

Agency review: The process that clients use when deciding to keep their current agency or hire a new one.

À la carte services: A single service (such as creative, media, graphic design, or PR) provided to an advertiser who is not a full-fledged client.

Bag man: A highly derogatory name for old-style account people whose only concern is keeping the client happy.

Bells and whistles: Special things presented in a new business pitch to impress prospective clients.

Below the line: Specialty agency services like sales promotion, interactive, or public relations.

Billings: A dollar value used to define the size of an account and the monthly invoice that goes to the client

Blueline: A black-and-white proof of a print ad or brochure used to correct for errors before a color proof is pulled. (From the days before computers – some places still use them.)

Boards: Storyboards.

Book: A portfolio of work kept for job hunting or business solicitation purposes.

Boutique: An agency that specializes in only one type of service, such as creative, or one type of advertising, such as business-to-business.

Brand contact management: An attempt to manage all the ways that a brand communicates with its customers.

Brand equity: The strength of the brand in the consumer's mind and the dollar value it represents to the company.

Brand personality: If a brand were a person, how would it be described?

Brand Stewardship Report (MarCom annual report): A report that summarizes the contribution the agency made to the growth and vitality of the brand.

Brief: Creative brief.

Buy: A noun. Another name for a media schedule.

CD: Creative director.

Call report: Sometimes meaning a conference report, but most often a written summary of a telephone conversation.

Campaign brief: A larger planning document than the creative brief. It contains all parameters of the campaign.

Cannes: An international advertising award competition.

Capitalized billings: If all agency income were converted to 15% media commissions, how much media billing would that be?

Category: The product classification, like subcompact cars or regular cola drinks, assigned by a big research company like Simmons.

Category review: A detailed analysis of all players within a product category for purposes of spotting new-product, marketing, or advertising opportunities.

Cause related: When a charity is involved in and benefits from advertising promotion.

CLIO: Arguably the top advertising awards competition in the U.S.

Clean: A term used to refer to creative work that is simple and effective.

Closing date: When the contract and material are due in a print media buy.

Collateral: Brochures, mailers, and other printed material.

Comp: A comprehensive, full-size, detailed layout, as opposed to a "rough" or a thumbnail.

Competitive benchmarks: Competitive points of reference that the client's advertising needs to be better than or different from.

Conference report: A basic communications document that summarizes a meeting (or teleconference) between the client and the account manager. See Chapter 3.2, "The Conference Report and Call Reports."

Consultative selling: Making recommendations to the client and then being accountable for the results.

Convergence: Multiple-media packages offered by companies who own print and broadcast media.

Co-op: Advertising dollars made available by brands for dealers who want to advertise the brand on a local basis.

Copy/contact: An account manager who also does the creative work.

Copy platform: Another term for copy strategy; sometimes refers to the theme line or concept that unifies the creative approach.

Creative brief: The document prepared by the account manager and/or account planner to give direction to the creative team.

Creative cycle: The time from initial creative input meeting with creative team present until the time the client actually approves something.

Creative guidelines: A list written in the creative brief that states the functional expectations of the creative solution.

Creative Rationale: A document which tells why a specific creative recommendation is very good.

Creative shoot out: An agency review with heavy emphasis on creative ideas.

Creative strategy: The communications strategy part of the overall marketing strategy – how the creative objective will be accomplished.

Credentials presentation: Part of the agency review process where agencies present previous work and show off the expertise of key personnel.

CRM: Customer relationship management.

DP: Director of photography, aka "cameraman." Often found on the set of commercial shoots and large budget print photo shoots.

Deliverables: A term used by public sector clients to describe the tangible things they purchase from agencies.

Discovery: The input meeting and process of gaining input from the client on a new campaign.

Dog and pony show: A slick and comprehensive display of creative work intended to impress a prospective client or an important person from an existing client.

DM: Direct marketing.

DR: Direct response.

Execution: How a creative concept actually gets expressed in the ad.

Executional considerations: A certain type of creative input. Do's and don'ts. Sometimes includes legal restrictions.

FAB: Features, advantages, and benefits.

Flesh out (not flush out): To put meat on a basic concept, to demonstrate what it will look like when produced.

Full service: A term meaning the agency offers most, if not all, of the MarCom services an account needs.

Gatekeeper: Someone who manages the flow of information, materials, and people to and from the agency to the client.

Gross rate: A price for media space or time that includes an agency commission.

GRP: Gross rating points, also called "grips."

Grip: Someone on a commercial shoot who does the heavy work and set up.

Heavy breather: A senior agency principal who is especially good at presentations and client relations.

Hot button: Something that's important to the account or the target.

IMC: Integrated marketing communications.

Income: Agency revenue after all internal expenses are deducted.

Inoculation: During presentation, dealing with objections before they come up.

Insight: Important knowledge about the target audience that will translate to creative.

Intangibles: Those things that are hard to measure but are very important to the client-agency relationship.

Integration: Making the pieces of a campaign work together.

Killer creative: Strong, breakthrough ideas.

Layout: A computer-generated or hand-rendered visual used in concept presentations to show what a finished ad would look like.

Leave behind: The summarized written proposal left with the prospective account after the pitch.

Legs: A creative concept that has multiple executions over time.

Lifetime value (LTV): A calculation of what a customer represents in the way of sales revenue over a specific period of time.

MarCom: A term that grew out of the hi-tech industry. Short for "marketing communications."

Measured media: Any media where a third party provides audience delivery data. Traditionally, measured media have been radio, television, outdoor, magazines, and newspapers. The Internet is still working on acceptable third-party reporting.

Mechanical: A word from an earlier age that means the finished composition of a printed piece before it goes to proofing stage.

Media mix: All message vehicles (measured, new, nontraditional, collateral, and others) selected by the agency for a specific campaign.

Media objective: What the media buy is intended to accomplish in the way of audience delivery, cost efficiency, or tactical considerations.

Mock ups: Another word for medium to tight layouts.

Net rate: A price of print or broadcast media that does not include an agency commission.

Network: See "agency network."

New business: Soliciting and competing for new accounts.

One Show: The creative awards competition jointly sponsored by the Art Directors Club and Copywriters Clubs of New York.

One stop shop: An agency that offers all the communications services that a client needs.

Open ground: Finding a creative approach or marketing concept that no one else is using.

Performance bonus: A financial bonus given to the agency for reaching preset goals for an ad campaign.

Pitch: The act of presenting, especially in a new business context.

Point of view: A certain creative style or approach to advertising.

POP: Point of purchase.

POS: Point of sale or point of service.

Pro-bono: Professional services provided by the agency free of charge to charity or public service accounts.

Promotional mix: All the various communications vehicles to choose from: measured media, sales promotion, public relations, events, etc.

Proactive: Being ahead of the client. Example: offering unsolicited ideas.

Propeller heads: Techies who design the back-end of Web sites and sometimes try to design the user interface.

RFP: Request for proposal. The basic tool used by public sector clients to describe the work they need done by an agency and the process for agency selection.

Seamless: Making the agency seem like a well-oiled machine to the client. No hitches, no bitches, no muss, no fuss.

Shoot: The filming of a commercial or a still photograph session.

Shoot out: A creative competition for new business.

Shops: Another word for ad agencies.

Short list: The list of finalists in an agency review.

Shot list: The list of shot or set-ups that the director will cover during a film or video shoot.

SKU: Stock keeping unit. Every different item in a product line has its own SKU code. Twelve different items = 12 different "Skews."

Spec: Speculative creative work. Done at the agency's expense in hopes of winning a new client.

Specialty items: Coffee cups, golf balls, and anything else you can put a logo on.

Status report: A progress report issued periodically by the agency. See Chapter 3.5, "The Status Report."

Strategy: Broad strokes of how goals are to be accomplished.

Suit: An outmoded nickname for account managers.

Tactics: Specific actions. The details of how strategies are going to be executed is often called a "tactical plan."

Tight: Describes amount of detail and specificity in a layout.

Thumbnail: A smallish, rough layout of a print ad or brochure.

Traffic: The department inside the agency that manages the movement of projects.

Trailboss: A project manager.

Value added: The value the agency brings to the client that the client could not provide themselves.

Vendor campaign: Special retailer advertising campaign that is paid for mostly by the brand being advertised. Not the same as co-op.

Write off: When the agency absorbs charges it normally would have billed to the client.

2.4 The Money Side of the Business

As account manager, you will deal with a lot more numbers than you probably expected. Sometimes you may even wonder what business you are in – advertising or accounting.

Chapter 3.7, "Billings, Budgets, and Financial Management," discusses the full range of account manager responsibilities relative to financial issues. The purpose of this chapter is to explain how agencies make money and how the evolution of agency compensation has had a profound impact on the importance of the account manager.

Financial responsibilities for account managers fall into these categories:

1. Revenue/Agency compensation
2. Billing
3. Budget management
4. Forecasting
5. Account profitability

Revenue/Agency Compensation.

The modern agency has several sources of revenue:

1. Media commissions
2. Production mark-ups
3. Retainers
4. Project fees
5. Hourly service fees
6. Performance bonuses

As the following discussion will reveal, media commissions once were the king of agency compensation. Now, many agencies like to have accounts that have 50% or less of their MarCom budget in media. Such a budget normally allows the agency to provide a wider variety of fee-based services.

For many account managers, especially young ones, the compensation agreement between the agency and the client is something that is hammered-out between the top management of the two companies.

Nonetheless, it's important that you understand how agency compensation works. You may not be responsible for developing the compensation agreement, but you will have responsibility for account profitability and might have to answer questions about it.

As agency profit margins have been squeezed and agency income migrates to a fee-for-service basis, it is more important than ever that time is used efficiently and managed effectively. The account manager bears ultimate responsibility for making this happen.

Media Commissions.

Until about 1985 most agency revenue was tied to the 15% media commission. Simply put, this media commission system of agency compensation provided the agency with $15 worth of gross revenue for every $100 in client advertising it placed in the traditional measured media (television, radio, magazine, newspaper, and billboard).

If, for instance, a full page in the *Wall Street Journal* cost $100,000, the agency would bill the client $100,000 for the ad, pay the paper $85,000, and retain $15,000 as earned income.

The history of the 15% media commission system dates back to the time when publications had to prepare ads for advertisers because there were no agencies. Publications then started to grant commissions to a new type of business established to create ads, the ad agency. The media commission was the driving force behind the creation of the agency business.

When radio and television came of age, they followed suit with the media commission to recognized agencies.

The result of the media commission system was twofold. First, some agencies maintained an allegiance to commissionable media when peripheral media, such as direct mail, might have been a better tool for the client. Second, advertising agencies became increasingly profitable.

Income increased as media prices rose, but the agencies did not necessarily have to do any more work for that increased income.

Clients got wise to this. At the same time, some agencies started to cut the commission rate as a way of attracting new business. Today, the media commission is still in use, but it is only one component of the agency income and is often now negotiated at less than 15%.

Production Mark-Ups.

The advertising agency owns no printing presses, no video production studios, no direct mail list brokers or research firms. Yet, in the service of its clients, the agency may purchase services from all of these companies and many more, such as trade show display builders, commercial artists, and radio voice talent.

Purchase of outside services – such as photography or video production – is the result of professional communications services being rendered by specialists inside the agency. In recognition that managing these professional services also needs to be compensated, the production mark-up was born. The production mark-up essentially says that the client will allow the agency to add a certain percentage to each outside purchase.

Production markups are a set percentage that normally run from 5% to 25%.

So a $10,000 photography bill to the agency becomes a $12,000 bill to the client under a 20% production mark-up agreement.

Unlike media commissions, which are computed as part of a gross media rate, production mark-ups are add-ons to a net rate. You need to understand the difference in how these two are computed.

Hourly Service Fees.

As media commissions have become smaller, the biggest change in agency revenue has come in service fees. As the agency has become more of a consultancy, the hourly fee has become more the accepted norm. Hourly fees for specific talents such as media planning, copywriting, art direction, and account management are set in the working agreement between agency and client.

As services are rendered, "billable" hourly charges are accumulated and billed at the end of the month, in the same way a law firm does it. The amount of hourly rate service fees billed to a client will vary with the load of work going through the agency. Sometimes this is applied against a set fee or retainer.

Service fees have the advantage of placing a monetary value on what agency employees do for clients and also making "billable" agency employees much more aware of how they use their time.

Project Fees.

Instead of having set hourly rates that are charged as work is done, project fees are (as the name would indicate) project specific.

They normally involve larger projects and are most common when the agency and the client have no continuing working relationship beyond the project at hand.

The agency looks at the specifications for the job, say a brochure. In addition to estimating how much the photography and printing will cost, they'll estimate how many hours will be required by the creative department, production and traffic department, and account service.

All of these billable agency hours will be added as a project fee to the outside production expenses such as printing and photography.

Unless the specifications of the job change dramatically, the agency project fee is set. If the agency can deliver the job using fewer hours than estimated, the agency makes more profit on the assignment. If it takes more time than estimated, agency profit is less and the estimator gets shot at sundown.

Retainers.

Much like the retainers of legal and accounting firms, agency retainers estimate the number and type of agency staff hours needed to service the account and then multiplies those hours by the hourly rate for each staffer involved.

Retainers can cover all people at the agency used in service to the client or can be limited to specific people such as account managers, media planners, or creatives. Retainers can also be the only form of income for an account or can be used in combination with commissions, mark-ups, project fees, and service fees.

A retainer is usually set on an annual basis, one-twelfth of which is billed each month as a lump sum "agency retainer."

Performance Bonuses.

In an effort to make agencies feel more accountable for the results of their work, some clients have introduced the concept of lower levels of compensation in some areas and big bonuses if preset and agreed-upon goals are met. Though risky, some agencies have taken up the challenge of the performance bonus.

The goals on which performance bonuses are predicated are things like increases in awareness levels, increases in brand personality recall, number of inquiries for information, sometimes even sales or market share.

For example, a client may insist on a slightly lower retainer but offer the agency a $100,000 performance bonus if campaign results exceed the goals set for it.

The risk in bonuses based on reaching a goal is that advertising is just one part of the marketing mix. Sales or market share increases, for instance, can be as much the result of aggressive pricing or new distribution as they are of a great ad campaign.

Even more, communications-based measurements such as brand awareness and benefit recall can't be totally attributed to advertising alone. Agencies with a performance bonus have used it as leverage to gain more control over the client's total ad budget. The argument goes like this... *"OK beloved client, we will happily take on the performance bonus challenge BUT with the following conditions. If we're going to be judged on performance, we want total control of all the elements that can affect the result.*

"That means the sales promotion business you have been giving to that sales promotion agency... we get it. That Web site design redo that is so badly needed... we do it. That new storefront design you were going to do in-house... we do it. That publicity being done by your PR agency... we get it."

If performance is going to affect revenue and account profitability, then agencies are demanding control of all communications-based activities. Point of sale, product placements, interactive, packaging, and more. If it carries a message and is a brand contact, they want it. And rightly so.

Assuming the agency has acceptable capabilities in all areas, the performance bonus can be a winning idea for everyone involved. The performance bonus also puts additional responsibility for account profitability on the account manager, who will be managing an expanded list of services being provided to the client.

BUZZ:

In Search of a New Definition.
by Noreen O'Leary, AdWeek, *April 22, 1996*

Selecting the means of (client) communication is one of the biggest factors changing the way account managers ply their trade.

At the very least, ad execs say, they face new pressures to be familiar with marketing disciplines ranging from public relations and direct marketing to promotions. *"It's not enough anymore to think just in terms of advertising,"* says Mullen Inc.'s chief operating officer Joe Grimaldi.

"It's not a matter of being a generalist," Grimaldi adds. "It's a matter of being an expert in more than one thing, to think broadly while never losing your expertise."

Even if the agency is not the provider of all the client's marketing services, account managers should position themselves as coordinators of those disciplines. "We don't have to own all these elements, but to the degree the agency controls the process, it will be all right," says Ed Wax, chief executive of Saatchi & Saatchi Advertising Worldwide. "But we have to have account people who are trained to think this way."

To shore up their position, Wax says, account managers need to be recognized for more than client hand-holding. "We need the smartest people we can find who will take as much responsibility in the final result as any of their peers," he notes. "We feel more and more that account people should have their own reels and books."

Dick Costello, president of TBWA Chiat/Day, notes that good account executives are often underestimated, since their role is now spread so wide. "The account person, in a way, has the toughest job in the agency because he's had to interact with client, creatives, media, research. With really terrific account people, they have to be good at twelve different things, unlike other good advertising people, who have to be good at two or three things."

In a way, account managers must regain their power and status by acknowledging they've lost some of it. Says Kevin Allen, a senior vice president at McCann-Erickson: "The challenge for young people coming into account management is for them to know they are an advertising/marketing person first."

Want the Best Service? Look for Great Work.
by J.J. Jordan, J. Walter Thompson

Where do account managers fit in the aggressively evolving equation of agency value? Before I try to answer, let me share the fundamental belief I have about advertising and client service: The best service is great work. All the good meetings in the world won't mean a thing if they don't result in the production of great advertising. Likewise, clients can forgive a lot when your work is suddenly selling their product off the shelves. In the final analysis, that's what they want.

So the big question for me is, how can account people best contribute to making great work?

First, they must know their client's business. Deeply. And they must know their clients. The sign of a good relationship is not being pals with the client, although that's nice. Rather, it's knowing what the client needs to do.

Planners can tell us about the consumer, about who we're talking to, but it's the account person who must help us understand what brand and business goals must be accomplished. If we don't get that right, we're screwed from the start.

Then, as strategic and creative work develops, the account people have to manage the process. Keep it honest. Keep it open. And most of all, keep it clear. Clarity is key. Again, not just with the client, but with us, too. And not so that the process becomes an end in itself, but so that the process yields the best work. Again, don't be seduced by good meetings instead of good results.

All of this sounds obvious, and yet we've all been in situations where some of this has been overlooked. I'd rather have an account manager confront me with some grim reality early in the process than have the client hit me with it as I'm holding up the storyboards.

If you're an account person, ask yourself: Was the process better for having gone through you? Is the work better for your involvement?

Did you help solve a problem and make a great idea actually achievable? Did you quell the misgivings of a vocal naysayer?

Did your insight into the client's business contribute in any way to the advertising and ultimately the brand?

Did you help a nervous client gain confidence in something that could actually help their business?

Did you help enhance your agency's reputation?

Are you personally proud of the work?

If you can answer yes to even a couple of these questions, you already know your value in the agency equation. And so do your creatives.

Underappreciated, until You Need Them.

by Jon Steel; Goodby, Silverstein & Partners

I began my advertising career as an account management trainee and was dismayed, after a mere week on the job, to learn from a copywriter that "advertising would be much better without account management." Actually, he used words of fewer syllables, some unprintable, but I got the general idea.

Over the years, I have heard the same opinion expressed many times, on both sides of the Atlantic, by creatives, planners, and even clients. The underlying reason for that hostility is difficult to figure out, but I have concluded that it has much to do with the way that agencies traditionally define the roles of their departments.

Creatives, we say, are responsible for the ads. Planners represent the consumer, and account management represents the client.

Unfortunately, that description is not only inaccurate, it is damaging. And particularly damaging to account people.

The person who represents the client will never be the most popular employee in the agency, especially among creative people.

And even clients, their supposed friends, will sometimes turn their backs, being more interested in the people they see as responsible for the ads and for the strategy (in other words, the ones who are most different from them). "Those," I was told by another agency's client only last week, "are the people who make things happen. Account people are peripheral."

In my own experience, both in London and at GS&P, that couldn't be further from the truth. As a planner, I work in close partnership with many different account people, and there are no clear boundaries between us.

We take joint responsibility for both the advertising strategy and the quality of the creative work that emerges, and while we bring different craft skills to the process, we share jointly in almost every part of the process. They are deeply involved in consumer research, I in the client's business; together, we develop strategies and creative briefs, in conjunction with our creative teams, and we both work with the teams as they develop ideas.

Some people have the idea that in a strong creative agency, like GS&P, account management is weak by definition. On the contrary, the stronger the creative product, the stronger account management needs to be.

The best account people are also the best advertising people, and their greatest value comes not from their performance against a narrow job description, but from their contribution to the process as a whole. Incidentally, I'd say the same thing about the best planners, media, and creative people.

From Fresh Ideas to Whole Campaigns.

by Roger Baron; Foote, Cone & Belding

Clients hire an agency for great advertising that builds brand value. Great account managers quickly realize that the agency is the sum of its parts, not just the media department or the creative department or the account management department.

Their job is to field and lead the strongest brand management team they can put together.

Finding creative solutions to marketing problems is too pivotal to be left only to people with "creative" in their title.

It demands creativity from every corner, the kind that comes from a well-oiled team of marketing partners working in sync.

What skills do account managers have who get the best out of their media department?

- They possess a fundamental understanding of their client's business. They "get it" and have a missionary zeal to "share it," to provide as much brand information and marketing insight as possible to their partners.

- They have a thorough working knowledge of the media environment and the media department's capabilities. They speak our language and never promise what they can't deliver.

- They have been trained to look beyond media's stereotypical role of number crunching. They view media planning as idea generation and media people as inventors of new communications platforms that can advance the overall marketing strategy and creative product, whether that means special sponsorships, unique out-of-home ideas, or the Internet.

- They understand the client's strategic and political climate. They know when and how to challenge us to push the envelope with new ideas. They're willing to fight for the great ones and steer us away from land mines.

The best account managers, the ones we really look up to, are good business people and good human beings: opinionated, direct, honest, and open to new thinking. They value the expertise we bring to the table. They don't just assign projects, they communicate regularly. They celebrate victories and manage defeats. They have a sense of humor as well as a sense of responsibility.

If you're looking for creative media solutions to turn communication into persuasion, bring us in early – at the first strategy meeting and, often, every step of the way from creative briefings right through to the final presentation. Many times, we've found that a fresh media idea early on can spark an entire campaign.

Finally, be entrepreneurial. Look to media – demand from media – the same innovation you demand from your creative people.

When the advertising is great, all they'll remember is your agency did it. And there will be plenty of credit to go round.

JUICY CASES:

2.1: We Like You, But.....

About a year ago, your agency won the high profile ad account of a company run with an iron fist by a flamboyant eccentric entrepreneur, who, historically, has been extremely involved in the creation of his advertising.

Your hope at the time was that this dynamic executive would step back and let his new ad manager and your agency apply your respective expertise to his advertising.

Hard as you've tried, things have not gone smoothly on the creative side, so much so that none of your creative people want to work on the account.

In your latest meeting with this client, he admits that his advertising style is too important to him to let go very much.

He comes to the conclusion that no agency is going to make him happy, but he really likes you. You're the first agency person who has figured out how to deal with him.

He likes the way you and he interact in spontaneous ad creating sessions, where you act as a sounding board for his ideas and make frequent tactful observations that influence his thinking.

He tells you that his ad manager is leaving and he's going to set up an in-house advertising department to do his technical ads. The agency will no longer get any technical assignments, but he still wants to keep you involved as a sounding board and idea source on his ads.

He's happy to continue to run all of his media though the agency and let you collect the media commissions as compensation.

What do you do about this situation back at the agency?

2.2: I'll Know It When I See It.

You inherit an account from a departing account manager who was not extremely strong in his craft. The client has a reputation for being difficult to work with.

The problem can be summed up as the "I don't know what I want, but when I see it I'll know it" syndrome.

The client has paid for most, but not all, of the time expended by the creative department in trying to come up with something he will like.

What's the real problem here, and what are you going to do differently?

2.1: Computing Account Income

Here is the income report for an account which generates revenue from a variety of sources.

Using the facts below, do the following:

a. Compute total account revenue by adding up all six revenue sources.

b. Compute gross account income by deducting direct expenses from account revenue.

c. Compute agency overhead allocation percentage by dividing account revenue by agency revenue.

d. Compute agency overhead allocation in dollars by multiplying the total agency overhead by the allocation percentage (c).

e. Compute account pre-tax profit by deducting overhead allocation (d) from gross account income (b).

Facts:

Media commissions:
   10% commission on gross media billings of $6,770,000 = $_____

Production mark-ups:
   10% mark-up on $2,000,000 net vendor billing = $_____

Total service fees:
   $100/hr blended rate on 400 billable hours = $_____

Retainer:
   $5,000 per month = $_____

Project fees:
   $36,000 + $14,000 + $10,000 = $_____

Performance bonus:
   $50,000 for each new percentage of the target audience who include the client's brand in their consideration set. The benchmark was 38%. The new tracking study scored a 42. = $_____

Total direct internal charges = $400,000

Total agency revenue estimated = $30 million

Total agency overhead of $10,000 to be applied to each account as a percentage of total agency revenue.

2.2: Building a Mix Master Matrix.

The purpose of this exercise is to show how different clients use different communications vehicles in their media mix.

To do this exercise, build a matrix grid. (There's a work sheet on the next page.) On the left, list all the MarCom types found in the promotional mix, Chapter 2.2. Then set up three columns. Select three organizations in your city whose marketing communications programs are likely to be quite different from one another.

Examples of organizations to choose from could include: a restaurant chain, a manufacturer of nationally distributed consumer products, the city government, the largest hospital, a manufacturer of nationally distributed industrial products, and a large nonprofit organization.

Visit or call the three organizations and interview the person in charge of marketing communications. Identify the communications vehicles from the promotional mix list that make up each organization's marketing activities. Show them in three columns on your matrix.

The point of this exercise is this: All three organizations you selected could easily be handled by the same agency and by the same account manager within the agency. Note the diversity of communications vehicles and fields in which that account manager must be an expert.

BURNING QUESTIONS:

2.1: What is the relationship between a Creative Rationale and the practice of "inoculation?"

2.2: What is the connection between "integration" and the "one stop shop?"

MEDIA MIX MATRIX ANALYSIS:

POTENTIAL MEDIA	Organization #1 Name: Type of Business:	Organization #2 Name: Type of Business:	Organization #3 Name: Type of Business:
Television			
Radio			
Newspaper			
Magazine			
Outdoor/Transit			
Brochures, CDs			
Direct Mail			
Sales Promotions			
Publicity			
Trade Shows & Seminars			
Multicultural Communications			
Co-op Ad Program (Indicate use or fund)			
Advertising Specialty Items			
Event Sponsorships			
Signage, Wallscapes, Vehicle Graphics			
Cause-Related Promotions			
Other (list)			
Other (list)			

3.0 TOOLS OF THE CRAFT

THERE ARE MANY TOOLS which enable the account manager to perform the invaluable role as overseer of the agency process. The ones I've chosen to include in this chapter are:

- The information management system
- The conference report
- Campaign and creative briefs
- Evaluating and presenting creative work
- The status report
- The brand stewardship report
- Billings, budgets, and financial management
- Letters, memos, reports, and proposals

"It's a brand new reality show on The Account Management Channel."

The choice of the word "craft" here is intentional. The account manager position in an advertising agency is like no other. While there's a lot of science and methodology in advertising, managing the agency process is an art, requiring equal parts energy, integrity, knowledge, insight, and intuition.

Let's look at the tools used in the art and craft of account management.

3.1 The Information Management System

A lot of what an account manager does is communication and project management – monitoring timelines, managing budgets, and generally making sure stuff stays on track.

In most ad agencies, the account managers handle more than one account. An account manager can sometimes have 20 or 30 projects active at one time. With this kind of workload, an information management system is critical.

While the status report gives the status of projects at a given point in time, there is a lot more information that account managers will regularly need at their fingertips.

This information can include background information and documents on current projects, budgets, plans, correspondence, past billings, and anything else that is often referred to.

Exactly how the information management system is set up is normally left to the account manager. The best advice for an entry-level position is to ask senior account managers how their systems work.

The purpose of this chapter is to describe basic components of a system and to suggest one that provides pretty good information capture and retrieval without being overly burdensome to maintain. We've also included a section on managing timelines.

While much of the content of an information management system is computer-based, there's a regular need to have instantly retrievable information during client meetings, staff meetings, or other times when you're not at a computer. It is also impossible to carry tons of file folders around. A streamlined, hard-copy system serves a valuable purpose.

The Client Binder.

This binder provides an efficient, ready reference. Some account managers take the client binder to all client meetings, especially those standing meetings where all the activity on the entire account is regularly discussed.

Exactly what goes into the client binder and for how long is a product of what is needed and efficient, but there are some pretty common sections for this resource.

- Copies of active project work orders
- Conference reports
- Status reports and project timelines
- Client's annual MarCom plan
- Master client budget and budgets for major campaigns
- Billings for the last three to six months
- Reconciliation of budget to spending

Client Correspondence File or Binder.

Here you keep copies of letters to and from the client, hard copies of important e-mails, and memos.

Project Files.

Each active project gets its own file folder where you can quickly retrieve background information, the work order, change orders, briefs, research, budget, timeline, and correspondence. Simply, anything that has anything to do with that project goes in the project file.

There is some duplication between project files and the client binder. This is because project files and client binder are often used in different ways in different locations.

Past Billings Binder.

Past billings are valuable to have for answering billing questions that may come up and when preparing budgets for future projects and campaigns.

Samples.

Samples are an important part of the system. Some agencies have an excellent system for capturing and filing samples of the many projects done for clients. Other agencies do not.

Samples provide historical information. They are valuable in showing agency work to new business prospects and for showing existing clients how a project (done for another noncompeting client) could work for them.

It's a good idea to put at least one sample of the completed project in the project file. If you are especially proud of the piece, take a sample home and put it in your book, along with some notes about the contribution you made to it.

This information will come in handy if and when you are looking for a new position.

If your agency has a good sample system, great. If it does not, you'll have to set up your own and keep it secure.

Managing Timelines.

How long it takes to complete a project is the product of many variables: level of staffing, familiarity with similar projects, availability of resources, motivation, etc.

I specifically have not included a sample timeline since there are so many types of projects and so many variables that they're hard to generalize. Through experience, you'll quickly get a feel for how long different projects take and what slows them down.

In general, it's safe to say a project can never be completed fast enough... while at the same time, the creative, traffic, and production departments think they performed miracles to get the same project done on time. The truth lies in between.

Agencies often perform miracles in getting projects done on time and on budget. As an account manager your job is to keep the need for miracles to a minimum.

Three practices will serve you well.

1. Keep records on how long projects actually take under the best and worst scenario

2. Educate your clients about reasonable timelines

3. Start projects early and allow for slippage, especially on anything new and unfamiliar to you, the agency, or client

The actual establishment of timelines should be a collaborative effort between various agency departments – mostly creative, production, and traffic. Your contribution is key – the deadline when the print ad needs to be sent to publication, the direct mail piece needs to go the mail house, the trade show display needs to be shipped to the convention, etc.

Assuming they accept the deadline as doable, the creative, production, and traffic people build the timeline by working backwards from the deadline and agreeing to interim deadlines for key aspects of the project.

Once that timeline is set, the traffic department is responsible for keeping the project on schedule. However, every seasoned account manager knows that part of their job is monitoring how others are doing theirs.

Some interim deadlines will be your responsibility, the most important of which is getting the client to quickly approve briefs, copy and layouts, production proofs, budgets – things that clients approve.

Remember, if you agree when setting the timeline that you can get client approval on something in two days and they take a week, it is not the production, creative, media, or traffic department's responsibility to make up the lost time.

3.2 The Conference Report and Call Reports

Meetings are part of doing business. Not every member of the agency team can attend every meeting with the client.

This practice would be very time-consuming, inefficient, and expensive. The conference report is a basic communications document that summarizes a meeting (or teleconference) between the client and the account manager. Even when other agency members attend a meeting, it is important that a single document become the official record of topics discussed, decisions made, resulting actions needed, responsibilities, budgets, and deadlines.

Some agencies boast that they "don't do" conference reports… as if they are above all that. Even agencies that say this need some system for documenting and communicating the results of important meetings.

Any agency that doesn't do this is looking for trouble.

So are their clients.

Clients who do not ask for conference reports put even more responsibility on the account manager to mind all the details.

To help illustrate the nature of the conference report, here is the transcript of a typical meeting between an account manager and her client. The transcript is followed by the first two entries of the conference report as the account manager would have written it.

As one of your case assignments, you can write the rest of the conference report.

The Set Up.
On the next pages is a transcript from a meeting between the agency account manager and the client contact, the VP of marketing for a major chain of espresso shops/coffee stores.

The agency and client have a standing meeting (always at the same time) once a week. There was no meeting last week because the account manager was on vacation.

Most of the time, the standing weekly meeting is held in the client's office. Other shorter meetings involving more agency staff are held at the agency. Here's an example of a meeting at the client's office…

Julie, the agency account manager, arrives at the client's office after stopping off at one of the nearby client stores. The client has asked her to play "secret shopper" and see if the store is promoting a new pastry item just introduced.

These two people, Julie and her client contact, have been working closely together for more than a year. Their working relationship is good and, as such, the meeting often starts with a little chit chat.

Client: *Hi, Julie, welcome back. How was Mexico?*

Julie: *It was great. That snorkeling park you told me about was even better than you said. Thanks for the tip. How's Wolfgang (the client's beloved dog)?*

Client: *Well, he had to have some surgery, but he seems to be on the mend. Thanks for asking. How'd the folks down the street do on the new pastry item?*

Julie: *Could have been better. You know, I've felt that you've needed a better in-store strategy for new food items... something that will call attention to new items and invite inquiry.*

Client: *Yeah, let's talk about this next week. We have more new items coming on line. We need a better system to merchandise them.*

Julie: *There's probably a good model out there somewhere that we could at least use as a reference point. How 'bout you authorizing up to 10 hours of time for our research team to go out and do a report. They could hit a lot of different stores and show what people are presently doing in this area.*

Client: *That may not be a bad idea. No reason to reinvent the wheel. They need to do a literature search of the food trade magazines, too, especially those in Europe. Two weeks?*

Julie: *Yes, I think they can do it by then. I'll let you know if there is a problem with that timeline.*

Client: *OK. Just make sure you get good pictures. I misplaced the agenda you sent me. What's on the docket today?*

Julie: *Here's another copy of the agenda. I put the flavored coffees Christmas campaign at the top. Two weeks ago I gave you a campaign brief on the new line of flavored coffees for Christmas.*

I wanted to make sure you were on board with the brief before the creative team started work on the radio, television, magazine, and point of sale.

Client: Yes, I looked at the brief again last night, and I have two concerns. We've never done flavored coffees before, and among coffee aficionados, flavored coffees have a gimmicky reputation, as well as being masks for inferior coffee beans. We want to make sure there is adequate "quality" branding in the ads. Second, these flavored coffees are intended to be year-round products. Make sure they are not labeled Christmas items... they are just flavors that are being introduced at Christmas.

Julie: Got it. I'll amend the brief accordingly, and we'll start the initial concepting immediately. Unless you hear from me otherwise in 48 hours, you can expect to see preliminary concepts in three weeks. I'll put a timeline for the campaign in the conference report.

Client: Great.

Julie: The media department should be booking fourth-quarter radio, TV, and newspaper. Are you ready to sign off on the preliminary spot-market media budget?

Client: You know, this spot-market media budget has grown faster than my ability to fund it. I can't afford to do the normal fall flight in all of these markets, and I'm not sure how to reduce the size of the list.

Julie: I understand. The spot market list is 30% larger than last year. You guys have been on a major expansion tear. Typically, we buy those markets where the Category Development Index (CDI) and the Brand Development Indexes (BDI) are both above 120. But as the number of markets has expanded so has the number of spot markets needing advertising support under this criteria.

We could raise the CDI/BDI threshold, and we could add a third component to the weighting model.

Client: Sounds like you guys have already thought about this some. Do your media people have a recommendation?

Julie: Well, we've talked about it a little. We need to crunch some numbers, but we might think about raising the CDI/BDI to 130 each and adding in a cost-per-rating-point index where markets need to rate at or below 100 compared to the national prime-time television cost per point.

Client: Come on, Julie, you know I don't understand all that media-ese. What would that do?

Julie: It would reduce the number of spot markets, favoring the best coffee markets with the best media cost efficiencies.

Client: Now I understand. Let's make those adjustments in your weighting model to see what the list of markets and the budget looks like. Can you have that to me tomorrow?

Julie: Probably not. I'll have to ask the media department first. I know your fourth-quarter buy is a top priority for them. I'll just have to see how long it takes to set up this new model and input the data for the new markets.

Here's the second color proof of a new POS counter card. I think it looks a lot better since we changed the color of the background. I'm glad we have the policy of always putting the POS in the darkest corner of the stores to see how it holds up. This one looks great under a spotlight, but the photo we got from your field people needed some help under less favorable store placement.

Client: I agree the photo looks a lot better, but the logo is still too small, and it needs to be moved up. Why do your art directors always make the logo too small on the POS?

Julie: It's because they want as much space as possible for the message. And since it's only in your stores, they reason the logo can be subordinate. But, unless there is some other graphic reason I don't know about, we'll make those two changes. Do you want see another proof?

Client: No, I trust you.

Julie: Is the quantity still 5,000 and the delivery date October 5th at Central Distribution?

Client: Better make it 7,500.

Julie: Here's some very interesting intelligence from the Southeast. This share-of-voice analysis shows that your major competitor in places like New Orleans, Atlanta, Louisville, and Charleston is not advertising nearly as much as we'd expected.

Client: Wow, that's major good news. Our sales report shows that revenues in those areas are at or above projection. Time to cut the advertising. Let's cut back on the radio and cancel the balance of the schedule in Southern Living magazine.

Julie: Uh, we can do that, but we signed a 12-time contract with Southern Living. They're going to short rate you to the tune of about $1,000 each for the ads you have run.

Client: Well, just have your media department tell Southern Living that if they ever want to see another page of advertising from us, they'll forget about the short rate.

Julie: I think we need to treat them with more respect.

Client: Whose side are you on, anyway?

Julie: Short rates are never fun for anyone, including the magazine. And they have done some nice editorial pieces that have helped your business in that region. I'd like to keep them on our side.

Client: Maybe so… Any ideas?

Julie: Let's see what their rateholder policy is. Maybe we can get away with buying a bunch of small ads that still qualifies you for the 12-time frequency discount. That way you can cut the budget and avoid the short rate at the same time.

Client: Works for me. Let me know how much we are going to save as soon as you can.

Julie: Will do. Are you going to attend the photo shoot next Wednesday?

Client: No, I have to go to the East Coast, but George will be there for any technical assistance you need. Just make sure you take a bunch of different shots so you get at least one I like.

Julie: Shot variety may be a problem. Last time you were gone and George was on the set, he got the photographer and art director all upset because he was trying to play director of photography on issues that were plainly not technical. Can you speak to him about his role and ask him to please go through me if he has any concerns on the photography. I'll be the arbitrator.

Client: OK. I'll talk to him.

Julie: Good. Thanks. The lighting crew will scout the location two days before. I'll call George to set it up.

Here's the latest Roper-Starch readership study for Sunset magazine. Your 2-color, nonbleed ad was one of the highest scoring ads in the book, better than a lot of the 2-page full-color ads. The creative people really outdid themselves on this ad. This would be a good time for a little rah-rah from the client.

Client: I agree. What do you suggest?

Julie: How 'bout I draft a quick note and you can put it on your stationery.

Client: Good. I'm really curious about the next two items on your agenda.

Julie: Which do you want to do first?

Client: Let's go with the research.

Julie: OK! Here's an article about a company that has developed a way to do perception analyzer testing online faster and cheaper than the traditional method (putting 50 screened people in a room and showing them commercials while they rate the spots with a dial). Since you are such a believer in concept testing, I thought this might pique your interest.

Client: Very interesting. But I'd be concerned about controlling the leakage of the concepts and also that the size and profile of their sample was appropriate.

Julie: Yes, I had the same concerns, so I called them. The visuals shown in the test are not downloadable or printable. Everything is real time. That's how they deal with the leakage issue. As for their sample profile, they prefer products that appeal to a broad profile of people with better-than-average education and income. Sounds like your customer base.

Client: Sample size?

Julie: 2,000.

Client: Cost?

Julie: About one-third the normal cost for a sample of 1,000.

Client: Turnaround time?

Julie: Less than a week.

Client: Wow! Are you recommending it?

Julie: I think the savings to be gained if this thing works are worth a little investment to test it. So I propose running parallel tests using the traditional and the newer online method, then comparing the findings.

Client: Sounds reasonable. Let me look over the article and think about it.

Julie: This next item is really interesting, too. My interactive department gave me this flyer about a company that sells e-mail lists on a spot-market basis. So that you can send an initial e-mail offer to people in, say, Charleston who have "opted in" to other e-mailing programs. It's a lot like buying a mailing list of people who have purchased mail order items before.

Client: I can see how spot-market e-mails could be very useful in new markets.

Julie: Here's the real kicker. They have a way of attaching a data-rich coupon to the e-mail. The coupon has the e-mail address imbedded in this Aztec coding. Recipients can print out the coupon one time only.

When they redeem the coupon, the information is added to a master e-mail database, so you know which e-mail recipient redeemed which coupon at which store.

Client: *Pretty amazing stuff. Are you recommending a spot market test for this?*

Julie: *Yes. I think we should do Richmond, Virginia. That market has the lowest BDI of any market in the Southeast. This is a really surgical strategy to boost trial.*

Client: *Good thinking. Work me up an estimate and recommend a coupon scheme.*

Julie: *You know my interactive department has been eager to work on your Web site for two years. These latest interactive tools are just the latest examples of how strategic they are. We know you have a major Web site update coming up. What's it going to take for you to give us a crack at it?*

Client: *I'll tell you what, Julie. I'll make you a deal. You get* Southern Living *to waive the short rate, and I'll do three things. I'll go for the online perception-analyzer test, we'll seriously consider the Richmond e-mail test, and I'll entertain a formal presentation from your interactive department.*

Julie: *Excellent!*

Client: *I have only one proviso on having your interactive department involved.*

Julie: *And that is?*

Client: *That you stay closely involved in any work they do. I don't want to have to work with any more propeller heads or train anyone on branding issues or company structure. I don't have time to play referee or educator. That's why I have you. OK?*

Julie: *Got it. I promise it will be seamless. And thanks for the opportunity. These people know what they are doing. How about we do the preliminary discovery meeting with you at the agency in a couple of weeks?*

Client: It looks like 3 o'clock on the 25th is open. Will you send me a set of questions and issues they want me to address?

Julie: Great. I'll confirm that date in the conference report and get them started on the questions.

Client: Now don't get too excited. I have a bone to pick with you. There is a problem with the latest billing. The photography bill on the latest ad series was much higher than what was budgeted. What gives?

Julie: Well, I'll have to go back and check the billing ticket, but as I remember it, we agreed to exceed the budget because we could get multiple use out of the talent if we did a "buyout" on the photography rather than paying the usage fees as we go.

Client: Oh yeah. I do remember that conversation now.

Julie: I'm sure I confirmed that decision in a memo or conference report. Do you want me to find it?

Client: No, that's all right. I just needed to make sure you're minding my money.

Julie: While we're on the subject of billing, we have more clients all the time going for one-line billing. They found that they were spending too much time going through the billing details just to double-check the work that I and my accounting department do. If they ever need the detail, we are happy to provide it on a moment's notice.

Client: I do spend a lot of time going through the billing when all I really care about is that the project and campaign budgets are held. Could you redo last month's billing and show me what it would look like in the one-line format.

Julie: How about we do your next billing in the new format? If you don't like it, we'll redo it in the long format?

Client: I'll need a memo from you explaining the change so I can pass it along to my bean counters before they see the new format.

Julie: OK. I'll draft something up, and you can tell me if it's what you need.

Unfortunately, I did not save the best for last. As you know, creatives can be restless people.

Client: Who's leaving?

Julie: Lev (the copywriter who has worked on the account for the last two years).

Client: What is with you people? You get a good writer on the account and just when you get them trained, they're gone. That really upsets me. I really like his work.

Julie: Yes, I know. So do I.

Client: Is he going with a local agency?

Julie: Yes. It's an interactive shop, and I don't think he is going to try to pitch you or the merchandise manager.

Client: Good. That's the last thing I need right now is to have to fight off another attempt from the merchandise department to have its own agency.

Julie: Lev gave us an unusually long notice, and he's leaving on good terms. I suggest we move up the development schedule on the hard-goods campaign while he is still here. Then we can have a little more time to break in a new writer on smaller projects.

Client: Do you think we can get all the creative done before he leaves?

Julie: If we start right now, the odds are good that we can.

Client: OK, but let's make sure the next copywriter is as good, if not better, than Lev. In fact, I want some input on who the new copywriter is and I want someone with coffee or restaurant experience.

Julie: We'll make this transition as seamless as possible. I'll set up a meeting with you and the creative director to discuss candidates and your involvement.

Anything else on your list today?

Client: *No. That's it for me, I've got a staff meeting in five minutes. I just wanted to say that between Stan (the account supervisor) and Amy (the account coordinator), I hardly knew you were gone last week. Just kidding. But they did a great job of covering for you.*

Julie: *Thanks. That's the way we want it. A couple of fun things to finish on a high note. The ad club is doing its annual painted chair fund-raising event again. Last year you expressed some interest in having one of the company interior decorators paint a chair for auction. If you want to do it this year, the agency will sponsor the chair.*

Client: *Good internal PR idea. Send me the details and I'll line up a decorator.*

Julie: *There is a new restaurant opening in our neighborhood. Would you and Jill like to join us for dinner a week from Friday?*

Client: *Sounds like fun. Let me check our social calendar and I'll get back to you. If I haven't gotten back to you in two days, I've forgotten. So ask again, OK?*

Writing a Conference Report.

The format of the conference report varies from agency to agency and from account manager to account manager.

The format is only important in that it allows the client and agency specialists to quickly find the items that concern them, that it is clear what action they need to take, and what their deadline is.

Conference Report Format.

Following is a typical format for a conference report.

Just as a hint in writing these reports, not everything discussed in client-account manager meeting is included in the conference report. Certain items are left out of the conference report because they are best left "off the record" and handled discreetly by the account manager and client.

Topic Heading.

This could be a single project, a media plan, a small campaign, etc. Generally, one item is dealt with in each topic heading. If you try to deal with too many projects, decisions, or action items under one topic heading, it becomes too hard to follow.

Major Background Points.

Brief details of discussion. Here you give management and others enough information so they can understand the context of the decisions and action items.

Decisions.

What decisions were made or were deferred.

Action Items and Due Dates.

1. For client

2. For each agency department involved

The important thing here is to organize (and art direct) the report so the people who have action items can quickly scan the report and see what's coming their way. In most cases, the conference report does not officially serve as a change order or memo detailing what needs to be done next. Likewise, just putting a client deliverable and due date in the conference report doesn't means it is going to be done. You'll need to remind and prod the client, too, in order to keep everything on schedule.

On the next page are the first two entries in Julie's conference report after her meeting with the client.

Conference Report:

1. **Flavored Coffees Introduction**

   Background, Discussion & Decisions:

   Campaign brief was reviewed.

   Client underscored the importance of two issues.

   A. They've never done flavored coffees before and, among coffee aficionados, flavored coffees have a gimmicky reputation, as well as being masks for inferior coffee beans. We want to make sure there is adequate "quality" branding in the ads.

   B. These flavored coffees are intended to be year-round products. Make sure they are not labeled Christmas items... they are just flavors that are being introduced at Christmas.

Action Items:

- Account Service/Planning. Revise campaign and creative briefs to reflect this input.

- Creative. Start creative work immediately. Concept presentation in three weeks.

- Traffic. Set internal working schedules.

2. **Pastry POS**

   Background, Discussion & Decisions:

   Inconsistency in promoting new pastry items is a continuing problem in the stores.

   Client is interested in agency suggestions on how to address this problem with nonhuman solutions.

Action Items:

- Research. Conduct a survey among a variety of retailers to see how new items are being presented.

- See if a good model already exists. Photographs required.

- Also need a thorough review of trade magazines covering food and retail with emphasis on what is happening in Europe.

- Paperwork to follow. Due date is two weeks.

Call Reports.

Not all decisions are made in meetings. Phone calls often contain substantial amounts of actionable information.

Agency e-mails or memos confirming important phone decisions are as important as good conference reports and a very good habit for account managers to adopt.

3.3 The Campaign and Creative Briefs

The development of every major campaign starts with a source document. These documents may have different names, but they serve the same critical purpose – providing needed input to the various specialists within the agency.

This "briefing" document is normally prepared by the account manager, and it is often referred to as a "brief." Or "The Brief."

This sample campaign brief is a compilation of the briefs that are used by different agencies. Formats will vary, but they generally contain the following information.

Campaign Brief Outline:
Client Information.

Name of product, brand, or division
Name of project or campaign

Target Audience Profile.

Demographic information (age, sex, income, education, race, etc.)
Geographic information (including spot-market strategy)

Psychographic information
(lifestyles, values, interests, beliefs, self-image)

Behavioristic information
(category usage levels, benefit hierarchy, media preferences)

Communications Goals of this Campaign or Project.

What is the general purpose of this project or campaign?

What changes in knowledge, attitude, and behavior need to be accomplished?

What is the definition of success?

Promotional Mix.

What is the media mix for this campaign?

What other elements (Internet, sales promotion, PR) are in the total promotional mix?

Budgets.

For media

For creative

For production

Timeline and Approval Process.

Start and duration of campaign

Tentative deadlines for creative concept

Tentative deadline for finished copy and layout

Tentative deadline for media plan

Level of detail needed for presentations

Stages where client needs to approve

Time needed for each client approval

The Creative Brief.

Creative people generally like some input beyond the campaign brief, and they prefer to have the information prepared in a fashion that is most actionable for them.

This additional input often comes in the form of motivational research, which helps the copywriter and art director understand the mindset and emotional makeup of the customers.

From the campaign brief and this additional creative research, the account manager and/or account planner will develop a written document to serve as both input and inspiration for the creative team.

This is most often called a creative brief, and it usually covers the following:

Audience Insights.

1. Based on the demographic, qualitative research and our collective experience, the most insightful target audience characteristics are...

   Here we talk mostly about psychographic and behavioristic characteristics. For example: What are the target audience's big issues... their needs... their pains... their challenges... their fears... their hopes? How do they feel, what do they think when they use this brand or category?

2. Why are some people in the target audience buying the product and others not?

3. What do they currently know and think about our brand?

4. What emotional and psychological barriers do we need to overcome?

5. Who is the real competition and why?

Product Insights.

1. What are the most important or unique rational benefits and emotional attributes of our client's product?

2. What is the competition's strong point?

Executional Considerations.

These are things such as the proper message tone, corporate posture, brand personality, current positioning, competitive flash points, legal taboos, hot buttons, concurrent brand campaigns, peculiar market conditions, specific client preferences, and other parameters that might impact the direction of the creative work.

Creative Strategy.

Based on the product, the competition, and the mindset of the target audience, the most compelling thing we can communicate about this product and why people should buy/try it is...

Often, the working answer to this last question is: *"This product is the best... or the product can... or the brand should be positioned as... or the product is specifically designed for..."*

This is the Big Promise in rough form.

These are not headlines. Rather, they are insights that will help the creative team find an emotional way to make the product distinctive and memorable.

How Long Is a Brief?

The creative brief is normally a page or two, but it can be longer depending on how deeply involved the creative brief's author actually gets in the creative process and how much research analysis is needed.

Don't leave out something important, but, generally speaking, the shorter the creative brief the better.

The purpose of the creative brief is to distill the input down to insights that the creative team can use to develop an on-strategy, creative approach. Here's an example of a brief that resulted in good, effective work.

A Sample Creative Brief: Ann Sacks.

The creative brief is an extremely important document. It's often the hardest for aspiring account managers to understand.

Background.

Let's put the creative brief in the context of a campaign for Ann Sacks, a high-end manufacturer of ceramic tile, stone tile work, and, now, very creative plumbing fixtures. They sell through company-owned showrooms, dealers, and catalog-direct.

It's also important to understand that, in its market, Ann Sacks is a very well-established brand, known for creative design and high quality workmanship. The job of the advertising is to introduce and reinforce an already established brand personality among high-end customers, designers, and dealers.

The information on the overall campaign brief was pretty straightforward – basically, the agency needed to keep a good thing going.

So let's move directly to the creative brief.

Target Audience.
Based on demographic and qualitative research and our collective experience, the most insightful characteristics of our target audience are:

- They are upper-middle and upper income.

- They hold at least one college degree.

- They are most often designing or actually building a custom home on a new lot.

- They truly enjoy the creative process of designing a custom home.

- They regard the designing of a custom home as an intellectual as well as a creative pursuit.

- In visits to showrooms, they tend to use the common phrase "see it in my mind."

The most important or unique rational benefits and emotional attributes of our client's product are:

- They stimulate creativity.

- Their design often provokes a visceral response.

- They are trendsetters, but tastefully so.

- Ann Sacks' customer service associates have a good sense of style.

- The Ann Sacks factory is totally geared for custom orders.

- A favorite question posed by company founder Ann Sacks is "How do you want your home to feel?"

Competition's Strong Points.
Competitor's ads show beautifully photographed products in finished rooms.

- They are sometimes faster on delivery and always less custom-order friendly.

- They are often cheaper.

Executional Considerations.

- The message tone should be intellectual but not snooty.

- The corporate posture should be almost nonexistent, only enough to convey the stability and dependability of the company.

- Brand personality should be creative and challenging in a friendly way.

- The positioning should be that of cutting-edge craftsmanship as the best way to deliver a customer's vision.

Creative Strategy.

Based on the mindset of the target audience, the nature of the product, the brand personality, and the competition, the most compelling strategy for the creative is:

- To show that Ann Sacks understands the "vision"

- To focus on the process of creating the custom home, rather than the finished product

- To intellectually agree that the process is part of the reward of designing a home

- To stay away from beauty shots

- To make the ads intellectually challenging

In most cases, the creative brief is reviewed with the client before creative work begins. This is good insurance against using an input that the client feels is technically or strategically wrong. I can't think of any reason other than agency ego that a well-crafted creative brief would not be reviewed with the client.

On the next page are the ads which came out of the creative brief. For a glimpse of how these ads might have been presented to the client for the first time, see the section on Creative Rationale in this chapter.

Each short headline combines with a provocative color photo to capture the mood and the creative spirit of the moment when Ann Sacks products are specified.

"Right here."

"I'm home."

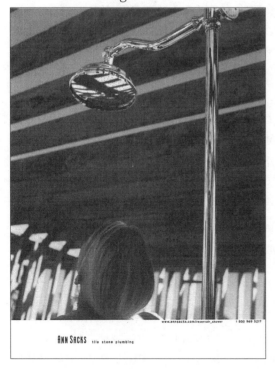

"Done."

"You see it, don't you?"

3.4 Evaluating and Presenting Creative Work

One of the toughest parts of being an account manager is critiquing the work of others. One of the best indicators you have arrived as a seasoned account manager is that you can do this and still maintain their respect.

It doesn't matter whether you personally like the creative proposal. What matters is whether or not it is on target, meets the objectives, and is it as good as it can be.

Sometimes, in spite of what you consider a very good campaign and creative brief, you will have major reservations about what is being proposed by the creative department.

How you handle yourself in this situation is critical to your ability to get the best work out of these people in the future. They want to feel whatever additional work needs to be done is a result of "mutual discovery."

Being Objective about Being Subjective.

First, this means any additional work required by the creative department is not the result of your inadequate input. Equally important is the way you handle your response to their proposals.

The word "objectivity" takes on special meaning in this situation. Advertising (especially creative) is subjective, and no one discounts the importance of your initial gut reaction to a concept as an ad professional or a potential customer. Did the headline and layout create a visceral response? Did it raise the hairs and make you want to enthusiastically thrust your fist in the air?

After that, there's the analytical side that your client expects. You have to find a way to take yourself out of the subjective equation, thus enabling your associates to accept your final critique as fair and enlightened.

The art of insightful questioning is a good one to cultivate. Nothing will expose weak work or confirm strong work faster than objective, intellectual challenge – insightful, probing questions about ideas and how they came about.

Early in my adjunct-professor career I was seeking a model for students that would formalize this task of "passionate objectivity." In the textbook *Advertising and Promotion: Integrated Marketing Communications* (Belch and Belch, published by Irwin), I found the creative credo as articulated by the D'Arcy Massius Benton & Bowles ad agency.

This credo is a wonderful, thoughtful set of standards for creative excellence. It also works quite well as a model for evaluating creative concept proposals and finished ads.

The D'Arcy/Ogilvy/Bernbach Model.

As I reviewed many sources in preparation for this book, I also found a list of creative standards written by David Ogilvy. Then I reread Bill Bernbach's notes on advertising creativity.

It seemed appropriate to add some additional creative standards from both of these legends, Ogilvy and Bernbach, to the model developed by the D'Arcy agency (now merged into Publicis). This model has come to be known as the D'Arcy/Ogilvy/Bernbach Model – D/O/B for short.

I know from experience in using the D/O/B model for years that creative people may not like what you have to say, but they will feel you were fair, objective, and rightfully passionate in your opinions.

An ad does not have to score high in each of these criteria to be effective, but an ad that scores poorly in most is probably not a strong piece of creative work. Not only do these criteria provide a model for objective evaluation of initial creative proposals, they also provide a list to justify the final creative product.

Know this model. Use it to form your own opinions about creative proposals and use it as basis for the writing the Creative Rationale.

The D'Arcy/Ogilvy/Bernbach Model:

1. **Does this advertising position the product simply, with clarity and relevance?**
   The target audience should quickly see and sense what the product or service is, what it does, and grasp some idea of how it fits into their lives.

   We must ensure that the creative execution does not over-whelm or obscure the message.

2. **Is the advertising an extension of the brand?**
   Products *do* something. Brands *are* something.

   Great brands have a personality that goes beyond features or benefits.

   Does this ad just talk about the brand, or is the ad itself an extension of the brand personality?

3. **Is the ad single-minded?**
   People's ability to remember advertising messages is enhanced by simplicity, clarity, relevance, and uniqueness.

   If we have determined the right thing to say and a unique way of saying it, why waste time saying anything else?

4. **Does the advertising make a "Big Promise"?**
   Our advertising should be built on the most compelling and persuasive customer benefit – physical, functional, or psycho-logical.

   Before we start worrying about how to say it, we must be sure we know what is most important to the customer. Does the headline and/or visual make a promise?

5. **Does the advertising contain a "Big Creative Idea"?**
   The "Big Creative Idea" transforms the benefit promise into a "creative" communications concept. It is the core creative idea that makes the ad *unique and potent.* The Big Creative Idea is a theme, a new word, a novel concept, or some other vehicle that is used to deliver the message in a memorable way.

6. **Does the Big Creative Idea have "legs"?**
   Long-term campaigns need Big Creative Ideas with staying power – ones that aren't faddish, and allow for multiple variations on the same themes over months or years.

7. **Is this advertising unexpected, different, or unusual?**
   Our clients should not pay good money for ads that look and sound like everybody else's in their category. We must be different, because sameness is suicide. Ads are not outstanding unless they stand out. Being bold, unusual, and different is imperative. Without using gimmickry, does this ad have the potential to make the audience say "Wow, that's interesting," or "Gee, I never thought about it like that"?

8. **Is the objective of the ad clear?**
   The purpose of the ad (to inform/introduce, to establish or change an image or attitude, motivate immediate action, etc.) should be readily discernible.

9. **Do the ads have a high degree of "visual or verbal magnetism"?**
   Great advertising is noticed and remembered because it is unusual to look at, pleasing or provocative, a nourishing feast for the eyes, and reinforces the verbal or written message.

10. **Does the advertising have inherent drama?**
    In some way, really memorable ads tell a story, dramatize a point, demonstrate something, create suspense, build to a finale, tug an emotion, or surprise us. Is there any drama here?

11. **Does the advertising have an emotional connection?**
    Really effective advertising provokes an emotional response by speaking one-to-one with a message that makes maximum appropriate use of the "fear of" or the "need for" appeals.

12. **Does this ad reward the prospect independent of the product?**
    Let's give the audience something that makes them glad they took the time to read or watch or listen… something that also helps our message penetrate and stick… a smile perhaps, a tear, a laugh, something that makes them happy to see the ad again or, best of all, a stimulus to inquire or buy.

13. **Is the approach right for the target audience and the medium?**
In order for the ad to be effective, the language, tone, and "attitude" must be right, and the ad should take advantage of the strengths presented by the media environment in which it will appear.

14. **Is the ad readable, and is the branding strong enough?**
Not everyone is young and has excellent eyesight. So let's make sure the copy is readable, the package is large enough to be remembered, and the client's logo is displayed with pride.

15. **Does it speak to current customers as well as prospects?**
One of the primary roles of advertising is to reassure current customers that they made a good buying decision and that brand loyalty is a good thing.

16. **Is there a compelling offer, a call to action, and a clear response path?**
Does the ad give an incentive to act immediately? Other than the Web site URL in the corner, is there a call to action? Is the response path clear? Have we tested the response path to make sure it's user friendly?

17. **Does the ad reflect the company's character and values?**
Is the ad just about the product, or does the company reveal itself in some constructive way?

18. **Does this advertising exhibit painstaking craftsmanship?**
Our work is art. The writing should resonate, the visuals should demonstrate top design, the music should embellish the emotional message. In other words, the work should sparkle.

19. **Does the ad have "Talk Value"?**
Does the overall concept of the ad have the potential of making the news, creating some buzz, starting a fad, or becoming part of pop culture?

20. **Is the advertising strategically driven and creatively consistent with the integrated promotional plan?**
Advertising is only one part of the promotional mix.

    The ad should creatively spring from a marketing strategy and fit into the larger promotional picture.

Prepared by D.L. Dickinson, Director of Advertising Management, Portland State University School of Business

Presenting Creative Work.

Learning how to speak and present in a business environment is very important. Advertising is a persuasion business.

Presenting creative work is an especially important skill that affects both personal and agency success.

Even when the creative people present their work, the role of the account manager is very important.

Presenting creative work has four basic stages or phases:

1. The Set Up

2. The Reveal

3. The Justification

4. The Close

1. The Set Up.

The "set up" is most often the purview of the account manager, even when the creative people do the "Reveal." The importance of the set up should not be underestimated. The worst thing you can do for a creative idea is slide it across the desk and say, "Here it is. Don't you love it?"

Wes Perrin likens the set up to lifting veils, probably because the set up is when the background is reviewed – the challenges, the objectives, the audience's mindset, the market environment, the strategies discussed... all the important stuff the client approved in the creative brief and then promptly forgot.

If involved in the presentation, the account manager typically will cover the psychographic and qualitative research findings and their strategic import for creative.

Also included in the set up are reference points such as the media environment in which the ads will appear and what the competition is doing.

Another technique I've seen used effectively is the showing of other ad campaigns that are stellar examples of a certain creative technique or campaigns that were excellent in reaching the client's target audience.

The set up provides the client with reference points that lead the agency to the creative proposal about to be revealed. The set up can also include references to the kind of creative approaches that should be avoided and why.

This kind of "creative inoculation" is especially helpful if you know the client is looking for a certain approach that the agency strongly believes would be a bad move.

Some clients may be impatient with the set up. They don't want to be "sold." They just want to see the layouts. In those cases, you need to get the client to sit through a short set up as a way to understand the agency rationale and as a courtesy to the agency team.

2. The Reveal.

Some creative people are terrific presenters of their work. Others are not so hot, even though their work is excellent. You are not going to be able to improve them. They are what they are. You just need to do the best job possible in your part of the presentation.

In the "reveal," those nicely matted layouts, storyboards, direct mail, promotions, etc., are enthusiastically presented in conceptual form, complete with headlines, copy, and layouts.

There should be a strong connection between set up and reveal.

When the creative people do not attend or present, have them coach you on how they would pitch the creative work.

3. The Justification.

After the reveal, there is discussion.

The client gives some initial reaction and asks questions.

This is when the account manager takes care to address any objections and reservations and enumerates the reasons why the creative is a great solution. (See Creative Rationale.)

Again, confidence and enthusiasm are paramount.

4. The Close.

Some clients like to have a little time to "get comfortable" with the creative. They may ask to keep the layouts.

Hopefully, the client can be trusted not to show the work around the office. A technique I found helpful in these situations is to have a bound written proposal that covers the set up and the justification and includes color photocopies of the layouts. The agency keeps the mounted work.

Other clients will approve the overall concept but want to study the copy. Great. Emphasize the importance of quick turnaround on approval so that the creative team has as much time as possible to do a good job on execution.

Some clients don't like to be negative in front of the agency team.

A positive initial reaction might be followed in a couple of days by a private not-so-positive conversation with the account manager.

The best insurance for success in this situation is:

- Having done a great job developing the creative
- Building a good case in the set up and the justification
- Anticipating the client's objections
- Believing in the creative work and sticking to your guns

In spite of an excellent job preparing the campaign and creative briefs, some changes may be needed before the client is ready to sign off on the creative work.

Such is the business. Client buy-in is important.

The agency wants the client to regard the ads as his own. This often comes when the client makes a small change in the ad.

Some creative people have a cow when the client wants to make any change. In reality, 80% of people who read ads never get past the headline, photo, and maybe a caption.

If the client wants a change in the fourth paragraph of body copy, it's a small price for the agency to pay in order to get client buy-in. After all, let's not forget who's paying the bills.

The Use of Roughs.

Different agencies work differently in regard to the polish they put on their work before it's presented to the client. In some cases the client is actually involved in the development of the creative strategy and primary concept or theme.

Being intimately involved in the creative process, the client sees firsthand all the rough thumbnail layouts, the creative strategy ideas written in the margins of the creative brief, and the headlines scribbled on the back of bar napkins.

This level of client involvement is relatively rare. Since creative concepting is the agency's forte, it generally does not want the client involved. Many clients, however, are very good at understanding creative concepts presented in rough layout and headline form.

This presentation normally happens at the agency if the client is invited in for a creative work session. Strategy is reviewed and roughs are presented in a sit-down-around-the-table format.

The client absorbs where the agency is going creatively and then provides objective feedback and direction for "tightening up" the concepts for official presentation.

This can be a very efficient way to work because it allows the agency to do the critical creative thinking and still involve the client while getting feedback and buy-in.

The drawback is that the client is likely to see some concepts that are way off. Or the client may want to start playing art director or copy-writer instead of waiting to see what the refined concepts look like.

Again, the level of trust the client has in the agency will determine the creative presentation style.

Presentation Skills Building.

If you can find a coach who understands the business world, get some lessons on making presentations: projection, nonverbals, body language, eye contact, humor, slang, posture, working with props, pacing, enunciation... those kinds of things. You can learn a lot in a short time, and the lessons will serve you well.

The Creative Rationale.

The creative team took the campaign and creative briefs and came up with creative approaches it thinks meet the requirements.

These various concepts are shown to the account manager, who evaluated them based on the input and a set of criteria such as the D'Arcy/Ogilvy/Bernbach model.

After some discussion and possibly some additional creative work, everyone agrees they have a good campaign to present. But there is still much to do before the presentation.

Though some may disagree, I believe that the creative is not complete until the Creative Rationale is written.

Working in conjunction with the creative team and perhaps the account planner, the account manager writes this document. As the name implies, it rationalizes the creative strategy being proposed and explains why it is the best solution for the assignment.

The written Creative Rationale may or may not accompany the presentation. Nonetheless, the discipline of rationalizing and defending the work ahead of time is great preparation.

The Creative Rationale Addresses the Following:

1. "The best way to convey the core message is through the overall theme line or concept of..."

2. "The best way to execute this overall concept or themeline is..." (Here is a detailed discussion of appeals, message types, and execution treatments being recommended. The Big Creative Idea is fully discussed here.)

3. "Lastly, we believe this is the strongest creative approach because..."

   (This section justifies the creative recommendations based on an assessment tool such as the D'Arcy/Ogilvy/Bernbach model.

Let's put the Creative Rationale in the context of the Ann Sacks campaign.

1. The best way to convey the core message is through the overall theme line or concept of "the vision."

2. The best way to execute this overall concept or theme is:
   - To show the products in the "vision state"
   - To depict the product as an emotional conduit
   - To speak in the language of the customer
   - To communicate that Ann Sacks is the company for those people whose new home will be the ultimate expression of themselves

3. We believe this is the strongest creative approach because:
   - It truly has a "Big Creative Idea"
   - It is totally unexpected and unlike anything else in the category
   - It makes an emotional connection
   - It has inherent drama
   - It establishes a unique brand personality
   - It is memorable
   - It has "legs"

Developing the complete package of campaign brief, creative brief, and Creative Rationale is a professional discipline that forces the creative strategy to be well thought out and, when the comments and questions come, defensible.

If you can't write a compelling Creative Rationale based on the work in front of you, maybe the creative approach isn't as strong as everyone thinks it is.

Giving Client Feedback to the Creative Team.

In the frequent situation that the account manager presents creative work and the creative team is not present, reporting client feedback becomes even more important.

Even when the creative work was loyal to the brief and presentation did a good job of setting up the work, things can go wrong.

When client reaction was not what was hoped for, the account manager needs superior diplomatic skills to rescue the situation.

The first step is to get a grip on why the client is not doing cheetah flips over the creative. Why don't they like it? What's not working? What scares them?

Now go back to the brief and measure client comments. Are the reservations executional, or is there now a strategic point of difference? If so, you're dealing with essentially new strategic input.

Actively listen and paraphrase what they're saying. Clarify. Make sure you can adequately relate the concerns to the creative team.

If the client has shifted direction and no longer totally agrees with the brief, then it's time to take a step back. If the new input (by way of client objections) is significant, it may be time to rebrief.

It's OK to bring client suggestions for executional fixes back to your creative team. But when you relate the suggestions, present them as "points of reference" that should further help the team understand the client's concerns.

3.5 The Status Report

Many agencies issue an internal weekly report on the status of jobs in progress. A status report is normally issued for each client or for clients grouped by account manager. These documents are often in the form of a spreadsheet, usually produced by the traffic or production department after weekly status meetings. Like this…

Client Project Name & Number	Internal creative concept due	Creative proposal to client	Client creative apprvl due	Initial prdctn proof	Shoot / Rec'g session	Final proof due	Post Prdctn date	Dlvry date	Comments
Snack Bar Trade Ad TMK-151-05-0506	5/16	5/21	5/28	6/ 8		6/ 15		6/23	Need to set up photo shoot for 6/10. Hero products with new packaging needed by 6/8. Three each.

Explanation of a project number

Every agency needs a numbering system to codify and track the many jobs that go through the agency. Called project codes, work order numbers, job ticket numbers, or something else, these codes help a busy shop keep things in order and serve other purposes.

TMK = Client code
151 = The number of work orders for this client when this ticket was opened.
05 = A project category so the agency can track billing by type of job.
0506 = The date when the job ticket was opened.

The decision to provide a client with a status report is driven by the client. Many clients trust the account manager and the account team to get the work done on time and don't want to be bothered with the agency's internal working dates.

The clients who do want status reports are those who have a lot of projects or have people in their own organization to which the progress of agency jobs is important.

So the status report serves the purpose of showing that the agency and the advertising manager are on top of things.

Clients who are some distance from the agency are also among those who like status reports, since face-to-face meetings are fewer. Status reports to distant clients are often followed by a conference call where the account manager, traffic manager, and client can review the latest report.

Status reports are valuable for one other reason. They help the account manager "ride herd" on the client, making sure that the client delivers on information, approvals, comments, product samples, and other things needed by the agency.

Much like the conference report, the format of the status report does not matter as much as its content and ease of use. The internal status report shown above could be sent to the client.

Or the account manager may choose to do a more narrative version. A narrative version of the same status report would look like this:

Snack Bar Trade Ad
Copy and layout presented 5/23.

Need final creative approved by 6/2, earlier if major revisions required in creative.

Photo shoot scheduled for 6/10 in town.

Need hand-selected "hero" products with new packaging delivered to agency by 6/8.

Final approval proof due on 6/15.

Delivery to publications scheduled for 6/23.

No problems anticipated at this time.

Note that items shown in bold are those which the agency needs from the client in order to make the various project deadlines.

3.6 The Brand Stewardship Report

In a small but growing number of agency-client relationships, the annual service contract calls for the agency to produce a report that summarizes the year's activities and results.

This document is called a variety of things, but most often a "Brand Stewardship Report" (BSR) or a MarCom annual report.

As the person who knows everything that goes on with the account, the account manager is responsible for keeping track of those things that will be reported.

As the person who is expected to be a superior business writer, the account manager also writes the report.

This is a significant and important responsibility, since the BSR must make both the agency and the client MarCom director look good.

Because it can be such a critical document, the BSR is often reviewed in rough draft by the senior agency management and the client MarCom manager prior to any official version that might be submitted to client top management.

Some items that would logically be found in such a report are:

- Market metrics
- Creative metrics
- Media metrics
- Public and trade relations metrics
- Interactive metrics
- Fiscal metrics
- Summary

In order to bring this document to life, let's look at a hypothetical BSR for a client that makes active sportswear and accessories sold through outfitters and other retailers across the country.

Sample BSR:
Annual Brand Stewardship Report – XYZ Sportswear.

Market Metrics.

The year just completed was a continuation of a successful brand building and market expansion campaign started two years ago. We know from attitude and awareness studies that brand awareness among the key customer profile is 15% higher than a year ago.

Brand personality recall among the same key profile audience is 10% higher, and the number of key profile respondents who would include the brand in a three-way consideration set has increased by 8%.

The sales-promotion-oriented introduction of the new footwear produced 7,000 hits on the Web site in the first 60 days.

This promotion drove product familiarization because it required a dealer visit or off-line study of the advertising in order to participate in the online part of the promotion.

Three markets – Seattle, Portland, and San Diego – improved their brand development index by 10% or more with only slight supplemental ad spending. All other markets were steady or saw slight increases in BDI.

Creative Metrics.

The new print campaign won a CLIO, a silver medal at Cannes, and top Kelly, awarded by the Magazine Publishers Association.

Readership scores on the new print campaign ranked in the top 10%, and were the highest-rated ads on two occasions.

Six major outdoor sports equipment brands gave our products prominent branded exposure in their print ads.

The point of sale display became so popular with consumers and dealers that it received premium placement in many stores.

Demand for the POS display required an additional printing.

The transition to the new garment tags was completed early in the year. The distinctive new tags are now featured prominently in all print and TV ads.

The mini-CD that is included in each hangtag created some buzz with its games.

The instant Web site activation feature on the CD has increased post-sale brand involvement. We know this because Web site visits through the CD can be tracked independently of other hits.

Media Metrics.
The share of voice analysis provided by Media Research Services estimates that our measured media campaign was at least 5% more efficient on a cost-per-target impression than the biggest competitor.

Though the measured media budget was essentially the same as year two, the estimated number of target impressions increased 7%.

The use of ads across the bottom of the weather page in *USA Today* was a major media coup, creating a lot of buzz with consumers and within the industry. Nothing like that had ever been tried before.

The agency's programming department was able to get the new women's outdoor vest placed in three episodes of *Friends*. With the prominent placement of the logo on this new product, the branding on the screen was very good and created early season buzz for the product among dealers and customers. We were able to use video clips and stills from the program in the second wave of hangtags and POS.

The three appearances on *Friends* garnered a 15 rating and a 25 share among the target audience and equated to about 27 million target impressions. The equivalent dollar value of this exposure had it been purchased as commercial time is estimated at $400,000.

Sponsorship of the nationally televised Extreme Team Relays has been a good showcase for the technology and durability of the featured products. ETR graphics are featured on the new garment hangtags for these high-performance products.

Public and Trade Relations Metrics.
Two strategies helped reach women in new ways. Involvement with the Race for the Cure has provided visibility and brand loyalty. The specialty item keychain/hiking whistle has also turned out to be very popular with woman concerned about personal safety.

The design of this item was very tasteful and the company branding on it was excellent.

The wallscapes in key markets have helped boost sales and dealer enthusiasm. Dealers absolutely loved having their name individually "sniped" at the bottom of the scapes.

The introduction of the new sunscreen shirt at the annual sportswear convention was better than expected. This was due, at least in part, to the highly memorable pre-show mailing and trade magazine campaign.

Reps report that the conversion to the new dealer signage and rep vehicle signage was 100% complete in the final month of the marketing year.

A potential major conflict with retailers was averted when a specially produced video was shown at the annual sales conference. This video appropriately showed the retailers that print advertising plays an important role, and to abandon print in favor of exclusive television advertising would be bad business.

Dealer activity in the co-op advertising program increased 20% over the previous year. While the associated cost of this program commensurately increased by 20%, the increase in dealer interest in funding local support of the brand is a very healthy sign.

The awareness of the new campaign and the ability to recite the new campaign sales theme is at an all-time high among marketing employees, reps, dealers, and customer service people.

The company's involvement with the national awareness campaign about the dangers of the drug ecstasy has given the brand another positive connection with active young adults.

Interactive Metrics.
The updated Web site that went online last year has grown without interruption every month in number of visits 60 seconds or longer.

Analysis of the search paths taken by these visitors has told us a lot about the people who use the site, including some new media possibilities.

More than 3,700 names were added to the database of high-end buyers. Ninety percent of these buyers "opted-in" for occasional e-mail contacts.

The experimental infomercial produced for airing in underserved markets produced two results. Dormant and nondealers started showing interest, plus the e-commerce side of the Web site actually reached the break-even point.

Fiscal Metrics.

Total ad spending was within the annual budget, with the exception of the spot market budget for the Northeast, which was exceeded because of a unique retail opportunity.

Sales per marketing employee is 3% higher than last year.

The company's share of market has increased 4%, and the market itself has grown 6%. The MarCom cost-per-market-share-point and MarCom cost-per-dollar-of-sales are both lower than last year.

Summary.

All in all, it was a very busy and productive year.

Progress was made on a number of fronts, especially in the area of promotions and the integration of the interactive strategy.

Some Final Thoughts on Brand Stwardship Reports.

The BSR for this client could easily include even more detail under more headings. Hopefully, this example is enough to provide you with a good idea of what a BSR is and does.

Remember, a Brand Stewardship Report is basically an historical document, but it should allude to future challenges and opportunities, which are usually dealt with in great detail in the integrated marketing communications plan.

3.7 Billings, Budgets, and Financial Management

As an account manager, you will deal with a lot more numbers than you probably expected. Sometimes you may even wonder whether you are in advertising or accounting.

This chapter explains account service financial management, in all its forms, and shows how critical this part of the job is to both the client and the agency.

Financial responsibilities for account managers fall into five categories:

1. Revenue sources

2. Billings

3. Budget management

4. Forecasting

5. Account profitability

Let's take them one by one.

Revenue Sources.

Chapter 2.4 deals with agency revenue and the various ways that agencies get compensated for their work.

The extent to which an account manager can alter the agency compensation agreement varies from agency to agency and client to client.

Generally speaking, the account manger should always be looking for ways to increase agency revenue as long as the client is still getting a fair deal.

Billings.

In the "Two Dozen Hats" section of Chapter 6 we discuss the role of account manager as accountant. Overseeing and approving the billing is a big part of that job. Billing is the industry term for the invoice the agency sends its clients every month.

Few things will mess up a good client relationship faster than bad billing. If there is a problem, the client doesn't call your accounting department, he or she calls you.

Clients expect immediate answers to any number of questions, all of which are coated with varying amounts of irritation and distrust.

Most billing questions fall into one of three categories.

Billing Problem #1: Lack of Information.

Clients who pore over the agency bills will often complain they do not have enough detail to know how much they paid for a specific aspect of a project.

Different clients have different hang-ups. Some bristle at creative fees. Some think the agency doesn't get the best deals on printing. Some don't like to pay for lavish food tables during big commercial shoots (although they really enjoy the spreads and the excitement on the set).

Many clients, especially government clients, insist on detailed billing including "back-up billing," an industry term for detailed itemization and copies of all supplier invoices for services and materials purchased on the client's behalf.

Other clients (with training and trust) come to prefer one-line billing. One-line billing means that they trust you to manage their money. As long as projects do not exceed budgets, they are happy to let the agency do its job and let you sweat the details. This is billing nirvana. Here are three examples that show the levels of detail a billing can take:

> **Level One (The One-Liner).**
> Project Code: TMK 151-05-0505
> Project Name: Three Snack Bar Print Trade Ads
> Services and Materials: $15,910
>
> **Level Two (By Category).**
> Project Code: TMK 151-05-0505
> Project Name: Three Snack Bar Print Trade Ads
>
> Agency creative and account management services: $4,500
>
> Agency production and art charges: $4,900
>
> Outside production charges including photography, illustrations, electronic files, and proofs: $6,510
> Total: $15,910

Level Three (Detailed).
Project Code: TMK 151-05-0505
Project Name: Three Snack Bar Print Trade Ads
Agency creative services:

10 hours of copywriting and concept time	$1500.00
10 hours of creative art direction and layout	$1500.00
2 hours of creative direction	$600.00
6 hours of account management	$900.00
Production art direction/supervision	$4900.00
Photography (McWalter Photography)	$4500.00
Illustrations (Way-out Graphics)	$1500.00
Electronic files, proofs (Prep-Expert, Inc.)	$510.00
Total:	$15,910.00

(Copies of vendor invoices attached)

As a rule, the less detail you can get your client to accept, the better off everyone is, as long as the overall budget is not exceeded. But… when clients want detail, they should get detail.

The billings are part of the agency service. They should be prepared in a way best suited for the needs of the client.

Trying to skimp on detail when the client wants detail will be interpreted as laziness, inflexibility, or evasiveness.

The best approach is to work with each client to see if, over time, you can wean them of their appetite for laborious detail on the billing. Many clients are happy to take less detail as long as they know that they can get all the details they want on any project, any time they want.

Billing Problem #2: Sloppy Billing.
The last thing you want is for a client to think your accounting is unprofessional and your billing lacks integrity. If there are math mistakes, vendor items assigned to the wrong job, or the wrong mark-up applied to a production invoice, you have problems.

Sloppiness is often the result of not billing projects right away, or even worse, waiting until they are totally complete.

Internal charges and vendor invoices pile up. Then, when they are finally billed to the client, neither one of you can remember what you did months or weeks or days ago. Not a pretty picture.

I had one project for a five-star resort client that took 32 months from the time the work order was opened until the last billing was done. It was a five-star nightmare.

Most agencies have adopted "in-progress" billing, where account managers have some latitude in delaying certain billing for good reason. But beware, memory and facts deteriorate over time.

When a project is complete and the last charges are noted on the agency billing, make sure there is not some other internal or vendor charge still lurking out there, ready to make you look bad on next month's billing.

Over time you will learn that certain agency people are slow to file their time sheets and some vendors are notoriously slow on their billing to the agency.

If these people were involved in a project, be extra leery before assigning the "final billing" notation.

Even details like the names of projects on the billing deserve attention. For example, over its life in the agency work process, a project may start out with one name and come to be referred to by client and agency as something else.

When the billing arrives, the client will expect to see the new name. But unless the account manager tells the agency accounting department to officially change the project name, the old name will appear on the billing, potentially confusing or even irritating the client.

The moral of these stories is to really scrutinize the billing before it goes to the client. Read it like a tough client would. Find the erroneous, vague descriptions. Find the incorrect "total to date." Find the projects that are marked complete but still missing a charge.

Don't give the client any reason to question your billing.

Billing Problem #3: Agency Charges Are Too High.

Actually there are two issues here:

1. cost of services, and

2. budget over-runs.

You may not be in a position to affect the compensation agreement between your client and the agency. Nor may the account manager be in a position to decide how much the agency charges for its services. This is often an arrangement that is worked out at the highest levels of the agency and client.

The real chore for the account manager then becomes making sure the agency services are rendered in an effective and efficient manner, thereby lending the maximum "professional value" to them. Everything done should be viewed from the value-added perspective.

The job of justifying how much the agency charges for its professional services should not be the account manager's battle to fight alone. Agency management should be ever vigilant to reinforce the value of the creative intangibles and the exemplary service that you personally provide. They can do this best when they are kept informed about the work that is being done on the account.

Best Practice for Dealing with Billings.

The best practice is to make sure that the billing is error-free, and when you know you are going to get a call challenging a bill, deal with it up front. I handled billing one of two ways. I would meet with the client and walk them through the billing each month, with answers ready for anticipated questions. This is always stressful but the preferred way to deal with billing because you can "read" the client immediately and know better which issues need follow-up.

Or I would write a summary memo for every billing, explaining those places where I expected the client might have a question or a gripe. This also worked well. It really depends on what the client prefers. The point is, if you make your billing bulletproof, your client will trust your billings, and you will have fewer divisive billing problems with which to deal.

Dough Flow.

Since ad agency profit margins are very slim, cash flow is very important. In this case, cash flow is functionally defined as "the agency having the account's money at or before the time their media and vendor bills need to be paid." When budgets deal in millions of dollars a month, the agency is in no position to act as a bank for its accounts. Even in smaller agencies, paying media and vendor bills and then waiting long periods for clients to pay the monthly agency billing is no way to operate a profitable agency.

Since cash flow management is imperative, a couple of systems have been developed to handle this need. Both have their strong and weak points.

In-Process Billing.

In this system, the agency bills the account for the expenses incurred during each month. The account pays the agency billing and the agency then remits to the media and vendors. Occasionally, the client will have a question about an item on the agency billing. Until that question is resolved by the account manager, the payment of the whole agency billing can be delayed.

Some clients will "sit on the billing" because they don't have time to review it in detail and approve it for payment. That's why the integrity of the agency billing (as approved by the account manager) is so important.

Sloppy billings and slow response to client questions can severely hurt agency cash flow.

Billing on Estimate.

In some parts of the advertising industry, mostly involving photography and broadcast production, the accepted practice is for the vendor to receive at least partial payment for services in advance. In order to accommodate this practice, the agency provides an estimate for the work it plans to do for the account.

Upon client approval, the agency turns the estimate into a bill, which the account pays. The agency then has the cash in hand to pay vendors who demand payment in advance and to pay other vendor bills as they are incurred.

At the end of the campaign production, the agency provides a reconciliation to the account, detailing how the money was actually spent. If there is any money left over, the agency gives a billing credit to the account. In most cases, however, the expenses exceed the agency estimate.

Being over estimate is quite legitimate, even when expenses are tightly managed. In the process of creating a new commercial or a new campaign, many creative decisions are made along the way. Some of those decisions will lead to the estimate being exceeded.

In those cases where the actual expenses exceed the cash the agency had to work with, the agency will have to bill the account for the difference. The problem here is that the client may make the agency wait until the project is totally complete before billing the amount over estimate.

Meanwhile, the agency has to pay vendors as the project progresses. Agency cash flow suffers in this situation.

Three disciplines help, all account management responsibilities:
- Realistic estimates
- Tight project financial management
- Quick final accounting on the project

Make Sure Your Agency Pays Its Bills.

While most agencies operate on a slim profit margin, they have to have enough cash flow and financial cushion to pay their bills on a timely basis. Sometimes agencies get a little behind on paying media and vendor invoices.

When this happens for a prolonged period of time, the media and vendors may let it be known that the agency is "slow pay."

This can be very embarrassing and uncomfortable for an account manager if the client pays the agency on time and the agency slow pays the media and vendors used for the account.

If your client pays their bills on time, it is imperative that the agency's accounting department pay the vendor and media bills for that client on time.

Budget Management.

Clients entrust hundreds of millions of dollars to their agencies. The keeper of the client budget is, guess who, the account manager. Since they often develop the annual ad budget, the account manager often understands the workings of the budget even better than the client.

Much like timelines, budgets are often made with incomplete input and the best of intentions.

Stated differently, the problem with budgets is that they are often based on the past, and the people who provide budget input are not the people who have to work according to it.

Developing the budget is a skill that is best learned under the guidance of a senior account manager or account supervisor. Most budget development has one foot in the past and one in the future.

The past shows what has been done before and what it actually cost. The future is what needs to be done and what it will cost (often with the past as a guide).

It's important to make sure next year's projects aren't underfunded by last year's assumptions. At the same time, it's also important that the people who actually are going to do the work – copywriters, art directors, photographers, producers, etc. – have some opportunity for budgetary input.

It's much harder for them to criticize the budget if they've had some input. They still will criticize, but not as loudly.

Annual Budget Setting.

There are various ways to set an annual budget. The most common is a historical percent-of-sales method, which simply takes the percent of sale volume spent on advertising in the past and multiplies this percent by the next year's sales goals.

In this method, the job of the agency is to tell the client how best to spend the money.

Another method of setting the overall budget is the share-of-voice or share-of-market method.

Both methods basically focus on media spending. They look at total category or client industry spending and then determine how much money the client must spend to achieve a certain percentage of total industry ad spending or a certain share of total industry sales.

Like percent of sales, these methods also assume a direct and predictable connection between ad spending and sales.

The budget-setting method that makes the most sense is the objective-and-task method. Instead of focusing on sales, this method focuses on the specific tasks that advertising does, like increasing awareness, changing attitudes, or stimulating certain behaviors. The cost of achieving such goals becomes the basis for the budget.

Once the budget is set, the account manager's job is to manage it in such a way as to achieve the most impact and make sure that the budget is not exceeded.

Part of managing the master budget is managing all of the component budgets for media, ad creation, research, and everything else that's in there. Clients don't like to "track expenses" or do budget reconciliations. They much prefer that their buttoned-up account manager do it.

Agencies that habitually exceed production and creative budgets do themselves great harm. Without being critical, you must understand that creative people and accounting are foreign to one another.

Creative people, in general, are concerned about the quality of the work first and the budget second. Regular communications about the budget and close monitoring of expenditures along the way are good ways to prevent cost overruns.

It may take a lot of work to break the cost overrun habit, but it can be done, and it is well worth the effort.

Estimates.

Smart agencies provide an itemized or one-line estimate for each project, large and small. An estimate is *not* a firm bid, it is the agency's best guess on what the project will cost ±10%. The client signs the estimate, and off you go.

The estimate is developed by an estimator who consults with the internal agency staff and relevant outside vendors.

Hopefully, everyone involved knows what their individual part of the estimate is and will live within it. But don't count on it.

You will encounter situations where the creative time estimated for a new ad is 5 hours and the copywriter wants 10. Now what? The answer is "that depends." Sometimes the copywriter will spend 10 hours and the agency will only bill for 5. Other times, the copywriter is told that 5 hours is all he gets. Other times you may have to try to explain to your client why the original creative estimate of 5 hours was unreasonably low and inaccurate. Not fun.

It's your job to make sure the estimate has integrity before the client signs it. Once signed, you have to live with it. History on similar projects is a good reference point for determining the dependability of an estimate.

Record Keeping.
Keep good records. If, for example, a certain type of project has historically cost around $10,000 and this time your estimate is 35% higher or lower, your internal alarm should go off.

Estimating the cost of creating something brand new is an inexact science. Nonetheless, billing should not exceed the signed estimate, except in situations where the scope of the project changed.

The client expects that the estimate is accurate and dependable. The time to deal with potential problems is at the estimate stage, not the billing stage.

If a project gets more expensive than estimated and a new estimate has not been signed, your client will likely want to know where, in his existing budget, you are going to find the money.

An occasional project may exceed its budget, but the overall annual budget had better not. As the keeper of his budget, your client will expect you to know its inner workings and what is going to be sacrificed if you need to find more money.

The "R" Word: Reconciliation.

Just knowing these aspects of the budgeting process should help make it better for you and minimize the unpleasantness of the next critical part of budget management, the "R" word: Reconciliation.

Remember, being an account manager means being a trusted steward of the client's money.

Creating customized solutions to client marketing problems is an unpredictable process. That's what makes it fun. That's also what makes budget management so difficult.

Clients, however, expect the agency to be buttoned-up when it comes to their money. Reconciliations are reports that compare actual spending to the budget, by project, by campaign, and by time period.

When something is more expensive than budgeted, the client needs to know. ASAP.

They'll also want to know where the money to cover the extra expense is coming from – cutting media expenditures, canceling or reducing other project budgets, or putting in a supplementary budget request (not fun).

Reconciliations are a good account management tool because they can help identify budget variances and potential trouble spots, hopefully in time to do something about them

Beware of the "W" Word: Write-Off.

There are many instances where the account manager does not want to bill the full number of billable hours spent on a project.

The reason could be that the agency spent more time on the project than budgeted or the account manager feels that the client should not be billed for some time the art department wasted when it made a mistake on the project.

The reduction in billable hours or absorption of other expenses normally billed is called a "write-off." Only high levels of management have the power to approve write-offs.

To get a write-off, the account manager must persuasively explain why the hours (or worse, an outside expense) should be written off and not be billed.

Justifying a reduction in agency income is not a pleasant experience, but every so often the account manager has to take the heat and management has to take the long view, deciding that a reduction is in the best interests of the client relationship.

Forecasting.

Agency management does income and profitability projections just like clients do sales and profitability projections.

The collective forecast for the agency is compiled from individual projections done by account managers as they forecast the activity level on their accounts for the next forecast period.

Forecasts tell management two things: how much revenue you expect your account to generate in the next quarter and how well you are managing your clients' budgets.

If your projections are consistently wrong, this tends to indicate that you have little knowledge or control over the budgets of your clients.

Account Profitability.

Billings are one thing, account profitability is another. It is quite possible to have a large account that is a loser and a smaller account that provides superior profits. In agencies that compute account profitability, it can have a major impact on the salary and career path of account managers.

So, it is important for account managers to understand how agency accounting works and how account profitability is computed.

While the way account profitability is computed is pretty consistent throughout the industry, there is some variation on the terms used in the accounting itself.

Pay special attention to the terminology and the definitions used by your accountants on your account.

Account Profitability Definitions.

Annual Account Billings:

The total sum of all the bills sent to the client for the year.

Account Revenue:

Total billings less all external expenses such as net media and vendor charges.

Account Gross Income:

Revenue less direct internal charges such as personnel working on the account. Accounting standards set by the 4As (American Association of Advertising Agencies) recommend that salaries not exceed 55% of account revenue.

Pretax Account Profit:

Gross income less overhead allocation (computed by determining what portion of total agency overhead should be applied to each account, based on each account's percentage of total agency revenue). The 4As accounting standards recommend that pretax profit be at least 20% of account revenue.

Capitalized Account Billings:

The amount of billings if all revenue for an account is the product of a 15% media commission. (Capitalized billings = total account revenue x 6.67.)

Capitalized billings are a way to express account size in a common language when agency revenue comes from nonmedia sources.

3.8 Writings and Meetings

Becoming a good communicator via the written word is imperative to success in advertising. Work hard at becoming a good writer. It will also help you be a better thinker and overall communicator.

As mentioned in "Fast Forward to Operator's Guide," this is not intended to be a book on business writing. There are good courses in business writing at almost every university or community college. You should take one.

There are also many books to help you with the mechanics of good business writing. Your agency may even have a style guide.

If not, your account supervisor will probably have some preferences and should be happy to show you what he or she considers to be examples of good business writing.

Build a library of good memos, letters, reports, and proposals. Writing gets easier with experience and good examples.

Short of any better direction, however, here are some guidelines to follow when struggling through your early efforts.

Fourteen Hints on How to Become a Better Writer.

The ability to write well in the business context is extremely important. Your credibility is at stake, and your career progress will be affected by your ability to write. If you have a chance, take a course on business writing. That way you won't have to learn how to write at the same time you're learning the advertising business. Here are some tips to help you along the way:

1. **Allow enough time.** Good writing takes time – time to organize, time to research, time to compose, time to edit, time to proof. Don't think that you can just sit down and bang something out.

   Start working on major reports and proposals earlier than you think necessary. This practice is especially important when you are writing on a subject new to you.

   It is safe to expect that you will need information, facts, or background that you don't have and maybe don't know where to find right away. Organize your piece early so you know what you don't know.

   Starting early also has another benefit. It puts your subconscious to work on the writing while you focus on more immediate things.

2. **Find the prime time.** Some people write better at certain times of the day. Find the time of day when you do your best writing and then block out that time.

3. **Know the purpose.** Especially when you are writing for someone else, it helps to know the intended outcome of the document: to educate, persuade, defend, recommend, etc. It might sound obvious, but many a rewrite has been done out of a need for repurposing.

4. **Be brief.** Cover the subject adequately, but use short words, short sentences, and short paragraphs. Remember, the longer it is, the less likely it will be read.

5. **Watch the tone.** Keep it positive and businesslike.

   Avoid slang, "inside" jokes, nicknames, code words, and other language that might embarrass your client or yourself if the letter went beyond its intended recipient.

   Avoid generalities and characterizations.

   Use superlatives and equally negative descriptions with caution. Don't qualify absolutes (e.g., "almost never").

6. **Be obvious.** Early on, indicate what the letter, memo, report, or proposal is intended to address, and, if needed, what it is not intended to address.

7. **Write it so it can't be misunderstood.** When you are not there, eye-to-eye, to monitor the receiver's understanding level, you must trust totally the accuracy and precision of your written word. Being understood is good. Not being misunderstood is even better.

8. **Be linear.** Address issues in the order that will make sense to a reader who is less informed than you. This is one of the most important characteristics of good writing, because you will not be there to clarify if the subject matter is presented in a confusing manner. Use topic sentences to open each paragraph and conclusion sentences to end each paragraph.

9. **Write for the ear.** Good writing sounds good. It isn't stuffy or formal. Get rid of the slang and sloppiness of some verbal communications but still maintain a style that sounds good when read aloud.

10. **Write in the second person.** Use of pronouns such as *we, our,* and *us* should normally be avoided.

    Organizations and people should be referred to by name.

    Refer to an organization as a single body. Things attributed to an organization are *its.* Things attributed to people are *theirs.*

11. **Art direct your work.** Make the document inviting, or at least not intimidating. Documents of any length, especially proposals, should be "art directed."

This means they should be visually treated with color, type variations, underlines, indentations... whatever aids initial reading and later reference.

Make sure the decimal points line up on columns of numbers.

Use subheads.
Use subheads to break up long sections.

12. **One draft is not enough.** Write it. Let it get cold. Then, rewrite it. You'll be glad you did.

13. **Watch your grammar, spelling, and punctuation.** While spelling is pretty set, the English language is wonderfully flexible in other ways. There are often preferred and alternative ways to express and punctuate. The key is to find writing and punctuation styles that work and stick with them throughout the document.

By the time you are a college senior you should know the rules of grammar and punctuation. If you don't, then a brush-up English course or a business writing course would be a good idea.

Here are a few of the most common student writing mistakes:

- Beginning a sentence with a numeral. Always write it out.

- Ending a sentence with a preposition such as on.

- Using *went* and *ran* preceded by *had*. (The correct usage is *gone* and *run*)

- Referring to the subject of a previous sentence by starting the next sentence with *this*. (In the new sentence, you need to state briefly what *this* is.)

14. **Get a style book.** The best advice to assist young business writers is to buy a style book. Publications such as the *Chicago Manual of Style* or the *Associated Press Style Book* answer many questions about punctuation, capitalization, abbreviations, possessives, etc.

Hints on Organizing.

Card Tricks: Anytime you are preparing to write a major document, there are numerous points you know you want to include. Write them each individually on index cards or Post-it notes. Then arrange them in order of appearance.

It will help you organize the document as you organize your thinking by identifying what else is needed, helping with transitions, and eliminating excess baggage.

The Brain Dump Technique: If you don't like the index card system, then take a deep breath and start typing. Don't worry about editing, spelling, or punctuation.

All you want to do at this point is get as many thoughts into the document as you can. Let it flow. Stay in the zone as long as you can. Don't interrupt for housekeeping.

When you are tapped out, print out your brain dump and organize it by page or paragraph in hard copy.

It's easier to see the whole work in multiple pages on a desk than on a scrolling computer screen.

Hints on Editing.

There are actually three levels of editing.

Level One Editing

- Overall, does the document seem to do what it was intended to do, or did it wander from its purpose?
- Is the content correct?
- Is the organization correct?

Level Two Editing

- Is the tone correct?
- Does it flow from one section to another?
- Is the writing efficient?

Level Three Editing

- Does it look good?
- Is the formatting consistent?
- Are the spelling, punctuation, and grammar correct?

Hints on Proofing.

Let it sit for a couple of hours before you proof it.

Print it out and proof the hard copy.

Read it aloud. Listen to how it sounds as well as what it says.

Writing Major Proposals.

Agencies write many different proposals and recommendations to clients. The varieties of Creative Rationales, media plans, packaging recommendations, research reports, and other documents make it hard to generalize about a format or style. Any good advertising textbook will have an outline for a major agency campaign proposal. Here is a short version.

Most recommendations start with some discussion of the scope and focus of the proposal... what it addresses and maybe what it does not.

The Situation Analysis describes the relevant marketing environment and competition. This section can include research findings and a SWOT Analysis focusing on the client's strengths, weaknesses, opportunities, and threats.

A discussion of Objectives and Strategy identifies what needs to be accomplished and sets the stage for how the actual recommendations are going to accomplish them.

The Recommendations section includes details of the plan – marketing and creative execution, roll-out strategy, timelines, budgets.

The recommendations are followed by the Rationale, which says why the recommendations are a good solution. In the Rationale, I have found it helpful to include some discussion of why other possible approaches to the problem are not being recommended.

This technique is called "inoculation." It helps support the strength of the agency recommendation and assures the client that thorough deliberations preceded the writing of the proposal.

Measurement techniques outline how the success of the project or program will be defined and determined.

Eighteen Tips for Being a Good Meeting Manager.

Meetings are a necessary part of the business. They can be productive and fun, or they can be something else. In an ad agency filled with high-energy, opinionated, stressed people with a lot on their minds, meetings are even more challenging.

Work hard and quickly to build a reputation for running short, productive, and efficient meetings. This reputation will help ensure that the people you need in the meetings will actually attend and show up prepared.

Entire books have been written on how to run a good meeting. But here are some tips on how to gain a reputation as a good meeting manager:

1. When trying to get a bunch of busy people together, give them three different possible times for the meeting and ask them to pencil in those times until you identify the time when most people can attend.

2. Make sure everyone knows exactly the purpose and the end product of the meeting.

3. Make sure everyone knows what they need to do before they arrive so they don't waste the time of others getting up to speed.

4. Remind everyone the day before the meeting.

5. Keep the meeting as small as possible.

6. If someone important can't make it, they should send a person who can speak for them.

7. The ending time and approximate cost of the meeting in terms of billable dollar value should be announced at the beginning.

8. Start on time and set a countdown timer.

9. Have a written agenda and set ground rules to maintain focus.

10. Be prepared to tactfully but assertively deal with the 4 D's (diverters, detractors, distracters, digressors) and anyone else who slows things down or tries to change the purpose of the meeting.

Your associates at the agency will appreciate the skill with which you deal with the time wasters.

11. If subject matter is flexible, try to organize the agenda by the people needed to discuss items. Then let people go as their contribution is completed.

12. Make sure important issues get the most time.

13. End on time

14. No cell phones.

15. Right after the meeting, spend a few minutes talking with the supervisor or account coordinator about how the meeting could have been better or conducted differently.

16. Issue an e-mail report, thanking everyone for their participation, itemizing the major decisions, citing new input, and repeating major postmeeting action assignments. Copy the account supervisor if he or she did not attend.

17. Pick a neutral spot or someone else's office for the meeting. Once your business is complete, or deteriorates into something unproductive, you want to be able to leave. Hard to do if the meeting is in your office.

18. Serve cookies.

BUZZ...

Blending Strong Creativity and Account Management.
Advertising Age; November 15, 1999

Dual Strengths: Jordan McGrath Clients Talk about the Versatility of the Agency.

We consider Jordan McGrath to be full partners in our business. They are excellent strategic thinkers, and they're heavily involved in understanding the consumer. They spend an enormous amount of time learning what turns the consumer on and what turns the consumer off in advertising.

I don't think you can create effective advertising by shooting from the hip. There must be a long-term learning commitment. You keep learning; you keep adapting; you keep picking up on what the consumer is telling you. And it's a big reason we've been working with them since 1985.

New Relevance.

These campaigns are created by some inspired people, and we have a wonderful working relationship with the agency at all levels. We have a tremendous respect for them; they're great folks.

Those working on our account constitute a small, very powerful team. Their quality starts at the top, with Pat McGrath [chairman and CEO], who knows our business well.

Also important to us are Stephen Badenhop [president], Ilon Specht [executive creative director], and Angela Pasqualucci [management supervisor], who is our main contact; Angela is absolutely top notch, one of the best partners we have.

Tim Penner, VP-North American Tissues & Towel, P&G.

Two Main Factors.

We've been working with Jordan McGrath for 20 years, and there are two main factors that have kept us together all these years. The first is their in-depth understanding of the Welch's brand and the equity associated with it. They've been a big part of helping us to build our very strong brand equity.

The other reason I like working with them is they are out to move our business, as opposed to creating advertising strictly to generate awards. Their approach is very product-focused, and the advertising has been very effective for us.

Their understanding of our business and our market is good. But what they contribute that's unique is their understanding of Welch's ethos – the essence of what the Welch's brand is all about and how it relates to the consumer.

Great Chemistry.

In addition, Jordan's people are great to work with. We wouldn't have been as successful as we've been, especially in the last few years, without a great chemistry between our staff and the agency's.

Sure, there's a bit of give and take. They will push us on issues that they feel strongly about, and they will listen to us when we have issues that we feel strongly about. Somehow, between us, we're able to be effective.

Of course, there has been turnover in personnel over the years. But there's been consistency provided through Rob Moorman [group director] and Denny O'Hearn [group director]. They're the two people on the account side who have done a great job for us. On the creative side, Grace McQueen [senior art director] has been a big factor.

It's almost as if Jordan McGrath's staff is a part of our company: they've been around here for so long, that in many respects we don't consider them an outside supplier. We have a very solid relationship.

Randy Papdellis, VP-Marketing, Welch's

Balance.

Based on our three years' experience working with Jordan McGrath (under our former name, TCI), I'd say they strike a nice balance between being strategically driven and being creative in their execution.

Another of their strengths is that while they do push back at the client, as many creative agencies do, they also listen well and adapt to constructive criticism. There's always push and pull in an agency-client relationship, and they do push for their point of view. But when the client communicates a particular point of view, they're good listeners.

In fact, I feel an agency is not doing its job if it doesn't stand up for its point of view. If they acquiesce too early, it wouldn't work well. But, at the end of day, Jordan McGrath's people do listen and take direction. And their ability to listen leads to good creative.

In this regard, Rick Bodge [management supervisor] has distinguished himself as the senior member on the account side at the agency. He really spends a lot of time reading the trades and staying up on our business. In fact, of all the agency people we work with, his command of what's happening in our difficult industry is as strong as anyone I've ever encountered. And Tom Wambach [exec VP-creative director] is good at pushing for strong creative, then responding to constructive criticism.

After we do the positioning work up front, we draft a creative brief, which they then re-interpret in their own style.

We agree on that, and then the creatives go to work against that brief. That way, you don't see executions that are outside the strategy.

Doug Seserman, Sr. VP-Marketing, AT&T Broadband & Internet Services

We like to involve our agency partners from the beginning, all the way back to strategy development and business planning. So Jordan McGrath works with us in developing the marketing strategy.

It's been a team effort, and the team seems to work well together. Dean Schwartz [group director], who supervises our business, has been terrific. He's a very clear strategic thinker. And Pat McGrath has come to our strategy meetings as well. It's not often an agency chairman gets involved in day-to-day strategy discussions. He pitches right in. Given his level of experience and his expertise, it's great to have him involved in our business.

Fred Huser, President, Novartis OTC

Range of Approaches.
What strikes me about Jordan McGrath is that both their account team and their creative team are terrifically talented. Some agencies may be stronger on one side or the other, but seldom in both areas. Jordan McGrath's terrific blend of creative and account talent makes for a very synchronized team.

They've handled our account for 10 years, and they are very actively involved in the toy industry and in the games business. Because we have a partnership relationship, they make it a point to actively participate in our strategic planning and in the overall process as we develop our product lines.

This approach starts with Pat McGrath and is pervasive throughout the entire agency. The agency provides a depth and breadth of talent, and they've dedicated this to our business. Their creative reflects this.

What I find appealing is they always approach an assignment from several different perspectives.

They will present a range of creative approaches that will address that assignment from a number of different angles, presenting rationales on why they are offering the different approaches.

Similarly, the account team will provide various strategic approaches and reasons why they are suggesting each particular approach. Clearly, this stimulates a client's thinking and enables you to think outside the box.

I've worked with a lot of agencies over the years, and I think Jordan McGrath is among the best in terms of the quality of our working relationship and the quality of the work they produce.

Dale Siswick, GM-U.S. Sales & Marketing, Hasbro Games

JUICY CASES:

3.1: Tight vs. Loose.

You're the account manager on an account that has been with the agency for a few years. A new senior art director has been hired and assigned to the account. This art director insists that all his layouts be presented in a comprehensive layout form (comps) and will not have any part of showing rough layouts to the client.

The client, on the other hand, is very good at visualization and doesn't need expensive comps to understand the concepts being presented.

In fact, comps have a negative effect. The client immediately sees them as an unneeded expense for which the agency is going to send him a big bill.

What to do?

3.2: A Matter of Interpretation.

You're an account manager with a brand new account that you were instrumental in landing. This new account is a government agency which, like most public sector clients, is process oriented.

As such, they are as concerned with the agency process of creating advertising as they are with the advertising itself.

Your first assignment for this client is a large direct mail and collateral project for one of its divisions. The MarCom manager who made the decision to hire your agency decides to let one of her promotion managers take the lead on this project and work directly with the agency. It turns out that this is the first project for which the promotion manager will be responsible.

Because you're the new agency working with an inexperienced client contact, you take pains to make sure the process is correct and to keep the MarCom director informed about what is going on.

A campaign brief is written and approved by the promotion manager. An informational copy is sent to the MarCom director, as are relevant memos and status reports.

In spite of your best efforts to do everything right on this maiden project, the presentation of the creative work is a disaster. The promotion manager rejects the work as being totally off target and starts making accusations that the agency did not listen.

You discuss the approved campaign brief with her and find that two critical words on the campaign brief have a totally different meaning in her mind than what they meant to you and your creative team.

After great reflection and soul searching you have come to a decision that the meaning this promotion manager has attached to those two pivotal words is unusual and unfounded, to say the least. The agency has thousands of dollars worth of billable time into this project.

What do you do?

AD-ROBIC EXERCISES:

3.1: Complete the Conference Report.

Review the agency-client meeting transcript in Chapter 3.1 and write the rest of the conference report started at the end of the chapter.

Focus on two things:

1. The format as presented in the chaper section

2. The selections of the items that, for seasons of sensitivity, do not get reported

3.2: Write a Creative Brief in Reverse.

Hot Shop Advertising Agency has a new client, Homewarehouse.com, an online home improvement store. The client did no research ahead of time to determine what target audience provides the most potential. The agency undertook research to narrow the target audience and figure out the best way to emotionally connect with them.

Based on the two scripts and the other background information provided, write a plausible creative brief.

Use the Ann Sacks creative brief in Chapter 3.3 as a template.

Include a discussion of demographic, psychographic, geographic, and behavioristic characteristics that would have led the agency to come up with this campaign. The media buy is also based on the agency's research findings. The spots are scheduled to air in markets like Portland, Seattle, Denver, Minneapolis, and San Diego.

Homewarehouse.com Radio Commercials
Spot #1: "Male Apology" :60

Announcer: And now a public apology to the women of America.

Character: Dear women, we are sorry for being insensitive to your needs. We are sorry for football season. We are sorry for not listening, even though we nod as if we are.

We are sorry for looking in the general direction of really attractive women. And the time in college we swore to never tell you about.

We are sorry for not noticing when you highlight your hair.

We're sorry for using the garage to store our tools instead of your car. And we're sorry we didn't use Homewarehouse.com like you said we should. They have a huge selection of home improvement products online at great prices. And their home pros would have told us that duct-taping the track light to the ceiling was a very bad idea.

So in conclusion, we are sorry for being big, dumb, self-absorbed man-apes who only think of ourselves when in reality we are put on this planet to serve you and you alone.

Thank you for being so understanding.

Announcer: This message sponsored by Homewarehouse.com... more home improvement (SFX: Knock, knock, knock) for less.

Look for our catalog in your mailbox.

Character: And we're sorry if we skipped anything.

Spot #2: "Contractor Apology" :60

Announcer: And now a public apology from the contractors of America.

Contractor: Dear people who's homes we've worked on, we are sorry for testing your patience and for being late. Not just late-late, but, you know, not showing up at all. We are sorry we can't be your own personal contractor who greets you in the morning with blueprints, a smile, and toasty Danish.

We are sorry for running our circular saw when we can clearly see that you are on the phone. We are sorry for using language that is foul and offensive. Most of all... we are sorry for saying that the job is going to cost $5,000 when in fact that sucker is gonna cost double that.

We should have used Homewarehouse.com. They have all the tools and supplies we need at incredibly low prices. In fact, you'd think we'd pass the savings on to you, but we won't because we're contractors and, well, we all want boats.

Announcer: This message sponsored by Homewarehouse.com... more home improvement (SFX: Knock, knock, knock) for less.

Look for our catalog in your mailbox.

Contractor: Oh yeah, we're sorry for our pants... you know, when we bend over to move the fridge.

BURNING QUESTIONS:

3.1:
Why is it said that account managers have to be as good with a pen as they are on their feet?

3.2:
Why is evaluating creative concepts such a delicate issue?

4.0 WANTS, NEEDS, AND EXPECTATIONS

ONE OF THE THINGS that makes the job of account manager so challenging is that parties important to your personal success want different things from you. Your client's wants are sometimes very different from what your agency associates need from you.

The senior management of your agency sometimes has yet another set of expectations. As usual, the key to success is knowing how to juggle these often disparate performance expectations.

This chapter contains five sections:

- What Clients Want from Their Agency and Expect of Their Account Manager

- What Creatives Want in an Account Manager

- What Media Planners Want in an Account Manager

- Straight Talk about Account Planning

- What Agency Management Wants in an Account Manager

"No, the client meeting is tomorrow. That was just the rehearsal."

4.1 What Clients Want from Their Agency and Expect of Their Account Manager

Since an important part of your job is to serve clients, you will spend the majority of your time making sure you and your agency deliver on the following expectations. As you progress through your career, it is helpful to have a yardstick against which to measure how you are doing.

Clients hire agencies to solve problems – tough problems in need of creative solutions that only agencies can develop. Each client brings their own pressures, biases, internal problems, and limitations that put a unique spin on the account manager's job of managing the agency's efforts.

The purpose of this chapter is to explain what clients want from their agency and therefore expect their account manager to deliver.

Short of a more formal assessment tool provided by agency management or your client, this list of client wants and expectations should serve you well.

A partner and collaborator, genuinely interested in and capable of building their business.

The relationship between agency and client is unique in business culture.

Some people liken this relationship to that of a client and its law firm, its accounting firm, or its management consultants. But the agency is expected to be a more proactive partner, leading the client rather than simply responding.

The agency-client relationship revolves around strategies and programs that will build image and generate revenue. Lastly, the agency-client partnership is unique because it is usually a lot of fun. Honest!

Smart clients know they need professional communications help and are willing to give you and your firm tremendous responsibility for their future success.

This is why clients are called clients, not customers.

When the relationship between the agency and client is good, you will be entrusted with information few people see.

Collaboration, objectivity, candor.

Three characteristics are present in every strong agency-client relationship: collaboration, objectivity, and candor. The contemporary model for a strong relationship involves the client in the agency work more than it used to.

The client review of the creative brief, the use of concept roughs, and even occasional client involvement in the creative process are indications that collaboration is good business practice.

Candor is another hallmark of a strong partnership.

Clients expect to be told what they can and cannot expect their advertising to accomplish and should expect to be told when and why the agency thinks they (the clients) are wrong.

You are not just making ads. You are building brands, effecting sales, and crafting the very voice your client uses to address its customers. This is no small deal.

The posture and demeanor of the agency should be creative but still professional, sometimes leading, sometimes equal, sometimes following, but always collaborative and always candid.

The senior management of your agency has convinced your client that your account team is the partner they can count on for the creative messages, integration, and leadership that will drive their share of voice, share of mind, and share of market. It is a very heady responsibility.

The account manager is the keeper of many flames, the candor flame being one of the most important. Clients need to hear the truth as the agency sees it.

The account manager is most often the messenger, the advocate, the taker of unpopular agency positions. Nobody said leading a client was easy work.

One cautionary note, however. The term "partner" may not set well with the egos of many CEOs and top marketing executives. They know they need a partner, but they may not be able to admit it. So be sensitive to the use of this term and go with something else like "resource" or "advisor," but act no less professional.

In order to be a capable and deserving partner in the client's business, the agency requires a strong business sense to complement its creative prowess.

Becoming a business partner is achieved through countless gestures and successes. For instance, going to client industry trade shows and participating in client industry associations. These are both seen as true demonstrations of a commitment to the client.

A philosophy of creating change, not ads.

"They get it" is a saying among clients who love their agency. It means the agency has a good business sense. The agency understands marketing, understands the client's business, and knows what business the agency really is in.

Advertising is not an end in itself. It's a business tool to create change in awareness, attitude, and behavior. It's normal for agency creatives to be in love with their ads.

The account manager must be in love with the impact the ads will have for the client in the marketplace.

Setting objectives is crucial to the account manager's role as "change agent." The more specific the advertising objectives are, the more focused the ads will be, and the probability of success increases.

Strong creative work.

Great ads are the most visible and tangible of the agency's products. Above all else, be committed and passionate about delivering strong, high quality creative work that is based on sound strategy and realistic objectives. This, of course, requires that you know when and why the creative work is the right work.

Clients believe they need strong creative work, but they might need some education to know it when they see it.

Evaluating the value of advertising is difficult and subjective. (Chapter 3, "Tools of the Craft," deals with the evaluation of creative work.) With the possible exception of direct-response campaigns, it is hard to isolate the exact impact of advertising. There are many factors that contribute to marketing success. Advertising is just one of them.

Don't assume your client fully understands or appreciates the strength and brilliance of the work your agency does for them. For many clients, if the work gets done on time, doesn't exceed the budget, and looks halfway decent, it's good work.

The level of involvement the client has in the creative process should be a mutually decided issue within certain limits.

Two driving factors in client involvement.

Two driving factors will be the amount of involvement the client actually wants and the creative director's tolerance for that involvement.

The creative brief process, when executed properly, should provide the client adequate involvement in the strategy review before work starts on any ads.

But some clients actually like to participate in the development of the ads themselves. This can be a very sensitive and problem-prone issue when the client is intimately involved in the creative work it has hired the agency to do.

Ultimately, the account manager is the keeper of the creative flame, ensuring consistently effective creative work. The client needs to trust you to know strong work, to be able to explain and defend it. If the work doesn't measure up to what has been done for the client in the past, or isn't work you would proudly show a new business prospect, then you shouldn't try to sell it, and you should not expect your client to accept it.

Team members who "own the customer experience."

Clients are often product oriented, consumed by issues of product features, production, pricing, and distribution. They hire an agency to stay in touch with the marketplace and add to the customer profile that is so critical to effective advertising.

While "owning the customer experience" is not the sole domain of the agency, the client should expect the agency will add significantly to the collective understanding of the customer psyche.

As discussed elsewhere in this book, account planning is a hybrid research and creative technique designed to ensure that the customer's perspective is represented in the creative process. So having everyone look at a campaign, or an ad, or a brochure from the customer's standpoint is a good thing.

Thinking like an account planner is especially important for agency teams that do not include an account planner. When no account planner is there, the account manager is responsible for making sure the customer is well represented in the creative and media strategy.

The ability of an account manager to own the customer experience and understand the marketplace comes through getting out into the field, observing, talking with customers, with retail sales people and dealers, using the client's products and testing the competitor's.

Occasionally an account manager, truly attuned to the client's customers and marketplace, makes a significant contribution in the area of product design, packaging, marketing strategies, and the like.

Integrated thinking.

Following closely behind strong creative work is the level of integration an agency should bring to a client's communications plan. The first thing a client will look at is the promotional mix – the choice of media being recommended.

It should be both creative and strategic in its make up. The next thing clients will expect is that all the pieces of the plan will be well integrated. Integration ensures that those elements of the recommended promotional mix work together well, follow a consistent strategy, and carry a consistent message.

As explained in Chapter 1.1, the "Evolution of the Advertising Agency," agencies are trying to be truly full service... to be able to deliver the services found in the promotional mix.

One-stop shopping is a good thing for client relations and the agency bottom line.

Briefing multiple resources can be a problem for MarCom managers who have a lot on their plate. So an agency that provides a wide variety of MarCom services and is good at integration is a valuable partner. Even when the agency does not offer a certain service (like PR or interactive) it is best that the agency take the lead in finding the best provider and managing that service for the client.

Being good at managing the whole promotional mix and integrating those services well for the client does three other things, all positive.

First, the director of marketing communications (your client), normally has many responsibilities beyond the ad program, so being able to rely upon one resource for everything is an efficient use of the client's time.

Second, from the customer's standpoint, better coordinated and meaningful advertising can enhance the brand experience.

Finally, from the agency's standpoint, the more services provided and controlled by the agency, the better the opportunity for effective integration and the more dependent the account is on the agency.

Clear and consistent communications.
Doing work for a client is one thing, tending to the business of account service is another. The level of responsibility, confidentiality, and money involved in servicing a client requires that the client know what is going on at all times with the projects entrusted to the agency.

As account manager, you are the conduit for these communications, the gatekeeper and the minder of the client's trust. Communications must be timely, complete, and accurate; questions and concerns must be responded to quickly.

The tools used to achieve effective communications include conference reports, project status reports, reports of all kinds, e-mail, and simple phone calls. Don't be stingy with these tools. The client will tell you if you are overcommunicating.

Two keys to communication success are:

1. attention to detail (write it down); and

2. providing what people need to know before they ask for it.

In general, the more you communicate, the smoother things go.

The smoother things go, the more trust you earn and the more the client will rely on the agency. The more trust and responsibility, the more space you get to do your job and the more important your growing account becomes to agency revenue. Think raise!

An agency team that's open-minded, listens well, and takes directions.

The most frequent reason for terminating an agency is "they don't listen." This accusation is most often lodged at a creative team that consistently brings forth proposals that (in the client's opinion) are off target or did not heed client direction.

Developing good listening skills is well worth the time for account managers. Some people in the agency might listen selectively for what they want to hear and for what's wrong with what the client is saying.

Agencies hurt their cause when they totally disregard a direction or suggestion made by the client. If not followed, client directions and suggestions still need to be responded to with well-considered explanations for why they were not taken. It's the diplomatic job of the account manager to make this happen. This is one of the most difficult jobs of the account manager.

Strong-minded creatives are a fact of life in the agency business. But, as account manager, your job is to always make sure your clients know their input was heard.

Sometimes this is a difficult job because the role of the agency is to lead the client to advertising that will stand out in the marketplace.

Stand-out advertising often seems risky to clients.

An account manager's role is to provide input and feedback to the creative team that ensures that the client sees the agency was listening.

Clients who have read this book unanimously agree on the importance of this point and say they rely on their account manager to be their "interpreter" to the agency. This occasionally includes filling in the blanks for what the client did not say.

At the same time, your role is to push the client to take reasonable risks in order to make their communications more effective.

Being responsive and assertive is an art that becomes easier as you gain experience and trust. Demonstrating that your agency listens well is the first step.

Creative thinkers in all parts of the team.
Ideas are your stock and trade. Clients hire agencies for ideas that will build share of voice, share of mind, and share of market.

Creativity can't stop with your creative department. Creativity must permeate the entire team. (Except, perhaps, the accounting department. There, less creativity is better).

Creative value added should be everyone's goal: media, interactive, public relations, it doesn't matter. The account manager's job is to challenge and motivate every team member to do their best creative thinking on every project or campaign.

Creative depth is wonderful. It doesn't always happen. But when that extra creative solution is needed, you and your team really need to deliver.

When someone (other than the creative team, of course) comes up with a stunning creative idea that really adds value to the campaign, make a big deal about it.

There's nothing better than to be able to tell a client that the new idea came from someone in the media department or an account coordinator or someone in the traffic department whom they have never met.

A team that is proactive.

"Staying ahead of the client" is the safe ground. Actually, it's the only ground. Account managers who sit around waiting for the next assignment from their clients aren't doing their jobs.

Thinking about ways to grow the client's business is part of partnership responsibility.

Looking for new markets for their products, finding new media, finding a communications technique used in another industry and seeing how it might apply, and pushing the client in the right direction – these are the things that clients need and expect.

Apathy and lethargy can set in after the account's "honeymoon" period. You must constantly check the intellectual energy level of your account team. With your intuitive talents and acquired skills, you need to keep your team and yourself pumped up – always proactive and always caring about the client's business.

Not every advertising and marketing idea you bring to a client is going to see the light of day.

Enlightened clients don't expect to accept every agency proposal. That's not the point, anyway. You build trust and appreciation with ideas that are well thought out, aggressive, and on target.

When one actually gets accepted and executed, you and your client both look good.

A team that can take constructive criticism and deal maturely with disappointment.

No one has time for a creative team that gets defensive or starts to sulk when a client criticizes its work. There is something wrong with the relationship if this happens regularly, and it's up to the account manager to fix the problem.

Creative work should be "on target" when presented, there should be no unpleasant surprises if the agency has done it's homework and has included the client in pivotal discussions along the way. Approval of the creative brief is one of these pivotal discussions.

Additionally, clients should feel that they can be constructively critical in an attempt to get to the best execution of the best ideas, as they see it.

Sure, there are going to be disagreements, but everyone is on the same team. The agency should welcome client comments and participation. It fosters client buy-in of the agency's work.

Dealing maturely with disappointment and set-back is also part of the business. Sometimes great ads and wonderful campaigns get killed regardless of their merits.

Changes in the marketplace and budget cuts are realities that client and agency often face together. Even worse, whole campaigns have been killed because the chairman got one negative letter from a stockholder or the wife of the CEO didn't like the new tagline. It can happen.

The agency-client relationship requires that the agency rebound quickly from disappointments and be ready to attack the challenge with renewed energy.

Genuine respect and appreciation for the realities of the client's job.

The job of the client always looks easy, until you take a look behind the scenes. Then you find that the client's job can be every bit as challenging as yours. Understanding the business reality of the client is sometimes sobering.

Political battles for control, conflicting directives, production problems, turf battles, budgets problems – you name it, they have it. The demands of their top management, dealers, employees, marketing, and production are often conflicting.

Sometimes it simply is not easy being a client. So what can you do? Listen, empathize, understand their problems, and look at everything you do for your clients from the standpoint of the challenges they face inside their own organizations.

While clients should always expect the agency to push them, the agency team, led by the account manager, should always respect clients as important to the agency.

You need to understand the environment in which your clients must do their jobs and respect their limitations, be they personal, organizational, budgetary, or otherwise.

You might wonder how an agency could afford to be disrespectful to a client contact, but it happens all the time.

In most cases disrespect is the result of an agency working with a contact who has no power to fire the agency. In this case, the agency can turn arrogant and make this poor client contact's life miserable.

It happens. One day the person who is being dissed by the agency may be in a position of power. Who will be the first to go? The agency.

Bad mouthing a client among agency associates does nothing but lower morale and drain creative energy.

A particular client can be a tough one and maybe not your favorite person, but if you want good work from your associates, showing respect and appreciation for the client is the best policy for you.

The old adage in the agency business is every client should feel like they're the agency's only client. Idealistic, for sure. Realistic, *not*.

But that doesn't lessen the importance of the point. Clients are the life blood of the agency and should be appreciated as such.

It doesn't take much to make a client feel important. Be responsive. Do good work. Spend their money as if it were your own. Trust and value their knowledge of their business. Treat them with respect. Say thanks.

How difficult is that?

Team members (especially the account manager) who are presentable.

The goal of an account manager is to become a valued member of the client's management team; to be recognized and respected within the organization as an outsider who is in the "inner circle" by virtue of advertising expertise, insightful customer knowledge, and a thorough understanding of their business.

The degree to which an agency is allowed to be visible inside a client organization depends on a number of factors.

These could include the importance of advertising to the client company, the self-confidence of the client MarCom manager, and how "presentable" the agency team is.

In most cases, the only members of the agency team who will have any significant visibility inside the client organization will be the account manager and a member of the agency's top management.

One of the prime characteristics a client looks for in an account manager or agency top management is salesmanship. An agency representative who can make persuasive presentations to the client's upper management is a true asset.

Being dynamic, compelling, authoritative, and articulate is good. Being able to blend in quickly with the client's culture is also one of the key skills of the account manager.

The "Chameleon Effect," as it is called, is easier for account people than it may be for others. Pay special attention to your client's internal culture and adapt to it.

This doesn't mean becoming something you are not. It does mean adopting protocols, dress codes, language, work styles, and other client cultural norms. When you do this, you are more likely to become an asset to your client contact and gain a position of importance within the organization.

There is something very special about being able to walk into a large client organization and assume a high level of acceptance because you've adapted to their culture. It's even better when you do the same thing in the afternoon with a different client and a totally different corporate culture. You've become a true chameleon.

If others from your agency are involved with your client, everyone should be sensitive to this issue of presentability. Even though agency people are expected to be a little different, they still are providing a professional service and should look and act like it.

Clients sometimes make funny judgments about people that could adversely affect the way they view the agency's work. Why let good work get penalized because some agency people insist on a certain type of appearance or behavior? You shouldn't.

Account team stability is also an important subset of presentability. Clients take a risk by introducing agency players (other than the account manager and top management) into their organization.

Frequent changes on the account team tend to decrease the client's willingness to give other agency people visibility, and frequent changes also impact the next issue: anxiety.

Agency service that is "seamless" and anxiety-free.
In addition to great creative work, the agency must be reliable in completing all manner of projects on deadline, on budget, and error-free. No easy task. Creating multifaceted campaigns from scratch can be a contentious, stressful process within the agency. But that's not the client's problem. They don't want or need to hear about all the problems you encounter.

The cantankerous copywriter, the error-prone media planner, the short-staffed production department, the agency's lack of cost controls – not the client's concern. Anxiety-free means that when the agency says something will be done, it gets done, on time, on budget, and error-free.

In the process of creating ads and meeting deadlines, a lot of subjective decisions have to be made and client approvals obtained. The client will want to know the account manager's "real opinion" on all manner of subjective issues, large and small.

It's the degree of trust in the account manager that compels the client to ask. It's a delicate art the account manager learns – to have an opinion and also speak for the agency.

It's part of being seamless.

It is normally acceptable for the account manger to have a preference for a specific approach among a number presented. But major disagreements on creative proposals need to be ironed out before anything ever gets presented to the client.

"Seamless" has at least six meanings:

1. Agency departments work well together, everyone on the team knows what is going on, and the complex internal communication is well managed.

2. Regardless of who in the agency does the creative or media work, it is always of the same excellent quality.

3. The agency is united on its recommendations.

4. Agency performance standards are impervious to personnel changes.

5. Even when the account manager is gone, things run smoothly. (Good luck.)

6. The billings are accurate and timely.

Clients hire agencies to do work that they can't do themselves and to make their jobs easier, not to give them more worries and grief. The last thing you want to do is add to the client's stress level by causing anxiety about your agency's internal problems or your ability to perform effectively.

Bottom line – make the agency's work one less thing the client has to worry about. On time, on budget, and error-free. No surprises. Keep your problems "in the shop" and solve them quickly.

Take total responsibility for results and make sure the client knows who to contact at the agency when you are gone.

At this point it is appropriate to talk about agency staff turnover. Account team stability can be a big, very big issue among clients and account managers.

Losing a key creative team member, a research analyst, a media planner, or an account coordinator means extra work for the account manager in the area of training and quality control.

Externally, when agency team turnover happens, the client will want to be reassured that there will be no gaps in service and that the new player on the team is actually a "plus" for the client.

A team that thinks big but minds the details.

If you want to be invited to the client's strategy table, you have to show you can handle the fundamental details of this incredibly detail-oriented business.

Media, creative, production, accounting, all the specialty services... an unbelievable amount of minutiae. An overlooked detail of the smallest nature can really dampen a client's enthusiasm about a new campaign and may cause you billing problems later.

So while account managers are supposed to see the big picture, they also have to make sure everyone is taking care of the details. Doing so requires that you understand the smallest details of everyone else's job.

Again, understand the small details of everyone else's job. (*Repetition for emphasis.*)

Checking the details will communicate two important things to your agency associates. First, you know what is needed. Second, you won't accept sloppy work.

Part of being detail-oriented is documenting everything and maintaining good files so that information and samples can be retrieved quickly. More on this later.

A team that will make the client contact look good.

Great agency work that is loved within the account makes your client look good. But beyond the work itself, the agency team should be dedicated to making your client look good.

This can take a variety of forms, but probably the most important is education. You are the communications expert. You are backed by a staff of experts. Your entire agency should be at the client's disposal to provide information, advise, and expertise.

When you have a close personal relationship with the client, you may be asked how you think they could be more effective. For clients, I've discreetly arranged a variety of skill enhancements and instruction. Presentation training, salesmanship, listening skills, public speaking, and media interviewing are among the topics.

The smarter your client is about communications issues, the better equipped they are to sell the agency's work inside their own organization when you are not there. So don't be afraid of smart clients. They're an asset to the agency.

Remember, your client contact has more audiences than just product users. Internal managers, stockholders, distributors, the business community at large, the news media, even government regulators may be among the people making judgments about your client, based on the work you do for them.

Clients get attached to people who make them look good, and they treasure an agency team that performs well under unexpected pressure.

A group of pleasant and interesting people.
Sometimes, working with the agency is the only fun a client has. The rest of the time it's stressful work surrounded by boring people. So if your client seems to enjoy hanging out at the agency and doing lunch with you and the creatives, there is a reason – pleasant distraction.

Make the most of it.

But remember, this is still a business relationship first, and your agency has been hired to provide important professional services.

Impeccable billings.
Consistently sloppy billings will almost always sour an agency-client relationship. There is no reason for this to happen. It takes a long time to overcome the client's distrust caused by billing errors. Clients spend more time combing over suspect billings and you waste time responding.

Your accounting department might scream, but everyone is best served by monthly billings which are accurate, complete, timely, and prepared in a way that best serves the needs of the client, not your agency's computer.

The level of detail in the billings will vary from simple one-line billing for each project up to U.S. government accounts, which require extreme detail and backup invoices from all outside vendors. If you want to get paid, you do the billing and you do it with same level of professionalism that you do everything else, maybe more.

Fair pricing.
How agencies make money is discussed in another chapter. Pricing is a separate and often touchy subject. How do you put a price on a creative idea? How much is an hour of media planning really worth? Why should the agency earn a commission on printing?

These are issues that management deals with when the compensation arrangement is hammered out at the beginning of the agency-client relationship.

As account manager, you may have little say over the compensation arrangement. Your job is to know your client's "money issues" and to make sure that in every way possible the client believes they are getting good value from the agency.

You need to show how good the work is, how efficient your team is, and add value wherever possible with ideas, efficiencies, and your own personal efforts.

Flexible work style.
Agencies are professional service organizations. Part of the service should be providing service in a way that best matches the needs of the client. This can range from the way creative proposals are presented to the way billing is prepared, from the frequency of meetings to maximizing agency accessibility by having the account manager work the same hours as the client.

Be ever watchful for the personal attention requirements and the opportunities to customize your services. As long as the customization doesn't hurt the quality of the agency's work, the general wisdom is to eagerly accommodate the client.

For instance, some clients have longer approval cycles than others. Not providing clients enough time to accommodate their approval process does two things.

It reduces the time available for revisions, and it makes the agency seem uncooperative.

From slow approval processes to specific billing requests, clients have internal administrative practices that can impact how the agency provides service. In the spirit of flexible work style, agencies should be as accommodating as possible.

If a client administrative process (and its impact on the agency) is far out of the norm, you have a couple of options. Try to find a happy medium.

Or say that the request can be met but will have to be billed as an extra service because it requires so much more time. You might be surprised what clients are willing to pay for if it makes their lives a little easier.

Involvement of agency principals.

Agency principals (owners and/or top executives) need to be active in each account. A lack of that top management involvement essentially says to the client that they are not important. Account managers should work to keep their principals involved. Conference reports, memos, and selected meetings are good ways to keep agency top management knowledgeable about what is going on with an account.

Agency principals are seasoned people with a wealth of experience. It's a shame they spend so much of their time concerned with administrative stuff rather than employing their expertise for the good of clients. They are great resources for account managers who understand the value of their involvement.

Anytime a client is planning a visit to the agency, it's important that agency principals are advised ahead of time that a client will be "in the shop."

The principals should plan to spend a few minutes with the client and be knowledgeable about the subjects of the day.

Busy agency principals really appreciate the efforts of account managers to keep them involved. Most will relish the opportunity to play a part in a client meeting or even pinch hit for the account manager, if they are adequately prepared ahead of time.

The client needs to know their account is important and if there is any problem on the account, they know who to call. Consistent agency principal involvement serves these purposes well.

An account manager who can be a trusted friend and confidant.

In this business, without trust you are toast. When you work with someone for a long time and you do it right, you build a relationship that goes way beyond business.

You often end up as friends. Graduations, birthdays, anniversaries, holiday parties, retirement parties, divorces, deaths – you share in the lives of your clients and they in yours.

For many executives, it's lonely at the top. They have no one in their organization in whom they can confide. Agency account managers often end up being that person. Why? Because they are outside the client organization, have proven they can be trusted, and are empathetic listeners. It is very fulfilling to be able to "check clients' oil" (ask how they are doing personally) when no one else even senses that something is bothering them.

Even if account managers are not yet confidants, they should always behave as if they could be. This is important, because the client is more likely to heed advice and value the opinion of someone who is genuine and trustworthy rather than "sales oriented."

You never know when a client is going to "need someone to talk to." Being there for them is a good thing.

The Annual Performance Review.

Agency managers (who are also good business people) know how important it is to periodically get a feel for how the client thinks the agency is doing. Some agencies avoid a formal performance review with the client, thinking that as long as the client is not complaining, everything is fine.

On the other hand, accounts such as P&G have formal checklists that guide the annual evaluation of the agency service.

Somewhere between doing nothing and being subjected to the client's own set of metrics lies the best approach to the agency performance review. The agency should take part in shaping the review.

The relationship of the agency and account, of the account manager and the client contact, is fundamental to success. This relationship can be stressed when subjected to a formal, across-the-table scoring process. Can you imagine a husband and wife doing this? Probably not, but business partners should and do.

So the best approach, especially with clients who do not have a formal annual performance review, is for the agency to take the initiative and do something effective, but not too formal.

This section, devoted to what accounts want from their agency, can operate as a checklist by which the agency can get valuable feedback from the client.

The annual agency performance review can also help the client feel that their opinion was solicited in a caring and actionable manner.

Proactive account managers will also do stealth performance reviews on their own work by constantly asking the client for feedback. This stealth performance review can cover everything from the preferred way to conduct meetings and present creative work to how they like reports written and billings prepared. The relationship sought is one in which the client asks for reasonable customization of services and the agency delivers it.

In some cases, a very "enlightened" client will ask that the agency conduct a client performance review. This is a very sensitive area, and the agency normally takes care not to be too critical. The review of client performance will include issues covered in Chapter 7.2, "In Search of the Ideal Client."

In the client performance review, the issues the agency cares to bring up are normally couched in this tone: "If you were able to improve on (pick an issue from Chapter 7.2), the agency would be able to serve you even better."

Who Is the Client?

The word "client" has two meanings – the client organization and the contact person. Contact persons can have a variety of titles and authority. One of the most fulfilling accomplishments for account managers is learning how to work with people on many levels throughout the client organization. When successful, the account manager becomes an integral part of the client organization.

In smaller accounts, an account manager may work directly with the president of the company, who may be a product visionary, an engineer, or a bean counter... but is usually not a marketing person.

In slightly larger accounts, you might work with a marketing manager, who is a glorified sales manager with little real training. Here, your expertise can fill a huge void where no other formal marketing and communications training exists.

The larger the client organization, the more layers of contact and decision makers there can be:
- Vice President of Marketing
- Vice President of Sales
- Director of Marketing Communications
- Group Brand Manager
- Brand Manager
- Brand Assistant

Exactly how the client organization is structured and how advertising decisions get made can vary from company to company, depending on the company's size, its industry, where the powerful personalities are, and the importance placed on advertising.

4.2 What Creatives Want in an Account Manager

Differences between creatives and account people are legendary and the subject of many amusing articles throughout the years. On the following page is a satirical view of what creatives think of themselves and account managers.

Creatives	**Account Managers**
• Never do bad creative	• Don't know good creative
• Multitalented	• Can be trained to write memos
• Zany and spontaneous	• Conservative and boring
• Free thinkers	• Linear thinkers
• T-shirts and jeans	• Suits
• His own man	• Yes man
• Stars	• Extras
• A legend in their own time	• A legend in their own mind

It's amusing. But there's a serious message behind this – if you can't work with creatives, it doesn't matter how much the client loves you. You will ultimately bomb as an account manager because you will fail to deliver to your client all the value your agency has to offer.

Your ability to work with copywriters, art directors, and creative directors will also be a barometer for how well you work with the other specialists in the agency. And great friendships are possible.

This has been true since an account man named John Young became friends with copywriter Ray Rubicam (Young and Rubicam) and Bill Bernbach teamed up with management guys Ned Doyle and Maxwell Dane (Doyle Dane Bernbach). Account man Stanley Resor even married his top creative, Helen Lansdowne Resor, and together they developed quite a little agency. It's called J. Walter Thompson.

Since the beginning of time, there has been conflict and friction between creatives and account people. But there's also cooperation.

The "collaborative" model for creating advertising and the growing sophistication of account management is quickly changing the old animosities.

Ask any seasoned creative director and they will tell you (sometimes begrudgingly) that the account manager can be the most important person in the agency because "the client trusts them."

In most cases, it is the account manager who expresses a preference about what creative team he'd like to work with. If you're a superior account manager (as defined here), it's the best creative teams who seek opportunities to work with you. Here's what they're looking for:

Someone who gives insightful input and can write a good campaign and creative brief.

The creative job is to find something new to say. Or, find a new way to say something old. Good input is the key to good creative.

You must understand how difficult the creative job is when they have nothing new with which to work. As an account manager, the more you dig for quality input, the more the creative team will deliver with good work.

Creatives truly need and appreciate account managers who can help them focus on the problem to be solved, thus lessening the likelihood that they will spend precious mental energy solving the wrong problem.

Chapter 3.3 provides a detailed discussion of creative briefs as the primary creative input document.

Someone who will have passionately objective opinions on creative work.

Advertising creativity is a very subjective thing. No surprise there. Opinions abound. Feelings are on the line. Surprisingly, most creative people want an account manager who has an opinion. When the opinion of the account manager is passionately objective, you approach creative nirvana.

Exactly what does it mean to be passionately objective or objectively passionate? Simply, it means that you have a strong opinion about something and that opinion is based on an objective and explainable point of reference. As an account manager, this is an important concept to remember in the evaluation of creative work.

What guidelines do you use when you evaluate the potential effectiveness of rough creative concepts? Strictly on how the client is going to react? Not if you are doing your job.

You need to find an assessment tool that helps you form an opinion about a concept or an ad where you are both objective and rightfully passionate about your position. (For an example, refer to the D'Arcy, Ogilvy, Bernbach model in Chapter 3.4)

Remember that objective passion is no guarantee of popularity. Sometimes you have to have the guts to stick with an unpopular position in which you really believe. Passionate objectivity also includes challenging work that, in your opinion, is mediocre. Asking hard questions exposes weak work.

Even if the creative people don't like your position, they will respect that you have thought it through and are willing to fight for it. Passionate debate on the issues is part of the creative process... a part at which account managers need to excel.

Someone who personally embraces their creative work.
"This is great stuff." Four words that will make a creative's day. Once you are happy with the work of the creative department, make it yours, love it, don't damn it with faint praise.

Display the layouts in your office until you have a chance to present them. Show them around the shop. Dig the work. Love the art that brings the message to life.

Someone who does a great job of presenting and defending the creative work to the client.
Creative people should always know they have the right to present their work, even though in many cases they won't do the actual presentation. It's an issue of confidence and morale.

In the majority of cases, the account manager will present the creative work. If you embrace the creative work, you are much more effective when you present it. Call on your creative team to coach you about how to present their work.

What do they think are the hot points? Is there anything that the layout does not quite convey? Why is the ad going to hold up well in its environment?

When you are the presenter, you need to milk the creative team for all the input you can get. This does two things. It maximizes your chances for success, and if you still bomb, it was not because their input wasn't used.

I think it's safe to say that creative people will subconsciously work a little harder for an account manager who they know will do a superior job of presenting their work the way they, the creative team, would present it.

The defending part of this "want" has to do with client-directed changes. Creative people not only deserve someone who will convincingly present the conceptual work but someone who will also successfully resist client changes when they believe the basic integrity of the idea would be compromised.

This is a true test of a good account person.

Someone who understands and respects the creative process. Creativity takes time and talent. Otherwise everyone could do it. "Just bang something out" – four words that *do not* make a creative's day. Everyone understands that not every project can win a CLIO or Addy or a Cannes Lion. But you don't need to make the work insignificant. After all, the client did ask the agency to do it.

The creative mind likes the challenge. It may just be a bill stuffer, but it's an opportunity to creatively make a statement for the betterment of the client. Respect the effort.

Breathing down their necks and hovering is no way to get the best work from creatives. It shows neither understanding nor confidence in the creative process.

Instead, try good input, inspiration, space, and time.

Someone who gives ample time for creative minds to work. Creative minds work 24/7. The creative subconscious works on one problem while the conscious mind works on another. It's the curse of being right-brained.

You never know when the "power idea" will come. Even the most productive creative team "hits the sand" once in a while. The one time you need a killer idea overnight may be the one time they can't come up with it.

Creativity takes time. The average turn-around time for copy and layout should be two weeks. There's a good reason for this.

It seems to be the optimum "simmering time" that a creative mind uses to work on problems – consciously and unconsciously – at one time.

You have your start-work meeting, and then even though the creative team goes back to working on something else, their subconscious has started to think about it. Then, ten days go by and they actually start serious work on your stuff.

The agency business is plagued with enough crash projects. You don't need to make the creative team perform miracles you don't need. Avoid bogus deadlines. Remember, *ASAP* is not a deadline.

Someone who can inspire.

Creatives like good sales people because good sales people inspire. The account manager's job is to put a spark under each project. This is your job, even though we all know that not every project is going to be the most important one ever done by the agency.

After all, how exciting can a bill-stuffer be? Nonetheless, it's important to try to find something about each project that makes it significant.

Creative people thrive on stimulation. Idea people are the ones they ask to "do lunch." Strive to be an "original thinker," a visionary, an idea merchant, and an agent of change. Throw the ideas out and let 'em go.

Someone who is creative in their own right.

Account managers whose creative outlet is a round of golf are not on the same wavelength as the creative folks. Not that there is anything wrong with golf. You are just not going to be "one of them."

On the other hand, if you enjoy creativity in genres other than advertising and actually do something creative (paint, write poetry, sculpt, make films), then you are likely to be seen in a different light by the creative team. The agency business is so stressful you need a creative distraction. Find one and use it to your advantage.

If you don't want to go the creative outlet route, it is even more important that you study advertising creativity. Read *Communication Arts* magazine and the *One Show Annual*.

Study the ads and talk to your creative associates about the work they think is good. You'll learn a lot and get to know your creative partners better at the same time.

Try to become an "idea" person who can creatively participate without getting in the way. If you're an idea person who doesn't care who ultimately gets credit for the idea, creative people will consider you an asset, a source of stimulation, an extension of themselves. *Cool!*

Someone who is willing to take risks.
Pushing the client is a recurring theme in this book. A strong account manager is the final decider of what will be presented to the client. Most clients are risk averse, even in their advertising.

Account managers who are confident enough in themselves and the agency's work to "stick their heads in the mouth of the lion" are going to have a lot of fans in the creative department.

Responsibilities shift in the creative department as people come and go and clients come and go. There is competition in the creative department for account assignments. And creative people do compete for accounts where the account manager is a reputed risk-taker.

Someone who knows how to work with creative people.
In addition to everything else said here, there are other traits that will enhance the success in working with creative people.

For this final segment, I borrowed liberally from Wes Perrin's excellent (but not currently available) book *Advertising Realities: A Practical Guide to Agency Management*.

Here are a few suggestions:

- Don't flaunt your education.
- Deal personally.
- Minimize paper and electronic communication.

- Get to know them as people with other interests. (They are normally good and interesting people underneath the egos.)
- Question.
- Be honest.
- Simplify.
- Have an opinion.
- Don't make fun or look down your nose at their sometimes "different" lifestyle.

4.3 What Media Planners Want in an Account Manager

First, it should be noted that there's a revolution going on in the media side of the agency business. Many small agencies are outsourcing the media function to media-buying services.

This is because media buying is becoming more complicated and because media is not quite the source of lucrative agency income that it used to be. (For a more detailed discussion of this phenomenon, see Chapter 1.2)

Whether the media function is done in-house or farmed out, the account manager is still responsible for the quality of the media plan. To a great degree, what the media department wants from account managers is much the same as what the creative department wants.

These commonalties include:

- Good input up front
- Respect for what they do
- Ample time to do a professional job
- Willingness to take a risk
- Enthusiasm for their proposal

The purpose of this chapter is to explore issues that are unique to the media function as they relate to account managers.

Keeping these in mind as you work with media planners will enhance your working relationship with them and the quality of the work they are able to do for you. Media planners want:

Someone who knows media basics.

Media people live in a world of numbers, indexes, ratios, cost-efficiencies, and effectiveness metrics.

They make decisions and recommendations based on these data.

If you're going to understand their recommendations and be able to present these proposals effectively to your client, you need to know media basics like:

- Cost per thousand (CPM)
- Rating points and cost per rating point
- Ratings and shares
- Net and gross
- Reach and frequency
- How to read SRDS for print media
- Indexes
- Media lead times
- Post buy analysis
- Frequency discount structures
- How to read Simmons, MRI, Nielson, and Arbitron
- How to read media flow charts

Media people are happy to teach you the rest of what you need to know, but they don't want to have to start with a blank slate.

Someone who provides good input.

Just like creative, clients can have strong opinions about media.

In addition to basics like target audience, timing, budget, and the like, the media planner needs to know any peripheral issues which could color their work.

This is especially important in the preparation of any defense that might be needed to change a flawed client attitude.

Someone who responds quickly to questions and proposals.
A good communicator provides quick and complete responses. A question that seems relatively unimportant to you might be mission-critical to the media planner trying to frame a creative media plan.

If it's asked, consider it important.

Once you have the media proposal, present it as soon as you are prepared. Media planners often have to contact media reps for the latest information that goes into a media proposal. Then the media reps call daily to see if there is any decision yet.

Receiving no word from the account manager on the status of a proposal that was the result of a lot of effort makes the media planner look bad and feel like it was just a waste of time.

Try to find a sense of urgency that keeps the client from sitting on a media proposal. For example, there may be a special deal with an end date or a closing date on a special issue.

If all or part of a proposal is rejected, make sure the media planner knows it quickly and knows why. It's the least you can do.

Someone who won't deal directly with the media reps.
Dealing directly with the media reps is not recommended, especially if you do so and then don't tell your media planner what was discussed or, even worse, what commitments were made by you or the client.

Media reps are a persistent bunch, and clients like to "do lunch" with them. Media reps often invite the account manager along to lunch with the client. This is good, because you can hopefully keep the client from making a direct commitment to the rep that might mess up something in the agency's master media plan.

If you're not invited to a meeting of the client and a media rep, you had better hope your client understands that his best interests are served by telling the media rep "all final media decisions are made by the agency."

Someone who will effectively present and defend the agency's media plan.

Clients sometimes have as strong an opinion about media choices as they do the creative work. When the agency does not agree with the client's media directives, this is a problem for the account manager.

Only in major presentations does the media director present the media plan. Normally it is the account manager.

When you expect a client to question an agency media proposal, the best approach is to prepare a rationale that explains why the agency proposal is better than what the client thinks it should be. In this case two plans (client-directed and agency-developed) may be presented together for comparison.

If the client wants to pay a higher cost per point and do something else that doesn't make perfect sense, at least the agency has fulfilled its obligation to give the client its best shot.

Someone who encourages creativity in media.

Media people deal with an incredible amount of dry data. They treasure the opportunity to be creative in their thinking.

It is the creative side of media which will multiply the impact of a good ad. Looking for new ways to reach the target audience, looking at new media and ad formats, or suggesting that a new audience deserves a test.

These are things that senior media people live to do.

Media people add value in two ways:

- First, by being tough negotiators with the media on price and positioning during the buying stage.

- Second, by thinking creatively during the planning stage. Encourage their creative thinking and be ready to embrace a good idea, regardless of how you think the client will react.

Clients need to foster creative thinking in media by designating a certain part of the media budget for experimentation... testing new strategies, trying new vehicles, being where the competition isn't.

Someone who will report results.

Media people genuinely want to know the results of the campaign. Unless you give them some feedback, they'll never know.

Measurement of media effectiveness is a tough call. There are many factors that go into the success of an ad campaign.

Media is only one variable. There may be no hard data to indicate that a new magazine was a good choice or that the extra 100 target rating points they recommended made the sale more successful.

How do you know? Sometimes, the best you can do is relate anecdotal information gleaned from the client, customers, or the medium.

Much advertising is done on faith and for competitive reasons.

While the client is interested in the overall effectiveness of the campaign, the media planner is more interested in the relative effectiveness of different media and vehicles within media categories... something even harder to determine.

Anything you can do to track results is normally good. In the case of media, it may be that each magazine in the plan has a different 800 number. Perhaps there is a way to count how many visits to the local dealers were created by each different radio station used.

Measure and report. Your media department will appreciate it.

How to Write a Media Plan.

While the agency media department is where the media expertise lies, there are reasons why the account manager might end up writing the comprehensive media plan. First, the account manager may be a better writer than the media planner, who is by nature a technical expert. Second, the media planner may not have the time to put the plan into the form the account manager wants for presentation to the client.

Even if the media department produces the written plan, it's important the account manager is able to explain and justify everything in it.

Since this is not a media textbook, you'll have to get one.

Or better yet, take a class in advertising media, so you understand the following outline.

Framework for a Comprehensive Media Plan.

Part 1: Advertising Objectives. (The Right Objective.)
Media plans should support a number of advertising objectives. For example, changes in marketplace knowledge, desired changes in attitude, or target audience behavior. Ad objectives go here.

Part 2: The Right Audience.
Here is where the audience(s) is identified, using four different profiling dimensions as applicable:

- Demographics – age, sex, income, education, ethnicity, etc.
- Geographics – region, state, spot markets/BDI, CDI, EBI, etc., city zones
- Psychographics – values, beliefs, lifestyles, interests, self-image, cultural heritage
- Behavioristics – product usage patterns, benefit hierarchy, media preferences

If there is more than one target audience, the strategic impression ratio should say what portion of impressions should be directed at each audience and why.

Part 3: The Right Medium.
Here is where the best media are identified, based on these criteria:

- Target audience preferences
- Suitability for the creative message
- Potential to generate trade support
- Ease of entry and exit, and flexibility for copy changes
- Budget realities (What can we really afford?)

If there are additional strengths that a selected medium brings to the campaign, they should be mentioned here.

It also helps to say why a plausible medium is not being recommended. This part is especially important if the client likes a specific medium that is not being recommended.

If more than one medium (like TV and billboards) are being proposed, provide a multimedia rationale along with some indication of how the media mix will work.

Part 4: The Right Exposure Level.

Here the audience delivery objectives (targets) are stated along with a rationale for the exposure levels being recommended.

Audience delivery is defined as the following:

- Number of impressions
- Number of rating points (GRPs & TRPs)
- Total reach and average frequency
- Effective reach and motivational frequency

If heavy levels of competitive ads are expected, a share-of-voice analysis might point to an upward adjustment of audience delivery targets.

Part 5: The Right Timing.

Here the media roll-out strategy is presented. A flow chart is normally used to show how, where, and when audience delivery objectives will be accomplished by each medium selected. Considerations include:

- Front-end loading
- Campaign duration
- Post-launch scheduling pattern
- Relation to seasonal sales patterns
- Simultaneous vs. sequential multimedia scheduling

Part 6: Right Cost.

Here is where a price is attached to the media plan. In many cases the budget is set arbitrarily by the client long before the media experts have a chance to figure out what they think it really should be. So the job is to do the best job of investing the given budget.

In the ideal situation, the agency is asked how much the media campaign should cost. The audience delivery objectives are "priced out" and that becomes the budget.

Since the price of media nowadays is pretty negotiable, the budget is an estimate that the agency thinks it can meet or beat, come time to actually buy the media. In addition to the total price, the budget section normally includes:

- Cost efficiency targets such as CPM and cost per rating point
- Expected media-contributed "value added"

4.4 Straight Talk about Account Planning

The client says, "This is my product."

The account manager says, "This is my client."

The creative team says, "This is our ad."

The account planner says, "This is my customer."

Quantitative Meets Qualitative.

Research departments basically work in two areas: quantitative and qualitative. Until the introduction of account planning as a formal agency discipline, the research department was the home of quantitative and secondary researchers. They specialized in analyzing Simmons and MRI data and ad tracking studies to glean insights into the marketplace.

Believing that emotions drive behavior, account planners are the newest discipline in the effort of advertising agencies to get inside the consumer's psyche.

Account planners are hybrids, part creative strategist and part qualitative researcher. The core of the account planning craft is the translation of qualitative research into the seeds of creative strategy. Their mission is to find customer insights, which consist of inner motivations, cheers and fears, symbols, beliefs, images, debunkable myths, prejudices, desires, and the emotional landscape of the brand.

Account planners provide the creative people with insightful and inspirational input on what makes the customer tick.

The intended outcome of account planning is that the advertising is strategically driven from the customer's point of view and executionally and emotionally relevant to the target audience.

Exactly where account planners are placed in the organizational chart is a subject of some discussion across the industry. Some planners say what they do is not research.

Hmmmm. Let's see. They do surveys, focus groups, and in-depth interviews. They do product-use video observation.

They ask for research databases on audience segmentation studies, and they study the "bleeding edge" to see what changes in society are five years ahead of us.

They study Simmons tables, tracking studies, cluster analyses, and study the research done by others in order to gain some new insight into the target audience. Is this not research?

In many respects account planners subsume the agency research function since the tools they use in the practice of their craft are all research, traditional and otherwise.

They analyze attitudinal tracking studies, sift through masses of data to find important trends, pore over focus-group and product-usage videos searching for a keen insight into why a product is purchased and how it is really used. Product-usage studies, product-velocity analysis, and ad testing are all tools familiar to the traditional, quantitatively oriented researcher.

The difference with account planners is their use of these tools to help the creative department come up with a creative brief that will result in a totally unexpected creative approach.

With no criticism intended, it's often said traditional researchers are passionate about research and clarifying the past, account planners are passionate about advertising and predicting the future.

Advertising is a creative process that benefits from the interaction of ideas, opinions, and personalities.

One of the key roles of the account planner is to challenge conventional advertising wisdom, to bring friction, provocation, and synergy to the process of making fresh and innovative advertising.

Considering the customer's viewpoint in advertising may sound like a BGO (Blinding Glimpse of the Obvious), but a lot of advertising talks about how wonderful the client is rather than making an emotional connection with the audience. This emotional connection is what account planners help to achieve.

Now that we've glorified account planning, let's examine the pitfalls of its application as they impact account management.

How the process of account planning gets done in an agency varies and is the subject of much controversy industrywide. Even within shops that have used account planning for a while, the process has evolved, and in some cases even been abandoned, due to the chaos it created.

In most agencies, account planning is a line function. Basically, this means it's directly or indirectly responsible for generating revenue. Clients generally like research because it is viewed as insurance.

But many clients have a hard time accepting that they should now pay for something they thought they were getting from the agency all along. A typical client question is: "Isn't this customer insight stuff what you guys said you were so good at to begin with? Why should I pay for it, when it's something you should have been providing anyway?"

Clients such as this will take a while to understand the newness of account planning and will probably never totally embrace it until they see the difference it makes in a campaign.

Some agencies that have made account planning a profit center do their best to sell account planning services to clients, but if a client does not want to pay for it, then the agency will do the best job of creating advertising without it.

The second big issue in the implementation of account planning is the degree to which the account planner is involved in development of the creative strategy.

Some creative directors will openly welcome the motivational and emotional insights and their creative implication. But if an account planner starts writing headlines, doing thumbnails, or employing other creative tools such as art, music, and film in the conveyance of their unsolicited creative suggestions, watch out for sparks.

In other shops, it is common practice for the account planner to use creative tools to make their point.

The second point of contention relative to account planners and creative teams is the role of the planner as creative sounding board. Evaluating and ultimately selecting creative concepts has been the purview of, first, the creative director and then the account manager.

When account planners are used, they rightfully should be involved in the evaluation of rough creative concepts.

After all, they are believed to be a one-person microcosm of the target audience. Thus, the additional filtering process can improve the relevance of ads. It can also be very contentious and slowing.

The creative department isn't the only function trying to figure out how to constructively deal with account planning. It can also make account management more interesting, not to mention more challenging.

In some agencies, the account planner sees the creative concepts before the account manager does. I never understood this practice. It carries a negative message to account managers that their extensive knowledge of the account and the marketplace are not important.

The bigger concern with this practice is that the account manager does not have the opportunity to spot a "kernel" of a great idea. If the account planner doesn't see the "kernel" and kills the initial idea, the client and agency both lose.

Of account planners, account managers often say, "Hey, isn't this my job?" The answer is *yes* and *no*.

Providing usable input to the creative team and being an objective sounding board for initial concepts have always been the jobs of the account manager, and they still are. However, the role of the account manager is changing, and once the working relationship is ironed out, the introduction of account planning can be a liberating experience.

First, the amount of research done by the account planner is impossible for the account manager to do, even if the account manager had the talents to do so.

Second, the interpretive skills that add value through the account planner are not always in the skill set of the account manager.

Third, since someone else now shares the primary responsibility of interacting with the creative team, the account manager can focus attention on larger strategic issues of what the client's whole MarCom program should look like and how it should be integrated for maximum results.

Remember, account planners are specialists with a fairly narrow focus. Account managers are generalists responsible for the big picture. Account planners do not want your job, and they'll be the first ones to admit that if they tried to be account managers, most of them would fail quickly.

Some say that the job of the account manager has been marginalized by the account planning movement. Again, the opposite seems true. The account planner, where used effectively, has added credibility to the whole creative process.

It is the account manager who can ensure that the work of the account planner is fully integrated and executed.

Account planners allow the account manager to spend more time thinking about overall brand strategy and campaign integration and less time dealing with subjective creative issues.

When done correctly, account planning has actually added another facet of sophistication to the role of the account manager as consultant and "integrator extraordinare."

The account planner and account manager must work collaboratively in order for the process to succeed. The creative brief should be co-authored, or at least undergo serious discussion between the planner and manager before it is presented to the creative team.

In many cases, the creative brief is reviewed with the client before it becomes official creative input.

As the first and primary point of contact with the client, the account manager must be "on board" with the brief before it is presented.

Practices vary, but most account planners don't present the creative work. Though they may set up the presentation by talking about research findings and strategic creativity.

Researchers at heart, most account planners feel their endorsement of an ad should only be on the basis of whether or not it is a good execution of a recommended strategy.

The account manager must hold the highest position of trust with the client. As such, the account manager is the first person a client turns to for reassurance if there is a concern about the creative approach.

The existence of good account planning work normally results in more effective advertising and a higher client confidence level in the agency's recommendations.

Account Planning When There Isn't Any.

Some account managers wonder what all the hoopla is about. These are managers who've always believed that consumers should be the focus of advertising.

When agencies don't have account planners, the account manager must perform this function. Account managers are expected to represent the client in creative deliberations, so wearing the account-planner hat at the same time is account service multitasking at its best.

The account manager does the client the greatest service by making sure the customer's voice is the agency's voice. So wearing the account-planner hat isn't an added burden, but essential for good advertising.

So how do you wear the account-planner hat when there isn't someone formally trained to do so? Good question.

The answer lies in understanding exactly what account planners do, which is to know more about your client's customer than anyone else. Anything you can do to understand the psyche, the habits, and mindset of the target audience will make your creative input better.

Gaining the respect and cooperation of the creative team is easier when your input is always good and your response to rough concepts is customer- rather than client-focused.

As a practical matter, many clients are preoccupied with issues of production, distribution, and pricing. So it does not take much for the agency, and specifically the smart account manager, to learn and know more about the client's customers than the client does.

The bottom line: when there's no account planner, you're it.

A Practical Example of Account Planning.

"The Campaign and Creative Briefs," Chapter 3.3, gives a blow-by-blow explanation of how the creative brief was instrumental in some very unusual advertising created by the much-admired Wieden+Kennedy agency.

A much briefer example of the value of account planning came in a project for a new retirement living facility where I provided the motivational research. I talked with and observed the first residents of the new facility, especially those who had moved from other facilities.

What I discovered was as surprising as it was enlightening. One of the characteristics of American society is that our elderly are not respected... as they are in other cultures.

An account planner would have known this going in, through research and study of the cultural backdrop of the customer.

When it came right down to it, the reason the new residents of this new facility were happy had nothing to do with the beautiful architecture, the great food, the free e-mail, or the marvelous activity program.

These were all nice features that residents got excited about, but the thing they valued most was the fact that the staff and local ownership were excellent listeners and communicators.

Because the staff had been professionally trained in listening, they could deal with one of the painful cultural realities in America – one that permeates retirement homes.

Elderly people, especially women, feel that no one listens to them and no one takes them seriously.

The campaign that resulted from this insight was different from anything done before. It was very effective because it resonated with the target audience on a key issue. That's account planning at its best.

If you're interested in account planning (you should be), there are two books you should consider. First and foremost is *Hitting the Sweet Spot* by Lisa Fortini-Campbell. For a Ph.D., she does an entertaining job of explaining ways to get inside the consumer's head. (Then again, she was also an agency researcher and the successful manager of an agency office.) Exercises at the end of this chapter were inspired by *Hitting the Sweet Spot*.

The other account planning book is more historical and anecdotal: *Truth, Lies and Advertising* by Jon Steel (AdWeek Books).

A Short Course in Audience Profiling.

Many clients actually know little about who buys their products and why. Gaining target audience insights is one of the most important contributions of ad agencies and specifically account planners. The better you know the target audience, the better you can communicate with them.

There are many ways to structure an audience profile. Following is a compilation of several different ones. At the end of this chapter is an exercise calling for a 20-dimensional profile of a Porsche driver.

Demographics
Age
Sex
Race
Marital status
Education
Household income
Number of people in the household
Employment status

Geographics
Region of the country
State
City
Neighborhood
Carrier route
Spot market ranking
Rural, urban, suburban
A,B,C,D county
Climate

Psychographics
Lifestyles
Interests
Values
Beliefs
Cultural heritage
Self-image

Behavioristics
Heavy, medium, or light user
Media preferences (What ad media do they prefer?
    Where do they spend their discretionary media time?)
Benefit hierarchy (why they buy)
Channel preference (where they prefer to buy)

4.5 What Agency Management Wants in an Account Manager

Concerns of agency management span the spectrum from agency reputation and account profitability to new business pitches and staffing levels. Their expectations of account managers are similarly diverse. While somewhat similar to the "wants" of creative and media, management's view of account service has its own orientation.

Management would not expect an entry-level account service candidate to excel at all of these wants and expectations.

This section explains how management will measure performance for anyone with five-or-so years experience.

The earlier an account manager shows strengths in these areas, the more promising the future will be.

The client relationship is one of the agency's biggest assets. Agency management wants account people they can trust with that relationship, ones who exercise good judgment, make good decisions, and represent the agency with distinction. Following are the building blocks of that trust.

Someone who loves advertising and loves what they do.
No question, advertising is a tough business. Account management is demanding work – gratifying and exciting, but demanding. In order to succeed personally and for the agency, you have to love the art and science of advertising. Management knows this.

If you love advertising but you do not enjoy the process by which it is created, then maybe agency account work is not where you want to be. Look into sales.

Someone who is hungry and willing to pay their dues.
Nothing is guaranteed in this business. Being hungry, working hard, and working smart paves the road to success.

There is no substitute for a strong work ethic and the understanding that the learning curve is steep and long. Hopefully this book will help shorten and flatten that curve.

Someone who can stay ahead of the client.

Account managers who simply react instead of leading their clients are account managers who put the agency at risk.

Management will look for signs that the account manager is thinking ahead and thinking strategically.

Someone who can increase client reliance on the agency.

Growth is worshipped in the agency business. If you're not growing, you look bad. There are three routes to growth:

1. Landing new accounts.

2. Helping clients increase sales so they spend more on advertising.

3. Increasing client billings by increasing the number of services provided by the agency. (This route can help the agency grow even if client budgets are static.)

The smart account manager is constantly looking for opportunities to provide additional services to the client. These can be services the client has been obtaining elsewhere or has not done before.

However, as a consultant, the account manager should never try to "sell" a service the client doesn't need.

Someone who can run profitable accounts, regardless of size.

The size of an account is not an instant or reliable determinant of its profitability. Many factors affect account profitability. The kinds of services obtained from the agency and the structure of the compensation agreement are two important factors.

Increasing the amount of services provided helps. Equally important are tight management of internal costs and limiting costly mistakes.

An account manager who stays on top of projects and manages budgets well is probably going to run profitable accounts, assuming the compensation arrangements are fair.

Another part of account profitability is managing the agency's compensation structure. As a client's needs change, there may be opportunity to change the structure so it produces more income for the agency.

Someone who "manages up."
It's very hard for agency management to stay abreast of what's happening on all the agency's accounts. The account manager who makes it a priority to keep management apprised will be highly regarded.

Conference reports are a good way to keep agency management and your account supervisor in the loop. If they have a question, concern, or idea, they'll respond.

E-mail or voice mail reporting of the results of important meetings are also good ways to report information that agency management may need as early as the next morning. (Perhaps an agency principal is playing a round of golf with the client VP of marketing.)

Sure, agency management likes to look important. They also like to use their years of experience. Every manager is going to have some problems. But management does not want to know every time the client is in a bad mood.

Conversely, they'd prefer to be brought in on a problem situation early rather than having to deal with a full-blown crisis.

Problem-solving ability and willingness to seek counsel from senior people are good indications that an account manager is future management stock. Letting senior management know what you need from them, when, and why is an important part of "managing up."

Someone who provides opportunities for client interaction.
In the section "What Clients Want," we discussed the importance of agency management involvement.

It shows clients they are important, and it gives agency management an opportunity to be involved and possibly make an important contribution. To bring in agency management effectively, don't just wait until there's a problem. It's better to look for opportunities to periodically use senior agency people in meaningful ways.

For example, there might be a new client project where a senior agency person has some expert experience. This would be a good opportunity for face time with the client in a productive context.

Initial campaign input meetings, sometimes called "discovery meetings," are another good way to bring in a management person, as long as there is good potential for them to contribute something to the campaign's development and perhaps participate in the presentation of agency work.

It's better for the account manager to "manage" the timing and level of involvement of agency brass. Be proactive on this issue. Look for opportunities to use management in limited but meaningful ways.

Don't use them just for window dressing.

Clients see right through this.

Someone who is an "agency first" person.
Some account managers sell themselves and their contributions hard at the expense of how the client views the rest of the agency team. What management wants is strong leadership characterized by the account manager's enthusiastic recognition of everyone's contribution.

If management suspects an account manager is taking too much credit, downplaying others, or flatly badmouthing the agency, they will suspect the account manager is planning to leave the agency and will try to take the account with them. All hell will break loose behind the scenes if this becomes a concern.

Being liked by the client and selling the agency team are not mutually exclusive. In fact, most clients really like account managers because of the high level of contribution that they get from rest of the team.

Someone who is liked and respected within the shop.
So much of the success in the agency business depends on working relationships. Much of this book is about working relationships first and advertising second. When you care enough to find out what others need and genuinely try to deliver, they know it.

Account managers are expected to consistently hand out recognition to others. When a creative, media planner, or some other specialist makes an effort to recognize the work of an account manager, management pays special attention.

Based on the critical role played by the account manager, this recognition happens much too seldom.

Someone who keeps their cool.
It is sometimes said that gifted account people come equipped with extra arms, eyes in the back of their head, a built-in clock, and ice water in their veins.

How else could they juggle so many projects, see 360°, manage time so well, and keep such a cool head?

If there's one thing that is predictable in the agency biz it is constant change and the need to regularly turn on a dime. You get used to it and build a work style that adapts.

Confidence and a cool head in the middle of chaos comes from knowing that you have a talented team and management behind you at the agency.

Someone who is going to be good at "new business."
Back to the growth issue for a moment. New business is the industry term for landing new accounts.

New business is important for a young account manager to understand because it is the fast track to advancement in the agency. Being such an important issue, new business has its own chapter – Chapter 7 – "The Business of New Business."

What management wants from account managers relative to new business is someone who can represent the agency well in a pitch and tell a salient success story based on the agency's work.

Agencies like to share success stories as a way to show how good they are. Success stories require you have the facts and samples. Smart account managers keep both good case histories and samples from past campaigns.

Someone who can be involved in the client's business but stay out of the client's internal politics.
It's a fine line between being a respected and welcome player in the client's inner circle and getting sucked into internal client politics.

Remember, the agency's objectivity and reputation are at stake.

There will be opportunities for you and the agency to take unpopular stands or be on the risky side of an issue. Consult with your account supervisor quickly. Let the agency's seasoned vets and senior management help you deal with it.

BUZZ...

Suits That Fit

by Robert Solomon, AdWeek, *May 8, 2000*

Abstract.

Great work is not enough to keep a client from walking.

Great work and great relationships are not mutually exclusive.

In fact, more often than not, great work emerges from a great relationship, not the other way around.

Agencies need people in all disciplines and departments as committed to building the client relationship as they are to delivering great work.

Agencies must understand what makes a great account person great, and use what they learn to train, mentor, motivate, and compensate the people with the greatest potential.

Now, here's the full text.

What Makes Great Account People Great?

I should have seen it coming. My agency did excellent work for this client – work fueled by invention, guided by insight, crafted with care and precision. Still, when the client called me into her office to fire us, I should not have been surprised.

Yes, we did great work. We also missed deadlines, exceeded budgets and avoided input as if it were a disease that would infect the advertising. Most important, we didn't listen and didn't hear the client's growing frustration.

The client told me that as much as she liked and respected our work, she could not withstand the pain of dealing with us. *"It's just too hard,"* she said. *"If I have to choose, I'd rather have an agency a little less talented but a lot more committed to getting the mechanics right."*

218

As she walked me to the elevator, she stopped and said, *"Good work, bad process."* By "process," I knew she meant not just budgets and schedules, but the whole relationship that governed, and ultimately undermined, the account.

That was a long time ago. But every time I read about an agency being dismissed by a client, in spite of terrific work, I am reminded of "Good work, bad process." Or to put it more broadly, "Good work, bad relationship."

I learned the hard way that great work is not enough to keep a client from walking. Since then, I've come to understand that great work and great relationships are not mutually exclusive. In fact, more often than not, great work emerges from a great relationship, not the other way around.

If I'm right, then agencies need more people in all disciplines and departments as committed to building the client relationship as they are to delivering great work. They especially need account people with extraordinary intellect, integrity, resourcefulness, diplomacy and presence to lead their accounts.

Great account people have always been a rare commodity. Today, agencies must compete with the lure of Wall Street and Silicon Alley, making it even harder to find and retain potential stars.

While agencies need to redouble their efforts to recruit new account-management talent to the business, they also need to focus on making the account people they have more effective.

Agencies must understand what makes a great account person great, and use what they learn to train, mentor, motivate and compensate the people with the greatest potential.

Creative directors must regularly acknowledge the critical role account people play in making the work. Senior management must lead the transformation from a culture of disdain to a culture of respect for account management.

And account people must be worthy of that respect by becoming better communicators, idea generators, business strategists, problem solvers and diplomats.

The agencies that do these things will find it easier to attract account management talent capable of nurturing client relationships that foster great work. The agencies that don't will want to focus on new business – because they're going to need to replace the client that just left.

Robert Solomon is author of *Brain Surgery for Suits: 56 Things Every Account Person Should Know* published by Strategy Press. He can be reached at robert@solomonstrategic.com

What Clients Look for in Ad Agencies.

by Ron Owens, Baltimore Business Journal, *May 20, 2002*

Seeing yourself as others see you is vital to any individual trying to make his or her way in this rough-and-tumble world. By all indications, ad agencies are not exempt from this law of survival either.

Advertising agencies try to be many things, often losing a sense of priority for what is really essential. What is considered most important can be arguable in the helter-skelter environment of day-to-day operations. It is possible to lose your way or take your eye off the prize.

The Lou Harris organization helps solve that dilemma with a poll (every other year) of over 600 client marketing executives representing the nation's leading advertisers. Part of this regularly conducted study clearly establishes attributes clients look for in selecting an agency. The findings of this broad survey taken over the last decade are definitive.

Over the years, what clients look for hasn't changed much, and the results of the latest study brought few surprises. Advertisers rate most important those services that they depend on an advertising agency to provide exclusively. Foremost on the client's rating scale – creative work that sells.

Creative Work That Sells.

Creative work that sells is the essence of our business. Hundreds of books have been written on how to achieve this, and people have earned a living traveling the world to lecture on the subject.

There are no magical answers. There are, however, some factors that are always present in effective advertising.

First, it must be based on the product user's need or self-image. Consumers want to know what's in it for them. If storyboards don't clearly address this concern, then it's better to start over.

Second, effective advertising always presents a fresh idea or delivers the familiar in a new way.

Responsiveness of the Account Group.

As a 29-year veteran in the account service, I know why this ranks so high. Clients look to account people as their representatives, their liaison, within the agency. They look to account people for rationality as well as for a business-like approach to problem-solving.

How do you get responsive account people? You hire people who could be successful in several different fields but have chosen advertising and the agency business. They relish the combination of business and the arts, living constantly with the unexpected, dealing with surprises and sudden change. They like to build a team, an image, a business, and they like the people in the agency business.

These people must be aggressive and highly motivated. If they are, they will quickly understand that helping clients meet their goals is the soundest way to build a career.

Careful with Client's Money.

An agency must regard a client's money as if it were its own. The agency must assume all prices – production, media, freelance, etc. – are negotiable. In commercial production, for example, it is almost always necessary to engage in competitive bidding.

In dealing with a client's money, think long-term. Nothing destroys an agency's marketing credibility faster than constant recommendations to spend more in both media and production. Yes, if more should be spent, the client should be told, but to build a long-term partnership, a client must also be shown how to cut costs.

I've told clients several times to reduce or even stop spending behind specific brands because it was the right thing to do – even though it reduced the agency's income for the short-term.

Creative Flair.

While agency creative people might rate this as the most important quality in selecting a place to work, less than half the advertisers in the Harris Survey think it is "absolutely essential." There's a reason for this difference. Clients see advertising as an aid in selling their products or services, but what agencies sell is primarily their advertising. Too often, agencies forget that advertising is a means to an end, and instead see their creative work as the end in and of itself.

For an agency to be successful from a client's point of view, it must deliver the top four attributes: advertising that sells, responsive account people, care with the client's money, and creative flair.

In order to become a long-term leader among agencies, however, all 12 attributes established by the study must be delivered.

How to Convince a Client That the Work Is Right.
by Jeff Goodby, Co-Chairman; Goodby Silverstein & Partners

An agency is only as good as its finest work. No one sees or remembers the meetings, memos, and phone conversations that may have resulted in the denigration of a brilliant piece. By the same token, bad agencies often possess a file of solid work that they were simply unable to convince a client to run.

At Goodby Silverstein & Partners, we are above all committed to the creation of great work. Therefore, when we are convinced that something is right, that it is truly a uniquely correct solution, we will do just about anything to explain and sell it.

We feel this way not for egotistical reasons, but for the benefit of our clients and their businesses. In the end, our clients retain us to guard the integrity of their marketing and advertising, to guide it intact through sometimes rocky political and legal waters.

It is in their interests that we hold strong opinions, that we push ourselves and the people around us because, as Pat Fallon says, *"The biggest mistake you can make is to spend all that money and find that no one even noticed."*

That said, it is important to add two things.

First, we are also deeply committed to the belief that a healthy advertising agency remains healthy and does its best work in the context of long, trusting client relationships.

This is a financial consideration, to be sure.

But it is also a creative consideration.

Great campaigns don't just run for a month or two.

They acquire their depth and dimension over time. They prove their correctness in the marketplace and earn widespread respect, not just among creative people, but in the business community and in the public at large.

The trust that develops between agency and client can allow the advertising to take more chances, to truly stand for something, to obliterate the competition.

Second, we believe that work forced upon a client under great duress is a time bomb. Such experiences greatly lessen the chances we will be able to sell that client more, equally challenging work in the future.

They lead to resentments that can bring a client to secretly hope that we – and the work we have forced upon them – will somehow fail.

Indeed, there are agencies that succeed through a succession of very short, stormy relationships that never really result in lasting, effective work for the client. For business and moral reasons, however, we don't intend to become one of them.

How, then, do we reconcile the need to sell great work with the demands of building long relationships? It is never clear and easy, but the following guidelines are key:

1. See things through the eyes of the client.

Look at yourself and your work from the client's standpoint, taking into account their business goals and personality. Is this the right work for them?

If they are uncomfortable, is that discomfort something that can be overcome in time? Have you really addressed and discussed their needs? What have you done to earn or merit their respect?

2. Use trust, not force.

Trust results in an atmosphere in which you can do more, even better work in the future. You will have a client who roots for the advertising to succeed, even to the point of favorably interpreting research. Moreover, your life will be simpler, your stress lessened.

3. The client can be right.

Always remember that clients have thought about their businesses 24 hours a day for years on end. They are sometimes liable to know something you won't. Appropriate their instincts and knowledge as a solid starting point and don't be too quick to dismiss their perspective or ideas. In fact, don't be proud about adopting them whole cloth. Until you announce otherwise, the world will think the client's best ideas were really yours.

4. Avoid arrogance.

You probably have every reason to believe in your talent and perspective or you wouldn't be working here in the first place.

Yet there is a fine line that divides confidence and strength from arrogance. Confidence and strength make for long relationships in which severe differences of opinion can be constructively hashed out. Arrogance results in short-term, often temporary gains, at best.

5. Create a partnership with the client.

If the client always sees you as an antagonist, you start every discussion with a disadvantage that must be made up in order to be successful. If the client sees you as a partner, half the job is done when you walk into the room.

Ed McCabe is one of the most cantankerous, opinionated, argumentative guys you'd ever want to meet. The clients he's done great work for are all well aware of this. Yet they to a person consider him a friend with their best interests at heart.

6. Start over.

This may be the most important point here. The greatest enemy of brilliant work is the loss of perspective. As a piece of work undergoes long changes and revisions, it can often be transformed beyond recognition.

Before any of the participants know it, the very things that made it worth revising are dulled or gone. Be honest with yourself throughout this inevitable process. Is this still great work?

If not, make your best appeal and then throw it away. (Sometimes the very act of offering this will galvanize a client to see the merit of your point of view.) It will be better for your work and the relationship. Besides, if there were only one way to do this stuff, it wouldn't be nearly as interesting.

[Note: This good advice is from the Goodby Silverstein Employee Manual, reprinted from *How to Put Your Book Together and Get a Job in Advertising* by Maxine Paetro. You can tell by the wisdom and good sense in this article why Goodby's agency has such a first-rate track record in both creative quality and solid client relationships.]

JUICY CASES:

4.1: Radio Heartburn.

You're the account manager on a local chain of restaurants that promotes its wood-fire grilling of steaks and seafood.

The other day you were listening to the radio, and one of your spots aired, followed immediately by a commercial for a heartburn medicine.

This unfortunate scheduling of commercials was made even worse due to the fact that the heartburn commercial started out talking about fire. Other production similarities made it difficult to determine where your restaurant client's spot ended and where the heartburn spot began.

Should you do anything about this matter?

4.2: The Creative Reassignment.*

You're the account manager on an account which recently appointed a new advertising manager who fancies himself a creative expert. He is consistently writing headlines, rewriting copy, and dictating the art direction, much to your dismay and that of the creative team.

You've been unable to stop this combination of creative ego and excessive client power. But, for the moment, the new ad manager seems happy with the agency's execution of his heavily reworked ads.

Seeing that his creative stars are getting frustrated, the creative director of your agency reassigns the senior creative team to other accounts and puts a relatively new team on this account.

When asked to explain his action, the CD says he can't afford to have his senior creative people frustrated and why should you care anyway if the client is happy with his own ads?

As the account manager, there are three reasons you should be seriously concerned about this situation.
What are they? Think big picture.

*Inspired by a case in *How to Get the Best Work from Your Agency* by Nancy Salz.

AD-ROBIC EXERCISES:

Account Planning and Gaining Audience Insights.

In her book *Hitting the Sweet Spot,* Lisa Fortini-Campbell discusses many techniques used to glean insights from a target audience. Three of the most interesting are the simple power of observation, the concept of brand personality, and last, the projective question as a method to see how people think.

4.1: Self Analysis.

As inspired by *Hitting the Sweet Spot,* keep a day-long diary of every product and service you use. Be acutely aware of how you felt in anticipation of the product use, the use experience itself, and your feelings about yourself and the product after use.

Why do this? Because you are trying to get to the "emotional load" that is part of many products, even the most mundane, like toothpaste. After you have mastered the art of observation on yourself, start watching others as they purchase or interact with a product or service.

4.2: Defining Brand Personality.

As inspired by *Hitting the Sweet Spot,* make a list of five well-known consumer product brands from different product categories.

Give the list to ten of your friends and have them list three personality traits they would associate with each of the brands if those brands were actually people.

For example, if Nike were a person, its personality traits might include aggressive, arrogant, flamboyant, technology oriented, upscale.

4.3: Appreciating Our Differences.

As inspired by *Hitting the Sweet Spot*, interview three people who are quite different from you in age, gender, cultural background, education, income. Ask them a set battery of projective questions.

Projective questions can take a variety of directions but they are basically "blue sky" type questions.

- If a genie gave you three wishes, what would they be? Why?

- If you only had time to do one thing you'd never done before, what would it be? Why?

- What animal do you think you are most like? Why?

You and your friends can easily come up with a dozen of these questions. While your questions are interesting, the answers you get from your small but diverse sample should be even more interesting. People are truly amazing.

4.4: Who drives a Porsche?

Find an owner of a late-model Porsche and do a 20-dimensional profile of them. Revisit the profiling model found in Chapter 4.4 and select at least four dimensions from each of the four headings that you think are the most revealing audience characteristics.

BURNING QUESTIONS:

4.1:

In a unique sense, account managers compete inside the agency in three major areas. For what do account managers compete, and what techniques/tactics/behaviors are used in this competition?

4.2:

Give a multidimensional definition of "proactivity" and tell why it is so important for the agency to be proactive in its relationship with the client.

5.0 WHAT A RIDE!

THE PURPOSE OF THIS CHAPTER is to further explain, by vivid and detailed example, what it's like to be an account manager.

Two sections provide two different perspectives – "Journey of the Job" and "Fifty Hours on a Roller Coaster: A Week in the Life of an Account Manager." One (the journey) as a history of one project from start to finish. The other (the roller coaster) as a week-long snap shot of daily life as an account manager and an account coordinator. If this doesn't show you what life is like in account service, nothing will.

5.1 Journey of the Job

One of the best ways to understand the job of account manager is to follow a project from its very beginning to its very end. By seeing how many times an account manager "touches" a project in some way, you can better understand the many aspects of the account manager position.

Each activity mentioned here is an independent function, normally done separately from the others.

The title, "Journey of the Job," actually has two meanings. Projects in agencies are often called jobs. The enlightening journey focuses on the progress of a job. In so doing, the activities involved shed great light on a significant part of the account manager's job.

Depending on size and how they are organized, agencies may vary slightly on practices and processes. The evolution of a campaign, however, will be relatively similar in all cases.

Here are the steps where the account manager "touches" and has an opportunity to affect a project on its journey to the marketplace.

Let's assume it's May. The agency is about to embark on the creation of a nationwide spot-market campaign for one of its clients. The campaign involves radio ads, magazine ads, and some point-of-sale (POS) materials.

"I don't know. After a day at the agency, I find it sort of relaxes me."

Set the Annual Budget.

The client operates on a calendar-year annual budget, and the account manager is often responsible for generating the master budget.

The first time an account manager would actually touch this campaign is when it was budgeted the prior year during the fall budget process. The size of the budget allocation for this campaign would normally be based on the objectives of the campaign and historical costs for similar campaigns.

Conduct Some Grass-Roots Research.

Shortly after the annual budget is approved, the account manager is reading a newsletter from the futurist society to which the agency belongs. In it there is an article that has direct connection to the client's business and this campaign.

Some additional secondary research on the subject is done through an online news group, and then the information is passed along to the client. No one on the client side has seen this material, and it has long-range significance for the campaign in question.

Chalk one up for the agency being way out ahead of the client.

Early grass-roots research might also take the form of a focus group the agency pulls together with family, friends, and agency employees who will not be involved in the campaign. It's a quick, low-cost way for the agency to get it's bearings on the large project ahead.

Conduct "Discovery" Meeting with Client.

The discovery meeting is the primary input activity for writing the campaign brief. It is where the details of the campaign are gathered – the objectives of the campaign, detailed product information, new marketing data, competitive intelligence, the launch date, special needs of the trade, the spot markets to include, the budget.

Supervise Benchmark Research.

Advertising agencies do very little research themselves because they are often measuring some aspect of their own work. Agencies are, however, intimately involved in the design of the research and the selection of research companies.

Let's assume the product being advertised is not a new product but is going to receive a major facelift and significant ad support through this campaign due in large part to the grass-roots research you did earlier in the year.

It is reasonable to expect the client and agency would want to establish a benchmark for attitude and awareness to complement the benchmark sales number. The account manager will often select and supervise the research firm in the conduct of such studies.

Develop First-Draft Campaign Brief.

The campaign brief is the first attempt to reduce the assignment to writing. It is the guiding document for the work assignment.

The actual content and structure of the campaign brief is in Chapter 3, "Tools of the Craft."

Writing a useful campaign brief is a valuable skill since agency specialists will use the brief as vital input.

Review Draft Campaign Brief with Client.

This exercise is to confirm that what the account manager heard in the discovery meeting is what the client intended to convey. Dickinson Axiom #1 says that all input is incomplete, at least the first time around. This review step helps complete the input and resolve gray areas, nuances, and subtleties.

Activate Account Planner.

Not all projects deserve the attention of an account planner for that extra added dimension of customer insight. The importance of this campaign, however, justifies a planner's involvement, be it on staff or freelance. The revised campaign brief is discussed with the account planner, who immediately starts consumer behavioral/motivational research.

Attend a Focus Group.

When there is a research department or an account planner, the account planner will arrange for some qualitative research to be conducted. In this case, three focus group research sessions are to be conducted. The account manager and client normally attend at least the first session, in order to assure themselves that the discussion guide is addressing the correct issues and the moderator has a grasp of why the focus groups are being conducted.

It is quite common for an account manager to hear something in a focus group that he or she wants probed by the moderator.

Often when something is heard and then probed in a focus group it turns out to be a valuable insight, phrase, or idea. It is the account manager's own instincts and keen ear that made it happen.

Review Creative Brief with Account Planner.

The creative brief is an additional part of the campaign brief, designed specially for the creative department.

It is often shared with the rest of the team, but the creatives are the main users of this brief. (To see the actual content and structure of the creative brief, see Chapter 3, "Tools of the Craft.")

The account planner reviews with the account manager the results of the research and the conclusions drawn.

Assuming the account manager is comfortable with the conclusions and the resulting recommendations, the account manager will co-author the creative brief or take the one written by the account planner.

Open Agency Work Orders.

Nothing gets done in any department until the paperwork officially starts the process. Every agency's work order looks a little different, but it basically asks for the specifications of the project. Ultimately, each component of the campaign (print ads, radio ads, POS, Internet banners, etc.) will require a work order.

To get things rolling, however, some agencies allow a campaign to be started with one work order, and then as specific elements of the campaign become clear, separate work orders are opened.

Work orders are placed on the outside of the job tickets which follow the projects through the agency. The more information on the work orders the better.

Hold a "Kick-Off" Meeting.

For a major campaign, the account manager calls a meeting of the full account team. The full account team includes the production and traffic people whose job it will be to get the work done after the copy and layouts have been approved.

In the kick-off (aka "start-work") meeting, the work orders and the campaign brief are reviewed with everyone who is going to work on the campaign. An account supervisor might be invited to sit in on the start-work meeting if he or she participated in the discovery meeting or might play some role downstream.

Any major problems the account team sees in doing the work as described in the start-work orders are discussed at this meeting. Interim deadlines for creative and production are agreed to at this meeting by those responsible for the work.

Review Creative Brief with Creative Team.

Even though the creative team attended the start-work meeting, their presence there is primarily to get them to commit to the due dates.

The best time to give the creative team their input is right before they start serious work on a project. The account manager and account planner will sit with the creatives at a later date and review the brief and recommendations from the account planner on creative strategy.

The importance of inspiration should not be forgotten. Not every project can be the most important one ever created by the agency. Yet everyone likes to think their work is important and valuable. Show the creatives and others how this project fits into the bigger scheme of things and how their success will impact the client.

Inspiration and project importance are especially relevant on projects that are not ads. Some creatives love to do ads but hate direct mail, brochures, and the myriad things that are within the contemporary media mix.

Review Preliminary Creative Concepts Internally.

After a few days or a couple of weeks, the creative team is ready to show some preliminary concepts to the account manager. Depending on the agency, the account planner may either have already seen the conceptual work or will see it at the same time as the account manager.

The account manager may immediately embrace the creative work because he or she feels instinctively or intuitively that it is a strong creative solution. In this case, the account manager will direct the creative to "tighten it up," which means to do more comprehensive layouts and complete copy.

If the account manager has concerns about the creative work, then discussions will take place and additional creative may be done.

Being a good "critic" comes into play here. See the D'Arcy, Ogilvy, Bernbach model in Chapter 3.3, "Tools of the Craft," for some hints on critiquing.

Review other preliminary departmental recommendations. With the same care and objectivity that the account manager reviewed the initial proposal from the creative department, he/she now looks at what everyone else thinks should be done in their area of expertise.

The account manager is the one position in the agency that is supposed to have an operating knowledge of every communications tool.

In that way, the account manager can recommend the best promotional mix for each campaign. In addition to the media department, the account manager has asked other agency specialists to make recommendations.

Let's say the production department has a new POS vehicle they really like. The sales promotion specialist has an incentive that fits. The PR department has an idea on how to involve kids and dogs in "photo ops," and the interactive department has a new angle on spot-market e-mails.

These are all items that the client is not expecting to see in the presentation and will not expect to pay for without accepting the specific recommendations. However, the job of the account manager is to recommend what should be done.

Develop Production Schedule.

In conjunction with the production manager and the other creative team members who will do a lot of the production work, the account manager will develop a timeline for the campaign. This timeline will establish critical-path deadlines in order for the various elements to be delivered on time.

Such a timeline makes assumptions about the amount of time the client will need or will take to give approvals at various stages of campaign development.

Even though the client approves the agency's production schedule, the account manager still has to make sure the client and the agency meet their respective deadlines.

Develop New Budget.

Based in part on the grass-roots research done by the agency, the client has decided to give the product a major facelift for this year's campaign. Now that the needs of the campaign are better understood, more money may be needed than was originally budgeted.

There are three alternatives:

- The client comes up with some additional money.

- Additional money will have to be found somewhere else in the budget by cutting other projects.

- Expectations for the campaign will have to be scaled back.

Finding the money to pay for all the recommendations is another major issue. Sometimes, clients can find more money if they really like a new idea. Most of the time, the account manager has to find the money in the existing budget by cutting something else.

The client will look to the account manager for recommendations on how to do the internal budget gymnastics in order to produce this important campaign. It's called managing the budget.

Along with the new budget is normally an estimate for creative work to be done. The client approves the overall budget and, by signing the creative estimate, assures the agency they will at least get paid for the creative work, even if the project gets tabled later.

Prepare Creative Rationale.

In the "Tools of the Craft," Chapter 3.4, there is an explanation of the document called the Creative Rationale. As indicated by its name, the Creative Rationale is an attempt to rationalize and explain why the creative approach being recommended is a great solution.

Sometimes the Creative Rationale becomes a formal presentation document that the client can study after the presentation. In other cases, the agency just uses the points from the Creative Rationale as talking points during the pitch.

Many times, the client agrees "the concept works, run with it." Instincts prevail. Hoorah! Other times, clients need reassurance, and great weight is placed on the analysis of the creative work. This is when you really need a good written Creative Rationale.

Depending on the amount of documentation the client likes, the Creative Rationale may never become a formal document outside the agency. Nonetheless, the process is a good one to go through, guided by the account manager.

Rehearse Presentation of Creative.

Effective presenting is a true art, but knowledge and rehearsing sure help. Agency work should be presented with pride, passion, and logic. The account manager should make sure all these prerequisites are in place before anything is presented. The client expects a high level of polish, and the agency work deserves it.

Good account managers come prepared to do the best job possible to present the merits of the agency's proposals. Rehearsing is an important part of this preparation.

Even if another member of the account team will be doing the presenting, rehearsing will ensure a crisper, more effective delivery.

When the account manager is going to present creative, media, or other recommendations, and those specialists will not be at the meeting, it's a good idea to have the specialist rehearse the account manager on the merits of the proposal and exactly how it should be presented.

This does two things. First, it extracts from the copywriter, media planner, sales promotion expert, etc., their best rationale, including points the account manager might have missed.

Second, it shows the specialists you really care about their work and will give it your best shot in the presentation to the client.

Write the Integrated Communications Plan.

One of the most important contributions an account manager makes is the knowledge of what communications tools should be employed and how they should be orchestrated. No one else in the agency can do this. Everyone else in the agency is a specialist. You are a generalist, with the big view and the ability to write a good communications plan. The integrated communications plan has a variety of names, but always covers the same basics:

- The goals of the campaign
- The target-audience segmentation
- The audience environment
- Campaign brief

- Creative Rationale

- The media mix

- Roll-out strategy

- Budget

- Measurement methods

Writing a detailed communications plan is good discipline even if the client doesn't care about the details.

Writing the plan will bring up important questions on strategy and execution that need to be addressed sooner rather than later.

Writing a detailed plan also shows the client that the agency is serious and professional about the service it provides.

Present Creative Concepts and an Integrated Communications Plan.

Thorough knowledge of the work is only part of successful presenting. Knowing how your client likes to be presented to is another key component of success. Some clients like big productions in their boardroom, with the whole account team present. Others like to see preliminary presentations in their office with just the account manager.

Some clients need very detailed layout and copy to fully understand what's being proposed. Others like to sit elbow to elbow with the creative team and review thumbnail layouts and headlines.

Knowing your client's presentation preferences includes knowing who else is ultimately going to see the work you are presenting. If your client contact has to turn around and present your work to a management committee, make sure that you have provided the tools to do a good job in your absence.

There are many different philosophies on presenting and methods of presenting. The best advice is to observe the veteran presenters. Look for different presentation styles. Take a seminar in presentation techniques and experiment.

Obtain Client Feedback.

After the presentation of the agency proposals, everyone listens carefully to the client's reaction... what is said and what isn't said. Many clients, especially in the presence of the rest of the agency team, will be very diplomatic with their comments, only to tell the account manager later what they really think. Clients don't like to be the bearer of bad news. That's why they have account managers.

Many clients do not make immediate decisions about agency presentations. They like to "think about it." When it comes, the client's feedback is often given only to the account manager. It is important that you walk away from the meeting fully able to explain the client's point of view, specific concerns, and suggestions to the team back at the agency. "The client doesn't like it, we have to do something else" is not acceptable.

If the creative was rejected, there has to be a flaw in the input or the agency's work. Your job is to find it and fix it.

Unless the client changes are extremely small or of a technical nature, the best practice is simply to understand why the client wants them and then review this input with the creative team or other specialist.

There may be a very good reason why an innocent-sounding client change is not a good idea at all.

Review Needed Revisions with All Applicable Departments.

When client feedback is finally received and fully understood, the work can continue. The account manager is usually responsible for revising project-specific work documents to reflect any changes in strategy, emphasis, or project specifications.

On major campaigns such as this, the agency team would have another meeting where the required "adjustments" would be presented by the account manager.

These meetings can be very stressful if the original agency proposal was way off target. People can leave the meeting upset that so much time and effort was put into an original proposal that now has to be redone. The potential unpleasantness of a postpresentation feedback review meeting underscores the importance of doing it right the first time.

Present Revised Creative, Media Plan, and Production Estimate to Client.

Revised copy, layout, media plans, and other agency proposals are normally handled by the account manager alone in a meeting with the client. Hopefully, the agency did a good job of listening to client feedback and all the revisions are on target.

If so, the client will give immediate approval to proceed or will schedule a meeting for the account manager to present the campaign to a senior management committee or board of directors.

Now that all the production details of the campaign are known, the budget estimate can be adjusted and client approval obtained.

Obtain Legal Clearance for Ad Copy.

In some industries, all ad copy must "clear legal." Nutritional and performance claims are the most closely scrutinized by corporate counsel.

Present Approved Campaign to Client Board.

Presentations to management committees or boards can be characterized in one of three ways:

- Courtesy and informational: "This is what we plan to do."

- Sounding board: "What do you think?"

- Clearance: "Do we have your approval to proceed?"

The account manager, account supervisor, or management supervisor are usually the only agency representatives who present to boards and committees.

The account manager can achieve a special place in the client organization. Because of the ability to adapt to a client's internal culture, the account manager can become a valuable asset in helping the client gain internal acceptance of advertising programs.

Initiate Production Work.

Once past the "proposal and approval" stage, the next segment of agency service kicks in. Another full team meeting is normally called, including members of the traffic and production department. Approved copy and layout is handed back to the creative department and approved media plans are handed back to the media planner.

Now the job of producing the radio ads, print ads, and POS materials begins, as does the placement and negotiation of the media buy. Budgets, timelines, and deadlines are all confirmed at this meeting.

Accompany Client to Print and POS Photo Shoot.

Depending on the importance of the photography, the client may or may not attend the photo shoot. In the case of this national campaign where photography is quite important, the client would definitely attend the shoot.

Clients normally have preferences as to how a product is lighted or depicted. The agency art director should have a strong influence over the overall look of the shot, but it is good account relations to have the client there to approve the shots as they are taken.

It eliminates the problem of a reshoot because the client doesn't like some small aspect of the photography.

Also, the photographer and art director will often come up with another shot idea once they get "into the studio." It is helpful to have the client there to provide immediate feedback or advise on a technical aspect.

Photo sessions are normally tedious affairs with a lot of downtime while lighting is adjusted and "hero" products get final styling. Smart account managers will find productive use of this time.

If there is a standing weekly meeting between the account manager and the client, using the photo session downtime to accomplish this meeting is a good use of such time.

Accompany Client to Radio Recording Session.

For the same reasons it's a good idea to have the client at the photo shoot, it is usually good account management to have the client in major recording sessions.

The copywriter will work with the recording engineer and the voice talent to produce the approved script, but as in photography, new ideas can happen. The voice talent themselves might make a small suggestion about the way they "hear the script." Perhaps a certain passage that looked fine on paper "just isn't working." It can be good to have the client there to discuss concerns and immediately approve the fix.

Recording and editing sessions can also have a lot of downtime, so it's good to find ways to make the time productive.

After the approved spots are "in the can," the account manager is responsible for preparing new scripts called "as recorded" scripts for the client and agency files.

Present "In-Progress" Production Materials for Approval.

In-progress ad proofs, rough-cut commercials, photo contact sheets, digital mechanicals, and the like need to be approved by the client so projects can continue their timely progress toward on-time delivery.

This kind of stuff normally goes pretty smoothly, especially if the client has been involved in decisions along the way.

Every once in a while, however, something will happen that will affect a project. This could be a product modification, an unexpected competitive development, or any number of things outside the agency's (and perhaps the client's) control.

These unexpected developments normally have three negative consequences: time crunch, more expense, and stress.

Quick reaction, a cool head, and experience in handling the unexpected are hallmarks of the account manager. This is why account managers handle "in progress" approvals.

Prepare Periodic Status Reports for Client.

Most agencies have weekly status meetings where the creative, production, and media departments review the status of each project with one account manager at a time. A status report is issued after the meeting to reflect any decisions on deadlines.

Depending on its structure and content, the internal status report might be suitable for sending to the client. If not, the account manager will need to develop a "short form" version to keep the client abreast of project progress.

Present Final Production Materials for Client Approval.

At some point, the final proofs are ready and the radio commercial is completed. Before these items are produced in quantity and sent to the media, the client gives final approval. Final delivery details for collateral materials are reviewed with the client at this time.

Confirm final details to all relevant agency departments.

Once final approval has been obtained, there is one more quick meeting of the production team to confirm things like changes in the print quantity of ad reprints, or how many extra radio tapes are needed for the dealer packets, or where the POS materials are to be delivered. Details, details, details.

Accompany Client on a Press Check.

Many clients are especially picky about printed materials. In addition to approving all the photos and proofs along the way, they like to go to the printer at the beginning of a long press run. The agency production manager and art director are also there. Having the client there to approve the press proofs is a lot better than having 10,000 pieces that are too yellow for the client's liking.

Get Early Samples to Client.

It is normally good account management practice to get ad preprints, radio cassettes, final media schedules and other campaign materials to the clients before the campaign breaks.

Since there is normally little time between when the campaign is produced and when it hits the market, there is only a small window of time when samples can be delivered to the client.

Quick delivery of samples shows the client you are sensitive to their needs and are enthusiastic about the campaign

Store away some samples of your own in your personal file. In many agencies, the sample filing system is awful. If this is the case with your agency, keep your own samples, even if you have to do it at home.

Samples have a number of valuable uses, one of which is for future "new business" pitches. As stated elsewhere, new business is the fast-track to advancement in account service.

Be ready for opportunities to show past work on your accounts in new business "credentials" meetings. It's great when you and the work you managed is showcased to a new business prospect. You have to have the samples and the case history facts to make it a good presentation.

Report a Media Discrepancy to Client.

Advertising media occasionally screw up. An ad that was supposed to run didn't. The wrong commercial ran. Or the reproduction of an ad in a national magazine or local newspaper was terrible.

These are called "discrepancies." The client should hear about these mistakes from you before they hear about them from anyone else.

This requires that the advertising media involved know they need to contact the agency as soon as a mistake is identified.

The good media companies pay special attention to mistakes they make and act quickly with the agency to find the right remedy.

It is important that the agency be aggressive on spotting and fixing media discrepancies. It's embarrassing to the account manager and the agency if the client is constantly the one to inform the agency about media mistakes the agency should have known about first.

One of the unwritten Murphy's Laws of advertising is that "the client will always see his torn billboard before either the agency or the billboard company are aware of it. Always.

Part of making the client look good is to quickly advise them about discrepancies and to inform them about the remedy that your agency has already negotiated.

That way when the client's boss nails him about the wrong ad running or crappy color reproduction, your client can respond: "Yes, the agency has already advised me, and they've negotiated some additional free spots or a special position free of charge for our next ad as 'make goods.'" That's being on top of things!

Review Billings.

In Chapter 3.7, "Billings, Budgets, and Financial Management," there is a major section on billings. Suffice to say here that billings are very important for a number of reasons that have significance to the agency-client relationship.

Supervise the Preparation of Campaign Kits.

The rollout of advertising campaigns is often preceded by the distribution of campaign kits to dealers, distributors, branches, regional offices, and the trade media. These kits normally include a cover letter from the MarCom director, ad reprints, ad artwork for local use, media schedule, samples of collateral materials, radio tapes, co-op reimbursement forms, and an order form just in case someone wants to order more materials.

These campaign kits often are packaged in a slick folder with a catchy headline and graphic on the cover to lend some additional hype to the campaign.

The introductory letter in the campaign kit goes out under the MarCom manager's signature, but the account manager normally ghostwrites the letter. Depending on how visible the account manager is in the client organization, it may be appropriate that the account manager co-signs the letter.

Develop the Sales Conference Presentation.

Advertisers often have an annual sales meeting where sales reps, dealers, and marketing staffers get together to talk strategy, opportunities, and to see the new advertising campaign. The account manager is often the person who gives the presentation of this new ad campaign at the sales meeting.

The presentation is a combination of PowerPoint visuals, video, and an entertaining, motivational narration that is designed to get the sales people all charged up.

This presentation is yet another opportunity for the agency to be visible within the client organization and for the account manager to put an individual mark on the work.

Supervise Entry Preparation to Creative Competitions.
The campaign was a smashing success, of course, and there are samples for contest entries.

International creative awards like the CLIOs, Addy's, and Cannes may be important to the agency, but recognition within his own industry may be what really turns the client on.

Almost every industry (be it concrete products or medical equipment) has an association, and almost every industry association has an annual convention where awards are given for outstanding examples of marketing communication.

Good account management often means some involvement in the client's industry and participation in industry competitions.

Different advertising media such as outdoor, magazines, sales promotion, and direct mail also have creative competitions sponsored by their industry association. These competitions may be of more interest to the agency than the client.

Nonetheless, if the agency's work won an award, the client would make good use of that award inside the client organization.

The issue of who pays the entry fees to award competitions can be a touchy one. Normally, the client has no problem paying fees for his industry association competitions.

If the agency needs to charge a nominal fee for preparing entries for such competitions, many clients are OK with that, too.

If the agency stands to benefit the most from an award in an advertising industry competition like CLIO or Cannes, most clients are not eager to foot the bill.

Accompany Client to Award Ceremony.
It could be Cannes, New York, or Sacramento. Flying to a conference with the client to study his industry and pick up some hardware is a fun part of the business.

Take your ambassador hat along and be on the lookout for new business opportunities.

If you're doing award-winning work for one company in the industry, your agency must be good. Why not leverage the visibility to another noncompetitive company in the same industry?

Supervise Campaign-Impact Research.

At some point, the effectiveness of the campaign needs to be assessed. If attitude and awareness were the main measures of success, additional research will be conducted and compared with the benchmark study.

If brand recall or image repositioning was the point of the campaign, those would be the focus of the follow-up research.

Again, the agency doesn't do its own research when measuring the effectiveness of its own work. However the account manager is normally very involved in supervising the research and selecting the research company.

Research companies are normally hired to do both the benchmark research and the follow-up research so there is consistency in method and familiarity with the issues being remeasured.

Summarize and Report the Campaign Results.

Once the follow-up research is done, it needs to be reported. The research company will normally provide a summary report of the findings. If a more detailed analysis of the data is wanted, the research company can provide it.

The account manager may prefer to simply take the research and do his or her own brief analysis of the findings.

The campaign impact report will normally also cover other issues relative to the impact of a campaign. These issues might be more qualitative or anecdotal in nature but no less important in the client's opinion about the campaign.

If company morale improved, if dealers really liked the POS, if customers wrote letters saying they like the campaign, if the campaign received positive national publicity, these facts can be as valuable to the agency as a short-term increase in product sales.

Review Quarterly Accounting Report.

Many agencies do quarterly reports with revenue summaries and sometimes the gross profit generated by each account.

This report will tell the account manager and agency management whether the account has been profitable.

Depending on the sophistication of the accounting software, it can tell whether a specific campaign was profitable for the agency.

Such reports are good for telling account managers how well they're controlling variable expenses and managing budgets. They may also point to possible changes in agency compensation.

Deliver Short Presentation to New Business Prospect.

Agencies like to show successful work to new business prospects. Assuming this campaign was a big success, assuming the creative stood out, assuming there are good samples to be used, and the account manager is a good presenter, the account manager may be asked to make a brief presentation to a new business prospect in a "credentials" meeting.

This type of presentation does two things. It showcases the agency's work and also showcases the quality of people the agency has in account service.

Author Annual Brand Stewardship Report.

This is not a common practice, yet. But it is a very good one to start.

The Brand Stewardship Report summarizes everything the agency did during the last year to improve brand communication – including the campaign just completed.

To some extent, it's a compilation of campaign impact reports with other noteworthy stuff thrown in.

Knowing that a substantial report will have to be prepared at the end of each year, the account manager and others in the agency will be constantly looking for ways to increase accountability.

Clients generally like this kind of report because it shows that they did in fact get something for their money and the agency is taking its brand stewardship role seriously.

Summary.

You've just reviewed 43 separate activities involving one fairly simple campaign. It is not uncommon for an account manager to have two or three clients with similar levels of activity happening at the same time. It's demanding, important work – this managing the work of others.

Hopefully, this section demonstrates the many opportunities account managers have to put their mark on the work and to give the best of themselves to the success of each campaign. That's what makes it so worthwhile. It's your work, too!

5.2 Fifty Hours on a Roller Coaster: A Week in the Life of an Account Manager

"Journey of the Job" illustrates all the possible times an account manager can touch or contribute to a specific campaign in the process of shepherding it to its ultimate conclusion.

The time it takes for the whole "Journey of the Job" scenario to unfold (from the first budgeting to the MarCom annual report) could be anywhere from a few months to a year or more.

The average account manager in a small or medium-sized agency will handle three to five accounts on an ongoing basis.

At any time, this account manager actually could be managing two or three major campaigns, plus other small projects, an agency project, some advertising industry activities, and maybe a new business pitch. Wow! No wonder they say account managers have to be superhuman.

Let's create a hypothetical but realistic account manager by the name of Bill. His agency is a medium-sized shop in a top-25 metro market in the western U.S.

Bill has been with his current agency for eight years.

He graduated from college 10 years ago and did a two-year stint at a small agency as an account coordinator before joining his current shop. He's good at what he does and is viewed by management as one of the future partners.

His agency is a well-established shop with a good reputation and annual billings of $75 million. Bill handles:

- The state's second-largest medical and dental insurance company

- The top western brand of cheddar cheese

- A five-state, federally funded program promoting energy-efficient homes

- A regional brand of gourmet potato chips

- The country's leading manufacturer of automatic carwash equipment and carwash franchises

Obviously, with an account list like this, Bill never gets bored.

That's one of the beauties of advertising. Every client brings its own set of challenges, and every project its own set of opportunities to shine. Bill likes the diversity of industries and the wide array of media in which he gets to work.

Bill is assisted by Pat, a very capable and energetic account coordinator, who will soon take over a few of Bill's smaller accounts.

Since the best way to learn is to experience firsthand, let's put you in Bill's shoes and let you see at ground level what a very typical week is like for this seasoned account manager and his right-hand person.

Seasoned account managers who read this chapter say it's entertaining, true-to-life, and makes them tired just reading it.

Ready? You are now Bill, account manager extraordinaire!

Sunday.

Do some "secret shopper" research on a regional brand of lawn fertilizer. The agency's been invited to compete for the account. Since you've become sort of the agency packaged goods and retail expert, you will play a major role in the pitch (oh good) and you need to get fertilizer-smart real quick.

Write a rough draft of a cover letter to accompany the new campaign kits to 33 electric utilities in the energy efficient–home program. Send it to Pat at the office via e-mail. Pat will make a couple of editing suggestions and then output the finished letter.

Monday.

7:30 – Arrive. (Pretty typical)

Call a magazine publisher in New York regarding some free media merchandising for the cheddar-cheese account. The plan sounds good, but the client has to give the final OK.

Ask for a written proposal to be faxed by Wednesday. Pat sits in on the call and writes a quick e-mail to the media department updating them on this conversation.

Put the notes from the conversation with the publisher in the files for this week's Friday meeting with the client.

8:30 – Attend status meeting where every job going through the agency for your accounts is discussed with representatives of the media, creative, production, and traffic departments. Pat definitely attends this meeting, since monitoring project movement is one of the account coordinators primary functions.

9:15 – Sit down with Pat and review all the materials and final assembly instructions on the campaign kits that go to the electric utilities. Reread the cover letter before Pat faxes it to the client for approval.

10:00 – Review the discussion outline with the account planner for a focus group on the medical insurance account. Call the client for clarification on a new service that will be discussed at the focus group.

10:45 – Start preparing two work orders for signage and a radio spot for the carwash franchise client. Schedule meeting with the creative team and graphic designer for tomorrow.

11:15 – Do the first draft of the campaign brief for the potato chip client, who is about to expand distribution into supermarkets after being the category leader in natural-food stores. Ask Pat to schedule a start-work meeting with the creative and media team sometime tomorrow.

Noon – Walk across the street to the deli and pick up two lunches Pat ordered earlier. Make sure you get the insurance client's favorite beverage, a Starbuck's Frappuccino. Then walk three blocks to your client's office for a working lunch. These are good meetings.

High-rise building downtown with a corner-office view. Good loyal client. Good friend. You review a number of projects, including his comments about the copy and layout of a new brochure on case management. Overall, he likes the layout but some of the suggested photography is too general and the tone of the copy isn't quite right.

1:30 – Review a stack of preliminary billing reports, which need to be returned to the accounting department by tomorrow night. Meet with your boss, the account supervisor (AS) and explain why you think five hours of art director time ($500) should be a write-off and not billed to the insurance client. The mistake was only partially your fault, but as account manager you catch 100% of the heat. After a stressful conversation about how an art director can spend five hours doing the wrong thing, the AS signs the write-off and you in turn think to yourself: "It doesn't get much uglier than this. Later (in about three years), you'll be able to laugh about it."

2:00 – Meet with media planners on their newest spot-market budget for the cheddar-cheese account. The number of spot markets that deserve advertising support has grown faster than the client's ability to fund them. The agency has been asked for a market-weighting model that will put the money in the most important markets. You and the media department developed the model and now you see what the budget looks like using the new model. As part of the training process, Pat attends this meeting but takes no immediate action afterwards.

The new spot-market numbers are still not where the client would like them, but the new model is doing what it was designed to do, and you agree with the media planner to present it the way it is.

3:00 – Meet with creative team to review preliminary ad concepts for intro of the new line of flavored cheddar-cheese snack bars.

While in the meeting, you schedule a day when the creative team can join you for a trip to the newly expanded cheese factory and cheese aging room. You think the aging room can add some real substance to the reputation of the brand, and you want the art director to see it, too.

Besides, the creative team has not been to the "client's house" for a while, so it's about time you all paid a visit. Since this is one of the accounts that Pat will be taking over, she also will visit the client.

You especially like two of the thumbnails and headlines for the snack bar introduction and ask the creative team to proceed to full copy and layout on those two so you can present Friday. This is fun!

4:00 – Prepare a draft agenda for tomorrow's standing meeting with energy efficient–home client. E-mail the draft to Pat, who cleans it up, fills in a couple of blanks, and faxes it to the client.

4:15 – Make three update phone calls to clients, reporting on the progress of projects in the agency. Of course they are not there, so you leave short voice mails.

4:30 – Broadcast producer drops by to get clarification on an issue regarding residual payments to a radio voice talent.

4:45 – The agency intern arrives in your office.

You do today's time sheet. Then you, the intern, and Pat join the media department for an open house at a local radio station's new studios.

Tuesday.

7:30 – Arrive and deal with an hour's worth of e-mail that you didn't get to on Monday.

8:30 – Call the brand manager of a regional brand of canned chili in Denver. Your cheddar-cheese client is looking for a tie-in partner or two for a western U.S. cities FSI (free-standing insert in the Sunday papers). You already have a regional corn chip brand lined up for a nacho theme FSI if you can find a chili brand to sign on.

The brand manager is interested and wants details immediately, so you draft a proposal for him which includes spot-market media costs and production costs. You assemble the information and ask Pat to get it in the mail with a quick cover letter that she will write and sign for you.

9:30 – Take a call from the executive director of the local chapter of the American Advertising Federation (AAF).

You're on the committee that is judging the entries from the Minneapolis AAF club's annual "Excellence in Advertising" awards. There are some last-minute logistical problems that have come up, and they need your help in solving them.

Again, as part of agency training for community involvement, Pat listens on the speaker phone and plans to be part of the support crew on judging day.

9:45 – Meet with the copywriter and graphic designer to get started on this year's "winterize your car" promotion for the carwash client.

10:15 – Meet with the full account team to go over the initial details of the gourmet potato chip rollout into supermarkets. Use campaign brief to lead discussion of goals, timeline, budget, and preliminary promotional mix. Yesterday, Pat reminded everyone by phone of the meeting and what needed to be done in preparation for it.

11:00 – You are looking for a specialty item that your energy efficient–home client can give out at the annual regional energy conference. At your direction, Pat has borrowed three specialty-items catalogs from the sales promotion specialist at the agency.

After a quick review of the catalogs, you ask Pat to go through the catalogs thoroughly and flag 25 of the best ideas for you to look at.

11:30 – Take an excited call from your medical-dental insurance client who is mildly upset about a project being over budget on the last month's billing (which he has just found). You think you know why the project was over budget but you promise to look into it and get back to him in 15 minutes.

You look at old conference reports and find that the client agreed to do a "buyout" on the photography instead of a use fee. This costs more than what was budgeted, but provides unlimited use on a variety of projects planned at no additional charge. You have a signed estimate if he needs further explanation. So you call back and explain. He remembers. Crisis over.

Noon – Drive out to two different chain supermarkets to study their potato chip sections. With the approval of store managers, you take some digital photographs for the art director, who will be working on some POS ideas for the gourmet potato chip client, and for the graphic designer, who is doing some packaging revisions.

On the way back, stop for a quick burger at a regional fast-food chain that is featuring your cheese client's products in a "cheeseburger promotion." You think they did a lousy job of branding for your client.

In your opinion, this is another reason why the client should have let you handle the menu mention program instead of his food-service sales manager. You "borrow" a menu and tray liner to discuss this touchy issue with the client.

1:40 – Review Pat's suggestions for energy-related specialty items. You narrow the 25 down to 10. Pat makes photocopies of items and sets up a file folder for today's meeting.

2:00 – Meet with multimedia department on the presentation you are going to make to the regional energy conference.

This conference is the annual rollout of the new campaign for the energy efficient–home program. You've drafted the preliminary script. You walk the multimedia guy through the presentation, which will include PowerPoint slides, television spots, print ads, and a demonstration of the new interactive home energy planning game soon to be available on the program's Web site. The stuff looks really good.

You're jazzed about the quality of the agency's work. Pat will be taking care of a lot of the behind-the-scenes details of your presentation, so she sits in on this meeting.

3:00 – Review the notes from yesterday's meeting with insurance client on the copy and layout for managed-care brochure. Make margin notes on the copy, place Post-it notes on the layout, and summarize the major changes in a memo. Then Pat quickly makes copies of all the brochure layout pages, just for insurance. The creative team shows up just as you complete the memo. You go over the revisions with them.

No major problems on the revisions except the art director is more concerned than before that the photography budget may be too low, based on what the client wants to show in the photos. He's going to get a new estimate on photography.

4:00 – Energy efficient–home client arrives at agency for weekly standing meeting. Pat makes sure the chocolate chip cookies and the client's favorite flavor of iced tea are in the conference room.

While most of the account team and agency management are not involved in the meeting, you or Pat have made them all aware that the client will be "in the shop" and they may be called upon for something, or they are welcome to stop by and just say hello.

There's only one issue today that requires discussion with the art director, who, of course, is not in his office. You ask Pat to find him.

The meeting ends with a quick review of the monthly billing. You call a couple of small items to the client's attention.

6:00 – Do daily time sheet.

6:30 – Finish reviewing the rest of the preliminary billings. Return them to accounting department on the way out.

Wednesday.

6:30 – Attend monthly breakfast of a local group of supermarket and packaged-goods marketing execs.

8:00 – Return an urgent call from your carwash client. (Every call from this client seems like an urgent call.) This one is really big. Two big developments have made significant progress in the last week.

First, the most winning driver in Nascar has agreed in principle to become a spokesman for the franchise chain. Part of his compensation is for your client to build two car washes for him to own.

The other news is that a major brand of car wax has developed a new product that can be applied automatically in the car wash. This branded product will only be available in the franchise locations.

In addition to the normal stack of stuff you go through at the standing Thursday afternoon meeting, the client wants you to talk about a full-scale consumer campaign for the new cobranded waxing service with the driver as the spokesman. (The creatives are going to love this!)

Ask Pat to try to get everyone on the carwash account team together for an emergency meeting tomorrow morning. Tell them that it's a good emergency.

8:30 – Write a conference report on yesterday's two-hour meeting with energy efficient–home client.

10:00 – Attend a meeting of all the account managers, account supervisors, and account coordinators on how to better serve the clients. Special attention is paid to how account managers can do a better job of integrating all the services provided by the agency.

11:00 – Read an article on e-coupons, which have taken on even more relevance since the carwash call this morning.

11:30 – Review latest competitive sales and promotion expenditure data from Simmons on the cheddar-cheese category.

Noon – Have a working lunch with the team working on the lawn fertilizer new-business pitch.

1:30 – Start a semi-annual budget to billing report for energy efficient–home account.

2:30 – Do time sheet, then accompany energy efficient–home client to a studio session, where three new radio spots are being recorded and produced.

6:30 – Meet a fellow account manager from your old agency for a drink and to just catch up.

Thursday.

7:30 – Write and fax over the agenda for this afternoon's standing meeting with the carwash client.

8:00 – Pat was successful in getting the media planner, copywriter, art director, sales promotion specialist, PR person, and interactive specialist together for a quick brainstorming session on what the campaign might look like for the new carwash service/Nascar spokesman promotion.

Draft a preliminary "talking points" outline about alternative campaign directions for today's meeting. Multiple ideas allow the agency to show its expertise and nimbleness without locking itself in to any one concept so early in the campaign development.

10:30 – Talk to the multimedia/programming expert about getting your potato chip client's package on a popular game show, which is sold on a spot market syndication basis.

11:00 – Proofread the latest proof of a benefits brochure being produced for the dental side of the insurance client.

Noon – Grab a quick sandwich with one of the art directors who's going to be working on the fertilizer pitch. Informally talk strategy.

1:00 – Research company account exec comes in to talk about online concept testing of three new potato chip packaging designs. The graphic designer also attends.

Take the research company's proposal material and rework it for presentation to client.

2:30 – Meet with carwash client in his manufacturing office. Cover the agenda items. He likes the preliminary thoughts on the Nascar/cobrand campaign. He's especially intrigued with the online coupon idea and the Web site interactivity ideas.

5:30 – Review address list for the next agency promotional mailing.

6:00 – Do time sheet. Rush to catch rest of agency softball game.

Friday.

7:00 – Write conference report of yesterday's meeting with carwash client. Forward it to Pat via e-mail for clean up and distribution.

8:30 – Pick up cheese client and drive over to printing plant for a press check on new POS. While the printer is making color adjustments, walk three blocks down to a photo studio where some new packaging is being shot.

You walk back and forth twice between printer and photographer. During the walks and the downtime, you conduct an almost normal meeting where a stack of stuff is reviewed – including your presentation of the three snack bar ads now in comp form.

Noon – Do lunch with cheese client.

1:00 – Receive a call from Pat. The media department is in a tizzy and needs to talk with you. It seems that at noon today, a radio station in Cincinnati ran the wrong commercials for the carwash franchises there and all hell broke loose. The station takes full responsibility and will do anything to make it right. In your absence, the media department took the lead and negotiated a make-good package which includes 50% more spots, an on-air contest, and a remote broadcast from each franchise location. Sweet deal!

You immediately call your client, tell them what happened and what your media department has negotiated. They'd just heard about the flap and appreciate that the agency was way ahead on this one.

Client asks that you personally call each Cincinnati franchisee and tell them the good news, then follow up with faxes and e-mails. Pat faxes franchisee phone numbers to the photographer's studio.

2:00 – Make phone calls to Cincinnati while cheese client works with art director on photos.(Not optimal to be fighting a fire for one client in presence of another, but you do what you gotta do.)

3:30 – Press check and photography done. Drop client off at hotel.

4:00 – Show Pat how to write a media change order asking the media department to cancel the balance of the schedule in an LA magazine for the cheese client. The distribution they'd hoped for has not yet materialized. So the advertising is a waste of money.

Try to return as many phone calls as you can while you deal with another hour of e-mail.

5:00 – Gather the latest proofs for a 12-page carwash equipment brochure to take them home to proofread. Also in your briefcase are the most recent issues of *Ad Age, AdWeek,* and *Promo* magazines – plus two *Wall Street Journals* you couldn't get to this week.

As you can see, advertising agency life is never dull. Hey, who needs coffee with a job this stimulating?

The responsibilities described here may seem superhuman, but for a talented account manager, it's just an average week!

BUZZ...

Creativity, Stability Score High Marks.
Advertising Age; May 24, 1999

Clients Praise DDB's Commitment to Excellence.
Obviously, the best thing about DDB is the people.
They exhibit a passion and commitment to our business that makes it hard to differentiate them from our employees.

I think there must be something in the water there that puts passion and commitment into their people. I've encountered that in dealing with them since 1982, and it's common among people in their Chicago office, in San Francisco, in their offices around the world. They all seem to be service-oriented and committed to our business.

Overall, they understand our products, and they focus on what the products do for the consumer. They're not in fairyland in terms of getting excited about some incredible look or unusual music arrangement.

We have the pleasure of working with people at DDB who have been in the business for many years, so they have great experience and enthusiasm about our business. There are many who fit this description, but two I work with are Kenny Dudwick on the creative side and Dan Odishoo [both are managing partners, DDB San Francisco] on the account side.

These are two experienced people who are doing what they love to do, and it shows. *Passion* is the word I use. These guys call me regularly with comments such as: "We're worried about what's happening with this brand; what do you think of this idea?" Kenny especially is an absolute fountain of ideas.

They might be about how to run the business, when a promotion should run, what the packaging should look like. Nothing is off the table. That's what makes it fun to work with them.

This is really about partnership.

Our relationship with DDB is more like a marriage than a business relationship.

This is a marriage that works well, at lots of different levels, in lots of different places. So we're thrilled to be working with them.

Larry Peiros, Group VP, The Clorox Co.

They've helped us through the difficult transition we've had during the last few years, creating a universal theme around our *"Did somebody say McDonald's?"* campaign.

And they are a role model for us on how collaboration works. They're very involved with all of our calendar teams in terms of our processing for future planning and the strategies we use for planning. They start right where we do with our customers and our operators.

Larry Zwain, Senior VP U.S. Marketing, McDonald's Corp.

DDB is the only agency we've ever had. Over 60 years, we've established a real kinship, a close working relationship between our top management and their top management.

Their CEO, Keith Reinhard, worked on our account all the way back to the late '60s, and that has been a very stabilizing factor. He and our previous CEO, Ed Rust Sr., and our current CEO, Ed Rust Jr., solidified the relationship.

To this day, I think Keith maintains a fervent feeling for State Farm… and the feeling is mutual.

The agency's understanding of our values and our culture has cemented the relationship. Also, they understand our marketplace and how to deal with our customers.

The day-to-day working relationships with their account and creative people have been excellent. Currently we work primarily with Jim Cass [VP creative director] and Rick Fobs [VP-group account director, both DDB Chicago].

But everyone in creative and in the account group seems to understand State Farm agents, how they work and how they think. Overall, the main thing about our relationship is the comfort level, the kinship.

Tom Nelson, VP-Advertising, State Farm Insurance Co.

We're very pleased with their strategic thinking, their creative work, their media purchasing.

People such as Steve Swanson [group account director] on the account side and Linda Antonelli [group media director] on the media side have done a superb job for us over the years.

It's very much a partnership, where we share full information.

Steve Scott VP-Marketing and Brand Management,
Amtrak, National Railroad Passenger Corp.

Hershey added DDB as a second agency 21 years ago. Initial assignments included Kit Kat, Hershey's Syrup and Y&S Twizzlers. All three of these brands are still assigned to DDB.

We have always worked in a team environment with DDB, and our meetings focus on a lot of discussion and listening and molding of the advertising, rather than selling and buying of campaign ideas. Because most of the agency people have been on our account for a long time, they understand our background, so we don't have to do a lot of explaining.

And, nearly since the beginning of our relationship 20 years ago, there has been Peter Tate (now president of the New York office) overseeing the relationship and the work.

DDB's main asset, I feel, is the excellent balance among the account team, the creative people, and the media planners. Everyone contributes to the discussion, and this team effort has led to better strategies and better advertising.

Michael H. Holmes, VP/GM/Chocolate, Hershey Food Corp.

The best thing about DDB is the people who work on our business, starting with Keith Reinhard. Then there's Bob Scarpelli, who was on the original team that pitched and won our Bud Light account in the early '80s.

Also I should mention John Greening [exec VP-managing partner, DDB Chicago], the head account man on our business, who has been with us since 1977, when DDB took on Busch beer. Both of them have watched our business grow.

In fact, DDB has been able to maintain a core group of people on our account for some 20 years.

And that's very important to a business like ours – which is highly regulated, heavily watched, and which is always being asked to have great creative because we buy a lot of high-profile media.

These guys know the demands, the dos and don'ts of beer advertising.

DDB people are hard workers, who care as much about our products as we do. Honesty, forthrightness, and trust characterize DDB's people, and we enjoy working with them. We don't talk to them as our agency; we talk to them as our partners and friends.

Bob Lachky, VP-Brand Management, Anheuser-Busch

JUICY CASES:

5.1: Not Again!*
You're the account manager on a hi-tech account.

Your client contact is a "techie-turned-marketing-genius." He tries to keep agency billable hours down by writing what he thinks are exhaustive new product briefs. The briefs are exhausting in their product orientation but short on benefit and branding.

Meetings with the creative people are not needed in his opinion because of the "thorough nature" of the product brief.

He gets upset when you come back with questions from the creative department during the normal creative process. He thinks the questions are unnecessary and does not like to bother engineers or product developers with such questions.

What to do?

* Inspired by a case found in *How to Get the Best Work from Your Agency* by Nancy Salz.

5.2: The Renegade Creative.
You're an account executive with a "creatively driven" agency where the creative people have ruled for a long time. Management has just begun to realize the benefit of stronger account managers.

Recently you had a project for one of your clients where two concepts were presented to you by the creative team. You embraced one as the best overall solution.

You thought your rationale for choosing the concept was thoughtful and prudent. The creative director agreed with your assessment, as did everyone on the account team, except (as it turns out) the copywriter.

You presented the winning creative approach to the client, who enthusiastically embraced the concept.

The next day you leave on a two-day business trip.

In your absence, the unhappy copywriter does an "end run." He makes an appointment with the client and pitches his concept. While not embracing the renegade's concept, the client tells you in a phone call that he thinks the concept "has merit."

The copywriter gets a slap on the wrist from the creative director and is told not to do that again. But you're left with an embarrassing mess.

What issues does this case bring into focus?

What is your best way of dealing with this mess?

AD-ROBIC EXERCISES:

5.1: Memo to Management Supervisor.

You are an account manager who has been at the agency for three years. In your annual performance review, your account supervisor and one of the senior partners gave you good marks in most areas but expressed concerns about profitability on your accounts. It seems there are three areas specifically of concern to management.

1. The amount of creative write-offs is higher than the agency average.

2. There have been media and production deadlines missed, which have meant extra expense to the agency.

3. Most of your accounts are slow pay.

Management has asked that you write them a memo outlining your strategy for correcting these concerns in the next six months.

For this Ad-robic exercise, write the memo with specific attention to the problems that have resulted in the three areas of management concern and your objectives for improvement.

5.2: The Power of Observation.

Imagine you're the account coordinator on a new bread account just landed by the agency. Visit a large supermarket and observe 20 people buying bread from the bread section – not the in-store bakery.

Make a record sheet for each observation.

Based on what you see, make the best guestimate you can about the following observation components:

- Sex
- Age
- Marital status
- Shopping alone or with another person
- Shopping for self or family
- Length of time taken to make selection(s)
- Any other behaviors that give insight into how this person made his or her selection
- Type of bread selected and number of loaves
- Price of bread selected
- Any other observations about those observed that might give a glimpse into lifestyle or economic status?

Write a memo (up to three pages) to the account manager on what you learned and the conclusions about bread buyers that you can draw from your observations.

Burning Questions:

5.1:

Explain the account management function of "expediting the client." Give three examples of this function.

5.2:

Review "Fifty Hours on a Roller Coaster." What five activities were the most interesting or surprising to you? Explain why this is.

6.0 EVERYDAY SUPER-HUMAN

SOME PEOPLE SAY YOU NEED TO BE SUPER-HUMAN in order to be a first-rate account manager. It's certainly not an easy job. An account manager needs to play many roles and employ many personality characteristics in order to get the job done.

The purpose of this chapter is to shed some additional light on the human side of the job (super or otherwise).

- **"Two Dozen Hats"** discusses different roles that will be played in the execution of account management duties.

- **"Eight Traits of Successful Account Managers"** talks about the personality traits that senior agency people think young account managers need to focus on.

6.1 The Two Dozen Hats of Account Service

A good account manager is versatile, able to play many different roles, able to adapt to the changing situation, able to smoothly "switch hats."

There's a classic saying in the advertising business that the account manager is a chameleon, able to quickly "read" the surroundings.

I chose the "hats" analogy because the critical skill is the ability to analyze a situation (preferably ahead of time) and then effectively play the right role.

Quarterback	Facilitator	Researcher	Strategist
Consultant	Psychic	Account Planner	Critic
Accountant	Teacher	Ethicist	Reporter
Firefighter	Diplomat	Cheerleader	Performer
Entertainer	Ambassador	Event Planner	Salesperson
Entrepreneur	Friend	Janitor	Marathoner

"It all started innocently enough. I needed a second thinking cap, and then something new came up and before you know it…"

1. Quarterback.

The advertising agency is often likened to a football team, with the account manager as the quarterback. The bottom line is that you are responsible for making sure that everyone on the team understands the objectives and how everyone is to work together to achieve them.

This may sound simple, but by the time you fully understand all the hats and the contexts in which they are worn, the job of quarterback will take on new meaning. Keep in mind that the ad agency account manager has all the responsibility for success on an account and no authority.

Living by your wits, trusting your instincts, and knowing what role to play at any given moment are all critical. Quarterbacks never assume something is going to happen unless they've made sure that it'll happen. Even then, there's no guarantee.

Virtually nothing happens on an account unless it's initiated by the account manager. Research, creative work, media planning, and other activities are done at the direction and request of the account manager. Progress on projects is usually made as each stage is approved by the account manager.

Don't be deceived into thinking that account managers merely give orders and everyone obeys. It's anything but that.

The job of quarterback is often to make order out of chaos... taking a bunch of people with differing opinions and skills and successfully finding a solution that the client will like, that the agency will like, and that will do the job; that's not an easy task, even for an experienced quarterback.

Account managers must have command of a large playbook. Most often, it is the account manager who will decide what elements of the promotional mix will be employed in any given campaign.

Therefore, they must be knowledgeable about the latest trends and the newest media. It is also the account manager who writes the integrated marketing communications plan, which explains how the campaign will be executed.

There's one small problem with the quarterback analogy and it is that football games always end – even the Super Bowl. In the ongoing agency-client relationship, there hopefully is no end.

So the quarterback's job really involves managing multiple projects, multiple timelines, multiple budgets, sometimes multiple clients and a never-ending continuum of wearing those other 23 hats.

2. Facilitator.

The key to success in account management is to make things happen by fostering a productive creative environment and inspiring others to do their best work. To do their work, people usually need things from each other: information, time, stimulation, clarification, feedback, encouragement, and money, to name a few.

Your job is to understand what the people on the agency team need and to make sure they get it. This applies to the client also, since the client is an important part of the process.

Facilitation may include any number of special efforts on your part depending on the people involved, their work styles, their expectations, and the dynamics of those involved.

Facilitation often involves some sort of information system and the cross-checks required to make sure everyone is getting what they need.

It's the personal effort of the account manager to understand how people work best that makes for truly effective facilitation.

When you're a facilitator, you are the lubricant that keeps the work moving. This may mean preparing information for a media person or a creative who absorbs it better if it is presented in a different way.

Or it may be as simple as knowing a certain part of the day is best for the team to engage in a certain type of activity.

Or that always having cookies at your meetings may help guarantee everyone will be on time and in a relatively good mood, thereby maximizing the effective work time.

Sometimes the role of facilitator seems more like "expediter."

It may be personally making a delivery of some material that saves a few hours or driving to a printer in the middle of the night for a press check instead of waiting for the messenger to deliver a proof at 10 a.m. the next day.

The agency business runs on deadlines. There will be many opportunities to help move things along. Most of these opportunities are worth the effort. Take them on with a smile.

3. Researcher.

One of the things that impresses business school students in the introductory advertising class is the amount of research involved in all aspects of the ad business.

The five broad categories of advertising research are:
- Exploratory/motivational
- Quantitative/attitudinal
- Concept testing
- Ad performance
- Audience delivery

The techniques used to conduct such research are many. The account manager should be familiar with the uses of research in all of its forms: product-use observation techniques, attitude and awareness studies, customized Simmons abstracts, Neilsen cross-tabs, cluster analysis, Roper-Starch Reports, and online perception analysis, to name a few.

Depending on the agency's use of account planners, account managers may also be responsible for some level of creative research. Expect to add to your repertoire the new field of explor-atory/motivational research done by account planners. This includes brand-use video observation, emotional connection research, cultural anthropological studies, and futurism.

Being knowledgeable about research design and knowing how to interpret data are important. But the most important part of this hat, however, is knowing when research will help, what kind of research should be done, and ensuring that the research will actually answer the critical question or provide the needed insights.

Like any other tool, research has its place and its limitations. Clients and account managers tend to like research as a way to improve the likelihood of correct decisions. Creatives, on the other hand, tend to hate most research, especially concept testing such as focus groups, perception analyzers, mall intercepts, and the like.

Sometimes the client and the agency are best served by you, the researcher and quarterback, knowing when to say, "To hell with research. Our instincts tell us we have a great idea."

This might sound odd, but most veteran account managers can remember a project where work was delayed anticipating that some coming research was going to be helpful, only to find that the research did not add anything to the equation or simply confirmed what they intuitively knew weeks before.

4. Strategist.

Next to clear objectives, smart strategies are where good ad campaigns are born within the walls of an advertising agency. We're talking media strategies and campaign integration strategies as well as creative strategies.

Sometimes the strategies developed by the agency involve issues even earlier in the marketing process, such as product design or the need for repositioning.

There is some confusion about exactly what a strategy is in the context of advertising.

For purposes here, let's just say that a strategy is the way the communication problem is solved. Here's a quick example.

The winning pitch for the 2002 National Student Advertising Competition was delivered by Southern Methodist University. The client was Bank of America Investment Services Inc. (BAISI). While all other competitors emphasized saving and investing for the future, the SMU team's strategy was to show how BAISI could help clients enjoy life right now.

This was a simple, insightful, and winning message strategy!

Strategic thinking like this is the expertise for which clients retain agencies. Great ads and superbly executed campaigns are the tangible results, but the strategy is where it starts.

Strategy not only holds the program together, it is the foundation of all of the subsequent thinking and activity. It's the account manager who is ultimately responsible for strategic leadership within the agency and making sure that the creative work is "driven" by the strategy.

Your clients and agency associates expect you to think like a strategist. You'll be expected to develop strategies with the client and by yourself. As part of your ongoing responsibilities, you'll need to make judgments about how the strategies and executions developed by agency specialists relate to the big picture.

For example, the interactive component must be aligned with the creative work. Creative must be aligned with media. Media must be aligned with sales promotion.

There is only one person who can make sure that the strategies created by the agency all spring from a consistent and meaningful core. That person is you.

Writing strategy statements is an art learned both by example and practice. As your career advances, you'll have a chance to see well-written strategy statements. Learn from them.

Ask your supervisors for examples of strategy statements to better understand what strategy is and how it is explained.

Part of being a strategist is being a "systems thinker," someone who can think things through and "see the ripples." Advertising and marketing strategies have impact in the marketplace and within the client organization.

A systems thinker can see what needs to be done inside the client organization and its marketing channels in order to adjust to new initiatives or react to tactics of the competition.

5. Consultant.

The word "sell" is used a lot in the agency business.

You'll hear, "Boy, John did a great job of selling this campaign" or "Amy sold hard, but the client just wasn't buying it."

Well, agencies don't sell anything, except their clients' products in an indirect sense.

Agencies are service organizations retained to provide their expertise on programs customized to the client's needs.

Sure, you deliver products – brochures, radio spots, a product placement on *Friends*, but you don't *sell* anything.

Your job is to advise and consult in an area where your agency is the expert – integrated marketing communications. There's no inventory, no sales quota, no weekly specials, no deal sheets.

The word "sell" in a consulting environment has a different meaning. Clients don't automatically accept what consultants recommend. The best of proposals can be rejected.

Essentially, selling in the agency means that the work you presented was outstanding and your presentation of it left no doubt in the client's mind that it was excellent.

In other words, the advertising was inspired, strategic, based on objectives, and your presentation was articulate, complete, compelling, and polished.

That is selling in the ad biz, and that's what consultants need to do so clients will adopt and act upon their recommendations.

6. Psychic.

Advertising is one of the most intuitive and nonscientific of all business disciplines. One necessary talent can best be described as the ability to see the future.

The term "futurist" has taken on a whole different meaning in the area of motivational research, and I think the best term for accurately predicting coming events is "psychic." Both futurists and psychics work with scenarios visualizing possible (or probable) future events.

The "psychic" abilities of an account manager are ultimately wide in scope, and they grow with experience, sometimes painful.

In most cases, your psychic talents will involve predicting how people are going to react and behave. Problems or opportunities will arise from these reactions or behaviors. Knowing what to do if and when a certain situation presents itself is also part of being a psychic.

For example, you know the creative team assigned to a project likes to do "edgy," hip work. Your client, however, is conservative – and, more importantly, so is the target consumer. Your psychic powers predict that you could be in for some challenging times.

Clearly, you want to avoid certain scenarios. For example, you may need to make an extra effort to frame your input to the creative team in a way that will help them get in touch with that conservative target consumer.

One of the things that will help inspire you to that extra effort to work with your creative team will be that psychic ability – seeing the various kinds of disaster that can happen if they don't make that connection. It will also help both you and the creative team develop a presentation of the recommended concept that will address your conservative client's concerns.

In most cases, that psychic ability to see problems before they happen is an "experiential skill" based on the personalities and tasks involved.

It could be a television producer who habitually underestimates costs, a print production manager a bit too optimistic on delivery time, an art director who's heard "make the logo larger" too many times, or a client who's probably going to be in a bad mood because it's Thursday and he's always in a bad mood on Thursday.

Coworkers and clients provide you inexhaustible opportunities to predict and avoid future problems.

And don't forget the importance of visualizing successful scenarios, where clients buy good work for the right reasons, because it was well presented and honest concerns were anticipated.

Mastering the "psychic" can add immensely to your effectiveness and your enjoyment of the job. Throw away the tea leaves. Start observing behavior. Visualize possible problems and their successful solutions.

7. Account Planner.

As discussed in Chapter 4.4, "Straight Talk about Account Planning," the account planner is essentially a specialist at creative research and a strategist who makes sure the customer's point of view is adequately represented in the agency's work. This is done at the creative research input and rough concept review stages.

Considering the customer's viewpoint in advertising may sound like a BGO (Blinding Glimpse of the Obvious), but a lot of advertising talks about features and how wonderful the client is, rather than making an emotional connection with the audience. This emotional connection is what account planners help to achieve.

When agencies don't have account planners, the account manager performs this function. Account managers are expected to represent the client in creative deliberations, so wearing the account planner's hat at the same time is account service multitasking at its best.

The account manager does the client great service by always making sure the customer's point of view permeates the agency's work. Wearing the account planner hat is not an added burden, it is the essence of good advertising.

Chapter 3.3, "The Campaign and Creative Briefs," presents an award-winning campaign, an example of an advertising campaign that is the epitome of account planning–driven advertising.

So how do you wear the account planner hat when there isn't someone formally trained to do so? Good question.

The answer lies in understanding exactly what account planners do, which is to know more about your client's customer than anyone else. Anything you can do to understand the psyche, the habits, and mindset of the target audience will make your creative input better.

Gaining the respect and cooperation of the creative team is easier when your input is always good and your response to rough concepts is customer- rather than client-focused.

8. Critic.

One of the toughest parts of being an account manager is to critique the work of others. One of the best indicators you have arrived as a seasoned account manager is that you critique the work of others and they still respect you.

This happens when your critique is objective, compassionate, insightful, and instructional (think "teacher").

Theoretically, the way to limit the need to tell people that their work "needs more work" is to provide them with exceptionally good input up front.

Sometimes this works, and the proposals that come back from creative or media are right on target.

Other times, and in spite of what you consider a very good campaign and creative brief, you will have major reservations about what is being proposed by the creative department, the media department, the interactive folks, the sales promotion specialists, or the public relations department.

How you handle yourself in this situation is critical to your ability to get the best work out of these people in the future.

The art of insightful questioning is a good one to cultivate. Nothing will expose weak work or confirm strong work faster than objective, intellectual challenge – insightful, probing questions about ideas and how they came about.

The word "objectivity" takes on special meaning in this situation. Since so much of advertising (especially creative) is subjective, you have to find a way to take yourself out of the subjective equation, thus enabling your associates to accept your critique as fair and helpful.

At the same time, you must have an opinion. Creative people are passionate about their work, and they have opinions. They expect passion and opinions from you. The key to success is having passionate opinions based on the right set of criteria.

In most cases, the most successful opinions expressed by account managers will focus on these broad issues:

1. Whether or not the creative is "right" for the communications objectives set forward in the campaign brief.

2. Whether or not the creative is "right" from the point of view of the target audience.

3. Whether or not the creative is "right" for this client.

4. Whether or not the work is bold enough to be up to agency standards. (They're going to love you for that one.)

The importance of your initial gut reaction to an ad is always important. However, young account managers should also have an assessment tool to help develop a formal opinion.

I suggest you revisit the D'Arcy/Ogilvy/Bernbach model in Chapter 3.4 on evaluating and presenting creative work.

I know from experience in using the D/O/B model for years that creative people may not like what you have to say, but they'll feel you were correct, fair, objective, and rightfully passionate in your opinions.

My advice: Know this model. Use it to form your own opinions and to be the best "passionately objective" critic you can be.

9. Accountant.

There's a lot more "working with numbers" in account management than most people expect. The accountant hat has five sides:

- Agency compensation
- Billing management
- Account profitability
- Budget management
- Forecasting

For many people who enjoy the right-brain aspects of advertising, wearing the accountant hat isn't much fun, but it's critical to a strong, long-term agency-client relationship and advancement within the agency.

Chapters 2.4 and 3.7 deal extensively with what a young manager needs to know about the financial side of client service. So here is a brief overview:

Agency Compensation.

How agencies make money is interesting, complicated, and changing. Since account managers are judged, in part, on the income they generate, it is important that you understand this issue.

Billing Management.

"Billing" is the industry term for the invoice the agency sends its clients every month. Few things will mess up a good client relationship faster than billing problems. If there's a problem on the billing, clients don't call your accounting department, they call you. They're already upset that you, the person who is supposed to look out for them, let the problem slip through. They'll expect immediate answers to any number of questions, most of which are coated with some amount of irritation and distrust.

Account Profitability.

Obviously, profitability is the goal for all accounts. Account managers should know about agency accounting and how account profitability is computed. Detail and a case problem can be found in Chapter 3.7.

Budget Management.

Managing the client's money is a large responsibility. Because you are often the author of the client's annual advertising budget, you know more about it than even they do. Managing projects to see that they stay within budget and keeping control of the overall budget is a job they have entrusted to you.

Forecasting.

Agency management makes decisions about staffing and employee compensation based on revenue and expense projections. Where do they get the revenue projections? From account managers.

Account managers are supposed to have a handle on the plans and activities of each account. They are best equipped to accurately forecast the amount of account spending in future quarters.

10. Teacher.

The definition of teacher in this context has two parts. In Chapter 2.1 of this book we talked about the account manager's responsibility for "making a better client." The role of teacher is fundamental to this process. The client is not the advertising expert and may have opinions, expectations, or work styles that are counter to the development of great ad programs.

As teacher, the account manager's job is to educate the client in ways that improve the agency's ability to do its work effectively and efficiently. Among these is to help the client understand what makes good advertising and to help him develop an appetite for it.

One of the eight traits in the following section is a "devoted student of the craft." The student and the teacher are inexorably connected. The best teachers are devoted to the study of their craft and knowing it better than anyone else.

It's said the best teachers are the most devoted students.

This holds true in advertising also. Account managers are expected by clients to be a professional consultant and expected to be the source of all knowledge by the rest of the agency team and management. This takes constant study.

Advertising is a rapidly changing field. New media formats, new forms of compensation, new alliances, new technologies, not to mention new campaigns breaking all the time.

If a client asks you about a new trend in the business or seeks your opinion of a new campaign, you'll want to know about it!

As a student of your craft, *Advertising Age, AdWeek, Promo, Communication Arts, American Demographics,* and the *Wall Street Journal's* "Media and Marketing" column should be part of your regular diet.

Don't just read and recycle, save some of the best. It's a good idea to start a file where you put interesting and pertinent articles.

Sharing your readings with others is a great way to reinforce your role as teacher and student. Clients like the fact that you took the time to read and share a pertinent piece. It shows you're thinking about them.

They especially appreciate it when an account manager reads an article about something seemly unrelated and can make it useful in the context of the client's business.

Bigger clients expect you to stay abreast of contemporary issues, trends, and events in their industry. This you can do more easily nowadays with customized computer news group services where you can quickly review marketing and communications articles in specific industry trade journals.

You should also consider keeping a "brainfood file" – a scrapbook of favorite campaigns, strong promotions, unusual uses of media. You need a collection of good creative work of all sorts.

Together, the articles you save and the brainfood scrapbook will serve to inspire you when you need ideas, and they will renew your passion for great advertising.

The second definition of teacher is internal to the agency. If you want to move up the account service food chain you have to demonstrate to management that you're management stock. A manager's job is to "grow" people.

Among other duties, this means paying attention to the aspirations of others. Teaching people who are eager to learn is one way to get more important assignments. In considering people for promotions, management will consider the void that will be created if you get a new and larger account assignment. Teaching others around you to do their job better will make it easier to put someone in your old job as you move up.

Some account managers will play the "knowledge as power" game, not sharing their knowledge because they are insecure. Your reputation should be one built on sharing your wisdom and giving others a chance to spread their wings.

Your reputation will follow you, and those who seek knowledge will seek out opportunities to work with you. Good teachers and eager understudies are good business.

Teaching has its delicate political side. For example, make sure your account supervisor knows the kind of responsibilities you're handing off to an account coordinator. This way, you've established a practice that someone in authority has embraced.

11. Ethicist.

Yes, advertising people are expected to have scruples and be concerned about things like ethics. The topic is not widely discussed, but, like any social science and business discipline, advertising provides it's own opportunities for ethical judgment.

The account manager is most often the person who will make the decision on ethical issues. Advertising's ethical issues and questions often fall into three categories:

- Those involving advertising claims
- Those involving media and vendor charges
- Those involving client billing

The ethics of advertising claims is a very gray area on the fringe.

Outrageously deceptive claims are easy to spot these days. It's the subtleties that can get you.

It may be product performance that is technically possible but in practice very difficult to achieve. (Some clients love these.)

Or it might be a creative treatment that infers competitive superiority when none exists. Or the implication that the product contains some important ingredient that it doesn't.

These are only three areas where the account manager must be vigilant about the ethics of claims. The guiding policy is that anything that could be remotely interpreted by a customer as an attempt to deceive is bad business for the agency and the client. This can be very touchy when the client has provided the input and insists that such truths be shaded.

The best advice a trusted account manager can give to a client who wants to shade the truth is that it will hurt them in two ways.

First, the ads will likely be exposed in the media for their deceptive tendencies, and the client will get some very bad PR.

Second, when ads are based on weak or potentially deceptive claims, it keeps the agency from creating a more meaningful and effective message.

The bottom line: don't let your agency or your client near anything that could blow up in your collective faces.

Invoicing from media and vendors sometimes provides ethical challenges. To explain, let's assume that an invoice comes in from a photographer used on a recent client project. The invoice is slightly higher than it should be, based on the amount of work done.

Does the agency contest the bill or accept it and bill it through to the client? The right answer is contest the bill and insist on a new, lower invoice. But if the agency adds a production markup to vendor invoices, then agency income will be reduced by doing the right thing. Hmmmm.

Same with media invoices. Let's say an invoice from a magazine is based on a six-time frequency schedule instead of the slightly lower nine-time rate. Does the agency ask the magazine for a corrected invoice or let it slip through?

After all, "it's only a small difference and if we ask for a new invoice, the agency does more work, gets a smaller commission, and won't receive the income for another month." What do you think?

The ethics of billing practices is an equally sticky issue. Some examples of such practices include billing the client for more hours than were spent on the job, allowing a higher agency commission or mark up than is correct, or not passing credits on to the client. All are serious breaches of client trust.

Many errors in billing practices are not intentional and get pretty far along the billing process before they are detected or questioned. Because they are well into the billing process, the account manager will not be a popular person when issues mentioned above are questioned.

But, as stated in other parts of this book, agency billing practices must be squeaky clean. There's no faster way to lose client trust than through billings that lack integrity. Unpopular or not, the account manager is responsible for the ethicality of the billing.

Better that the billing is delayed and redone than sent out with anything that doesn't pass ethical muster. Too much rides on the client relationship for it to be any other way.

12. Reporter.

On larger accounts with full-time agency staff, the client relationship often extends beyond the account manager to include media, creative, and production people on the account team.

This is a good situation when the client has personal relationships with more than one person at the agency.

In the majority of cases, however, creatives, media people, and others at the agency live an insulated life. They have very little actual contact with clients or the client's marketplace.

Most other agency personnel are equally void of information on how their work performed in the marketplace.

Account managers must be sensitive to the account team's need to know. If the account manager does not report back on how things are going, the other people in the agency will make one of two assumptions… neither of which is positive.

They'll assume you don't know how the agency's work is performing because you do not care, or they'll assume you do know how things are going and don't respect them enough to share the news.

The fact is that much goes into the success of a MarCom program, and the agency's work is only part of it. Directly attributing results, good or bad, to advertising is risky. Anecdotal evidence of success, client comments, and new attitude and awareness studies are all good things to share.

Feedback may be nothing more than "the client loves it" or "sales are flat, but the client doesn't blame us." Your associates are genuinely interested in the impact of their work. You need to feed them with feedback.

When the news is good, the account manager gives other people credit for the success. When the news isn't so good the account manager tries to assess what could have been done better without assigning blame.

Another aspect of reporting is the conference report.

Whether agencies use conference reports or some other method, the need is the same. The agency team needs regular updates on the latest discussions and decisions that occur in periodic meetings between the account manager and client.

The conference report, whatever the format, handles all this information in one package. The account team, including senior management, needs to know, and it's your job to report.

The next beat for the reporter is the status report.

Some agencies use a formal status report and some don't. Again, the format doesn't matter. Somehow the client needs to be regularly updated on the status of projects moving through the agency.

If the agency's internal status report is not appropriate for client consumption, the account manager will need to create one that is.

Budget-to-billing reconciliations are reports prepared by the account manager to tell the client how actual expenses are doing compared to allocations.

The Brand Stewardship Report (BSR) is another example of the account manager's work as a reporter.

You'll find discussion of conference reports, status reports, reconciliations, and BSRs in Chapter 3, "Tools of the Craft."

13. Firefighter.

The advertising business is like no other in terms of its fast pace and the demands that it puts on everyone to adapt quickly to change.

Sooner or later, the "wheels fall off" of something and you have a bona fide crisis on your hands. As a psychic, your job was to anticipate the myriad ways almost everything can go wrong and to do two things:

1. figure out a way to avoid the crisis in the first place; and

2. have a back-up plan.

Every organization, every team, has its weakness. Someone on the team has underestimated the cost and time it will take to complete a project – or the agency is putting too much reliance on an untested vendor. Someone wasn't back from maternity leave in time to finish the project. A talented copywriter who often offends the client is assigned to the new campaign. These examples and many, many (did I say many?) more are crises just waiting to fall in your lap.

Being a good "preventive firefighter" is something that can only come through experience and by getting burned a few times. As your experience grows, so will your ability to see the people and situations that could cause problems later.

To shorten this learning curve, watch what seasoned account people do. In status meetings watch how they focus in on specific issues, activities, or people who are mission-critical.

What do you do when a crisis does erupt?

First, keep your cool. The last thing you want is a reputation as someone who gets rattled easily. You want a reputation as someone who is cool and resourceful in a crisis.

Second, quickly get all the facts so you know how and why the crisis occurred. Learn from it. Expect that poor communication is at the root of most crises.

Third, don't immediately take on the responsibility for fixing the problem, especially if it was someone else's screwup.

Most people have enough integrity and professionalism to want to fix a mess of their own making. Your job is to make sure they fix the problem if they caused it. I'm not saying to fold your arms across your chest and be uncooperative in getting the crisis solved. Being understanding and helpful is good teamwork and will make people want to reciprocate when you screw up (nobody's perfect).

But don't be quick to take ownership of someone else's mess.

Counsel with your senior account people. Watch how they fight fires. Gather the facts and try to develop possible solutions for discussion. Don't ask your supervisor outright for solutions or ask them to go to bat for you unless you think the crisis is large and growing or there are cross-departmental lines being drawn in the sand over the situation.

Once the crisis is over, thank whoever fixed it, even if they caused it in the first place. Everyone unintentionally messes up. You will. And everyone benefits when an unexpected fire was effectively extinguished with cool heads, professionalism, and a bit of appreciation for dessert.

Fighting fires sometimes comes in the form of settling disputes.

Not all times are harmonious in the difficult world of the advertising agency. Creatives may disagree with the media department's recommendation.

The interactive department may have disregarded the branding strategy developed by the creative team. There is a lot of opportunity for disagreement among large egos on issues that are very subjective.

These disputes end up in the account manager's lap. If on top of things, the account manager can see the mess coming (think psychic) and start refereeing the resolution immediately. If the account manager is not on top of things, the mess may arrive in an advanced stage with tempers frayed and a lot less time to settle things productively.

Many referee situations come about because people do not pay attention to detail and input. As a result, members of the same team go in different directions.

Keep in mind that not all parties will be happy with every problem resolution. You can't please all of the people all of the time. You want the reputation of one who considers all sides and leads the parties to the best path, even if it's not the easiest way out.

14. Diplomat.

As account manager, your job is to get things started on the right foot and keep them moving along efficiently. This way, your agency does good work, you make deadlines, and you stay within budgets. Everyone is happy.

Sometimes this means wearing the hat of the diplomat.

Creative people can be arrogant, clients can be pushy, media people can be boring, production people can be bitchy. Your job is to be sensitive to the chemistry of the agency team as they interact with each other – and especially with the client.

You know your client better than anyone else. You know that if he introduces himself as Robert, the agency people best not call him Bobby in an attempt to be friendly.

You know whether the client is a morning person or an afternoon person. You know what pleases them and what ticks them off. You even have a pretty good idea how they're going to react to specific proposals.

Likewise, you know your agency team. The copywriter likes to use profanity, the interactive guy sometimes forgets to bathe, and the media person speaks a special language (called mediaese), which requires an interpreter.

As diplomat, you orchestrate these subtleties and work around them, or you live with the consequences.

Things can go wrong in a subjective world. A meeting that should have been a snap starts taking on a sour tone. The presentation room has bad karma. Creative people start debating in the middle of a presentation.

The agency owner is late to an important client meeting, and when he does arrive he talks too much. Call in the diplomat.

Combining psychic and diplomatic skills will help ensure you won't have to apologize to a client, won't have to smooth ruffled feathers internally, won't be blamed for not properly preparing your team, or won't be seen as handling an awkward situation poorly.

Diplomacy will mean that occasionally you have to sugarcoat candor, but honesty is still and always the best policy.

15. Cheerleader.

To be happy in account management you have to be happy giving a lot of praise to others and receiving little yourself. Cheerleading comes in a variety of forms. Here are some examples:

- Sending out a memo or e-mail praising the creative team on a successful pitch of a new campaign

- Praising the account planner for a key insight that moved a reluctant client to take a risk

- Putting a media planner in the spotlight for a stellar piece of media negotiating

Agency people thrive on recognition. Give it to them.

Cheerleading can also be broader, like making sure the whole agency sees a finished campaign in its entirety, you presenting the campaign at the local ad club, sending samples of a new campaign for one client to other clients.

When the agency people with whom you work see you recognize and embrace their work in these ways, they really appreciate it. Cheerleading is a good thing.

16. Performer.

You should work very hard on your presentation skills and your ability to handle difficult situations with style. This may not sound like performing, but it is.

Advertising is seen as show business by most people outside the industry. Advertising agency people are expected to be "out there" and to be fun people to be with. If you are a good presenter and have the ability to be a bit theatrical at the right time, not only will the client enjoy working with you, but the creative people will appreciate it.

There are many seminars available to hone your standup skills. I suggest you also get involved in an improvisation group. These groups are great for teaching you how to be quick on your feet, making the most of opportunities, and how to lighten up. Why not show that your agency's creative powers aren't all in the creative department?

Part of being a good performer is knowing your material so you can let your personality show through. Call on creative to coach you on how best to present their work. Chapter 3.4 provides some tips on presenting creative work.

17. Entertainer.

Taking clients to dinner, to the symphony, on fishing trips, and other social engagements is a fun part of the business.

Positive client relations are built by the mutual enjoyment of the association in a social setting. It's an important part of getting to know each other on a personal basis and a way for the agency to say "thanks for the business."

One-on-one business lunches allow the client and account manager to "come up for some air" and get a few things covered over the lunch hour.

Pizza and beer after work with the client and account team lets the client know that some nice folks are on his team and lets the account team see the client in a less stressful environment. Arnold Worldwide in Boston calls this the "pizza factor."

Policy on entertaining varies from agency to agency and by size of client. In virtually every case, the key to successful client entertaining is to do things that the client likes to do.

This criteria alone will compel you to find out what interests your client outside of their professional life. It could be vintage cars, gardening, reggae… who knows? I'll tell you who knows – you do!

Most entertaining is at agency expense, and entertaining is never billed to the client. Once in a very pleasant while, the client will unexpectedly pick up the tab for a dinner that was initiated by the agency. This is normally a good sign that the relationship has reached a strong level of appreciation. It's also the sign of an enlightened client.

Paying special attention to the client's spouse or significant other is a good account management policy. Almost as important as knowing your client's outside interest is knowing the interests of the spouse or significant other. It can't hurt when the spouse enjoys the time spent with the account manager, who is often accompanied by his or her spouse, but not always.

An overworked advertising executive (your client) really appreciates when the agency gives him or her a ready-made "date" with a spouse in need of a little attention, especially when it involves doing something the spouse really enjoys.

Discretion and appreciation are good hallmarks in entertaining. Keep in mind that it is still a business relationship first and always. Keep it that way. There have been times in my career, very few I'm happy to say, when on a business trip, a client consumed a little too much fermentation and suggested that maybe the agency would like to find him some entertainment for the night or even score something else.

The same could happen to you. Something strange happens to some people when they leave town. Business travel is where client entertaining can get really "interesting."

If ever confronted with one of these situations, have a diplomatic exit ready. (And you thought you were in the advertising business.) Do not go along. In the bright light of the next day, it will not reflect well on you or your agency.

The advertising business is much less booze-oriented than it used it be, but you'll still encounter clients who overindulge. It is not your obligation to match these people drink-for-drink. I tried that once early in my career with a client who obviously had a hollow leg. There was no other explanation for where he was putting all the drinks. If you're in for a long evening with such a client, sip slowly and eat.

One last tip on entertaining: don't try to buy the business with lavish entertaining. Someone can always outspend you, and good clients are inherently distrustful of big spenders.

Nothing takes the place of earning the respect and appreciation of your client through stellar work. It makes the entertaining even more enjoyable.

18. Ambassador.

We're not talking client relations here, we're talking being an ambassador for the agency in all other situations. The account manager is expected to be at the forefront of the agency's new business and community visibility efforts. More than any other position in the agency, the account manager is expected to be the consummate agency ambassador.

Literally, you never know where the next new business opportunity will come from. It could come from a casual encounter with an old acquaintance at the supermarket or a passing comment you hear in the middle of a service-club board meeting. You're expected to represent the agency's professionalism and expertise at all times. Remember, new business is the fastest track to advancement in the agency business.

More than any other position in the agency, the account manager is also expected to be visible in the community.

This responsibility can take many forms, but most often it takes the form of service on boards of directors of community organizations.

Advertising agency and marketing people are the third most sought-after board members for almost any organization, for obvious reason.

Accountants and lawyers seem to be the most sought-after professionals for board membership. Good grief.

The organization through which an account manager is an ambassador can be the Rotary club, the symphony board, children's special advocates, or the art museum board. You get the picture.

Normally, the higher profile the board, the better for the agency. Just make sure you have a genuine interest in the organization and that agency management embraces your participation.

19. Event Planner.

Much of what an account manager does is event-driven, especially presentations, trade shows and campaign rollouts.

Many of the arrangements for events can be handled by someone else, but if anything goes wrong, guess who gets the call. The coffee service was not ordered (oh no!)... the directions weren't sent out (everyone is late)... the ad reprints did not get to the sales meeting on time (agency looks dumb)... you get the idea.

While event planning is a specialty, the kinds of events that an account manager plans are the smaller affairs, but also very important.

The moral of the story is that delegation is good, but you should never abdicate. Check and re-check. Have a back-up plan for anything that looks shaky, especially when you're dealing long distance and your event is in a very large city or a very small town.

20. Salesperson.

Most of the time your job is that of a consultant, focusing all of your intellect on telling your client exactly what you think should be done regardless of ramifications to the agency.

Good account managers and good agencies don't try to sell clients advertising programs that are not needed or steer clients in a certain direction because there is more agency profit in it.

But let's face it, even with the amount of research done, advertising is still a business that requires belief, intuition, emotion, and risk-taking. That's what makes it fun.

The first example of selling is persuading the client to mount a campaign or to take on a project that you, as a consultant, truly believe they need.

Second, there will be situations where any action is better than none, one strategy is as good as another, and any of the agency approaches will work. In those cases you'll want to "sell" the one that is best for the agency.

This could be the campaign that will render more income to the agency given the same budget. It could be the campaign that allows the agency to gain expertise and work samples in a new medium. It could be the creative concept that will play best in the next new business pitch.

In situations where, in your opinion, everything else is equal, sell what's best for the agency, according to whoever is making that decision or your own opinion.

If you sell a creative approach the creative people really love, you will be a hero in the creative department.

If your net income for an account goes up because you sold a revenue-rich campaign, agency management will cheer.

If you sell a concept that is a steppingstone to another piece of business, this fact will not go unnoticed.

21. Entrepreneur.

Throughout the articles, academic studies, pamphlets, and speeches I reviewed preparing this book, some authors likened the account manager to an entrepreneur. I've always resisted this analogy.

To me, entrepreneurialism has a strong strain of independence that seemed contrary to the team environment in which account managers practice their craft. That said, I now agree that there are some aspects of entrepreneurialism consistent with, and indicative of, good account management.

The primary aspect is that of making things happen. Like entrepreneurs, account managers definitely must make things happen, especially on projects that are outside the norm. The ability to make things happen is a skill that relies heavily on improvisation, creative thinking, flexibility, and nimbleness.

Every seasoned account person has at least one example of the entrepreneurial spirit as it applies to account management.

While I've stayed away from personal stories in this book for a reason, this story will demonstrate the point I'm trying to make.

For some years, I handled a growing chain of upscale restaurants. In one of my weekly meetings with the co-owner of the chain, he lamented to me how they were in competition with another chain of restaurants for a prime location in a new mall in upscale Walnut Creek, California. No matter what he did, he could not make any progress with the developer, and he was fearful of losing the deal.

Out of curiosity, I asked who the anchor department store was for the new mall. He did not know. We concluded our meeting, and I went back to my office with a gut feeling I could be a deal-saver for the client. I called the mall developer. Nordstrom was going to be the anchor store. The week prior I'd been at a local mall where one of my client's restaurants sits next to a Nordstrom store.

I called my client and asked him if his restaurant was on good terms with that specific Nordstrom store. He immediately said, "Yes. Why do you ask?" I proposed that he ask the president of

Nordstrom to write a letter of recommendation saying how much the store valued my client's restaurant as a neighbor.

Then we would wrap the letter in a special Nordstrom gift box and have it delivered to the shopping-center developer.

My suggestion was followed by 10 seconds of dead silence on the other end of the line. (Any idea what 10 seconds of silence on the phone can be like with a sometimes volatile client?)

The silence was finally broken with the words, "Incredible idea, and I think we can pull it off. Let me get to work."

Two hours later my client called me back. The president of Nordstrom agreed to do the letter and suggested we write it for his signature. The real estate broker representing my client in the Walnut Creek deal was so excited by the idea that he asked for six gift-boxed letters to cover everyone involved.

My client asked me to write the letter, which I did before the end of the day. The client made two small changes and faxed the draft to Nordstrom headquarters in Seattle.

The letter was typed and signed the next day.

A restaurant manager in Seattle picked up the letter and FedEx'ed it to me. I visited the local Nordstrom store and got six boxes plus their finest wrapping paper and tissue. The six boxes were shipped the next day to the real-estate rep in California. Then we waited.

Another five days passed, and it was time for another weekly agency-client meeting. When I arrived at the client's office, there was a big banner out front thanking me for the "brilliant" idea and the personal service rendered in getting it done. They made a very big deal over me. It was awesome, and they didn't even know if the letter had done any good. They just appreciated the idea and the follow-through.

The next day the client got word that the Nordstrom letter was exactly what was needed to seal the deal. It gave my client the foothold on Northern California he'd been seeking.

The account guy pulled through for the client on, of all things, a major real estate deal. When you're truly involved in your client's business, you never know when you'll have the opportunity to be an entrepreneur. Hope you enjoyed the story.

22. Friend.

When you work with someone for a long time and you do it right, you build a relationship that goes beyond business.

You often end up as friends. Graduations, birthdays, anniversaries, holiday parties, retirement parties, divorces, funerals. You share in the lives of your clients and they in yours.

For many executives, it's lonely at the top. They have no one in their organization in whom they can confide. The account manager often ends up being that person.

Why?

Because the account manager is outside the client organization, has earned trust, and is an empathetic listener. Even if not a confidant, the account manager should always behave as if he or she could be. You never know when your client is going to "need someone to talk to."

23. Janitor.

The account manager's life is filled with meetings, presentations, late-night work sessions, and other mess-making activities. An activity is not complete until the site is clean.

So guess what? You get the responsibility of making sure the mess is cleaned up. Don't come off like a prima donna, too proud to help clean off a conference table, put the leftover food neatly in the refrigerator, or stack the chairs.

In its "Rules of the Road," Foote, Cone & Belding expresses this hat this way: "Wash windows – Willingly."

Pitch in. It's the "team player" thing to do, and your support staff will respect you for it.

Oh yes... will the last one out please turn off the lights?

24. Marathoner.

Now that you're totally exhausted wearing 23 hats, there is one more. Like the distance runner who is mentally and physically trained to go the distance, the account manager will regularly have the opportunity to go the extra mile.

The extra mile can take many forms, but the result is always the same. It's all about the relationship and taking special care of the client.

We're talking about the extra bit of field research you did that leads to a key marketing strategy. Or the extra creative concept the creative team came up with that sparks a whole new campaign.

Or the extra phone calls you make to see if the client's dealers were happy with the new promotion. Or the extra detail you included in the agency billing that saved the client an hour of review time.

The "extra mile attitude" is established by the account manager and should permeate the account team. The key to having the extra mile mentality pay dividends in the agency-client relationship is to make it visible to the client but not make a big deal out of it.

Clients will get it and will appreciate the extra effort when they constantly get more than they asked for.

Two Dozen Hats – Still Only One Head.

How does a young person learn the two dozen hats? The first step is to be aware of them. You're already on your way.

The second step is to watch veteran account managers do their jobs. Hopefully you have people who know what hat to wear and when to wear it.

6.2 The Eight Traits of a Successful Account Manager

To some extent, natural talent and aptitude determine success. Some skills and traits are easier for some people to draw on than others. To a larger extent, however, focus and determination carry the day. When you discover you're not strong in a key success trait, you work on it.

Here are eight basic personality traits and skills. If they don't come naturally, they can be learned.

This may sound like a lot of "motherhood and apple pie," but it's the result of a survey among senior agency people – the ones who hire young account managers. This is their list:

#1. Good Communicator.

- Has good written and verbal skills
- Is a good listener, for what is and isn't being said
- Provides objective and actionable input and feedback
- Regularly and frequently keeps everyone informed
- Anticipates listening and interpretation errors of others
- Manages expectations
- Polished and persuasive presenter of the agency's work
- Is accessible and quick to respond to requests
- Never assumes anything
- Confirms everything

#2. "Buttoned Up."

- Returns phone calls
- Is punctual
- Does homework and comes prepared
- Is always organized (has a written agenda and back-up documents)
- Stays focused
- Pays attention to detail
- Manages timelines and budgets closely
- Always follows through
- Is good at paperwork
- Starts projects early and gives ample lead time

- Produces clean billings
- Runs a good meeting
- Rehearses
- Proofreads
- Keeps good records and samples
- Writes complete, accurate, and timely reports
- Has an acceptable "pinch-hitter" when gone
- Documents everything – conference reports, call reports, discussions with vendors, etc.

#3. Team Player/Team Leader.
(Knows how to drive the bus from the backseat)

- Knows how to inspire the best work from others
- Leads the team to set goals
- Deals well with chaos, surprises, and the unexpected
- Can manage own ego
- Is a "constructive dissenter"
- Delegates and clarifies roles
- Accepts responsibility for mistakes
- Is quick to recognize the contributions of others
- Is results-driven and process-oriented
- Prepares others for client meetings
- Pitches in on the grunt work
- Makes the client part of the team
- Focuses team attention on problems before they get larger
- Is an activist and doesn't try to lead an account from a desk
- Doesn't make commitments without consulting the agency team first
- Seeks opportunities to train others and expand their capabilities

#4. Good at Building Relationships.

- Spends time getting to know people

- Knows and uses the client's products

- Looks for ways to make the client's job easier

- Looks for ways to make the client look good

- Keeps the client informed about the competition, the market-place, and the customer

- Gets involved in the clients "circle" – trade associations, social circles

- Appreciates the client contact's problems

- Is empathetic and responsive

- Can keep a secret

- Adopts a work style that best serves the client

- Always brings something of value

- Pays attention to personal things and does the little "extras"

- Is honest and dependable

- Treats the client's money like his or her own

- Is in constant contact with client

- Keeps the client informed about whereabouts and availability

- Keeps the client informed about the agency

#5. Devoted Student of the Craft.

- Knows 80% of what all other practitioners (media, creative, promotions, PR, research, account planning, production, etc.) know about their own specialty

- Studies cutting-edge campaigns done by others

- Is curious and inquisitive

- Studies the client's market, products, and competitors

- Investigates new advertising trends, techniques, concepts, and methods

- Shares interesting, pertinent information with associates and clients
- Regularly seeks enlightenment from agency specialists, associates, media reps, vendors, client, outsiders, etc.
- Keeps a file of articles and great work done by others
- Uses information and knowledge from other industries to "add value" to agency service
- Studies pop culture and "porous edge" cultural trends

#6. Good Strategic Thinker.

- Is analytical
- Understands the difference between strategy and execution
- Makes sure that strategy flows from objectives
- Makes sure that creative flows from strategy
- Has a "big picture" view of things
- Insists on a tightly integrated communications plan
- Is a "systems thinker" who understands the ripple effect of changes within organizations and markets
- Can write a strategy statement and Creative Rationale

#7. Creative in Their Own Right.

- Has an innate sense of curiosity
- Is able to grasp rough creative concepts and see how they apply
- Relishes the blending of business and the arts
- Has good creative instincts and understands "creative style"
- Comfortable in right-brain as well as left-brain situations
- Is a creative problem solver
- Is a self-starter and is good at self-renewal
- Has consistently high energy
- Sees a problem as an opportunity to push the envelope or try something new

- Does something creative in own leisure time
- Enjoys creative genres other than advertising
- Is an original thinker, a visionary, idea merchant, and agent of change
- Is passionate

#8 Good Personal Style.

- Has a strong work ethic
- Is pleasantly aggressive, positive, and upbeat
- Thrives on chaos and keeps a cool head
- Is flexible and adaptable
- Knows their shortcomings and doesn't take self too seriously
- Has high expectations for everyone, including the client
- Is respectful and diplomatic
- Is objective, open-minded, and fair
- Is trustworthy and trusting
- Doesn't "play games"
- Is willing to take a risk
- Has a sense of humor
- Always shows appreciation and is nice to the little people
- Doesn't mind "rolling up their sleeves" to get a job done
- Is self-confident but not cocky
- Is forgiving
- Has thick skin
- Likes to have fun

I'm a big believer in assessment tools. Albeit a bit long, "Eight Traits" is such a tool. A periodic review of how you are doing on these major traits will serve you well.

This can be done alone, with the help of a mentor, or maybe a trusted cohort – someone with whom you can engage in a caring exchange of "opportunities for improvement."

BUZZ...

Creative Suits.

by Warren Berger, Advertising Age's Creativity, *July/August 1999*

Who knew? "Suits" can be creatives in wolves' clothing. Or at least a creative's best friend. They may not be able to write or art direct worth a damn, but they have an unerring eye for talent and great ideas – and they champion both.

They're easy to spot at a client presentation: They're the ones who are passionate about the work, yet cool and persuasive, addressing both esthetic and bottom-line concerns. They're also the ones in the well-cut jacket and silk tie. They are, to use an old derogatory term probably coined by some rumpled and disgruntled copywriter, "the suits."

But the term doesn't seem appropriate for the most creative business-side agency executives. More and more these days, creatives at agencies acknowledge the critical role played by certain creative-minded business-siders in helping to foster strong advertising.

Pat Fallon of Fallon McElligott, Jonathan Bond of Kirshenbaum Bond & Partners, Patrick Hunt of Hunt Adkins, Bob Jeffrey of J. Walter Thompson, Roy Spence of GSD&M, Jack Connors of Hill Holliday, Tom Carroll of TBWA/Chiat/Day, and other "enablers" are often key players in encouraging, nurturing, and selling good work.

More Varied Backgrounds.

The phenomenon of the "creative suit" isn't new. Consider that Carl Ally, who helped ignite the creative revolution of the 1960s, came up through the ranks as an account manager. But it's probably true that there are more creative-driven executives out there today than in years past.

The creative suits "bridge the gap between account services and creative," says Tom Carroll of TBWA/Chiat/Day, and they are recasting the old image of the account guy as a bag-carrier or client golf partner.

They're also coming from various disciplines within the agency: Many, like Bond, Carroll, and Jeffrey, have been trained in account services; others are former hands-on creatives who've shifted toward the business side, like Jim Mullen of Mullen and Donny Deutsch of Deutsch Inc.; still others, like Jon Steele of Goodby Silverstein & Partners, have emerged from the account planning department.

According to Bond, "It almost doesn't matter what discipline these people came from"; what matters, he says, is their ability to cross turf lines. "In effect, we are translators," Bond believes. "To do this well, you have to understand creative ideas and concepts as well as any creative person, but you also must know how to explain to the client how all of this will translate into making money."

He notes, "You have to be able to think from both sides of the brain."

Pat Fallon, the co-founder of Fallon McElligott, may well be the "creative suit." As talented creative directors like Tom McElligott, Pat Burnham, and Bill Westbrook have come and gone, there's been one constant at FM: Fallon himself.

What separates Fallon and other creative suits from the run-of-the-mill business-sider? Patrick Hunt, who once worked under Fallon at FM, says that his former boss (who chose not to be interviewed for this story) possesses three qualities that are critical in any creative suit:

- The ability to recognize good creative work;
- a passion for selling it; and
- a rock-solid belief in its effectiveness.

"A lot of good account guys have some of those qualities, but Pat has all of them," says Hunt. But when asked to single out one of these qualities, Hunt picks the first: "I think I was most impressed by the way Fallon could always recognize a good ad immediately," he says.

An Element of Envy.
"A truly great account person needs to be able to see the bones," says Greg DiNoto, partner and creative director at New York's DiNoto Lee. "They should be able to understand and articulate the mechanics of an idea. You can't nurture – and you can't sell – what you can't understand."

But beyond just recognizing good work, creative suits tend to have an obsession with it. "A guy like Roy Spence is wildly passionate about the work, almost in an evangelical sense," says veteran copywriter Ernie Schenck, who freelances extensively for Spence's agency, GSD&M.

Schenck says that clients tend to expect that enthusiasm from creatives, but when it emanates from account-siders, he says, "it's infectious and extremely powerful."

Why are some account managers so passionate about creative work? A cynic might suggest they support and champion good creative for the same reason that a sports agent wants to rep Michael Jordan – because it pays to back talent.

But in reality, it can be harder and sometimes less lucrative for an account person to throw his persuasive skills behind quality creative, some say. "It's actually easier to sell bad work, because it's linear," says Jonathan Bond. "You can say to a client, there's the strategy and here's the ad to match it. It's much harder to sell something unexpected."

Bob Jeffrey, who championed great work at Goldsmith/Jeffrey and Lowe & Partners/SMS before becoming president at JWT in New York, may be typical of the mindset of the creative suit.

Starting out on the account side, Jeffrey immediately sought out Doyle Dane Bernbach, "because I wanted to work in a creative environment," he says. "I came from a liberal arts background, and I've always had the belief that advertising can be a form of art." Jeffrey adds that suits with respect for advertising's artful side tended to be more successful among DDB's account managers. "The agency would hire both BAs and MBAs as account people – and the BAs were usually the ones who survived," he says.

Bringing Down the Walls.

But even at creative agencies like DDB, there used to be a tendency to wall off account people and keep them away from the creative work.

No longer. Those divisions started to vanish, Weiss says, after contemporary creative agencies like Fallon McElligott and Goodby Silverstein began to create a more unified environment.

Plenty of traditional agencies kept their departmental barriers in place, but "what you found at an agency like Goodby was that it was all fluid between creatives and planners and account people, and there were no walls," explains Weiss. As Bond notes, these agencies have tended to take more of a team approach in developing and presenting work: "Advertising now is a team sport," says Bond. "It is not the creative superstar coming in to wow you. In a Fallon McElligott presentation, it's all about how Pat plays off Westbrook and [planner] Rob White and [designer] Joe Duffy – the client feels they're getting it from every angle."

Bond says through this team approach, FM gets the client to believe in the agency's creative process. "Pat is brilliant at getting the client's trust, not in himself, but in the agency. And then they'll believe in the work; otherwise, they might say, 'I like Pat, but I don't trust those creative guys.'"

Risks lurk further down the road, too. "You can go into a client and have great meetings, and you assume everything is all right," says Jeffrey. "Then they go into their own meetings later on, and suddenly all this doubt springs up. At that point, everything you're working on can unravel if you don't have a good account person, making the follow-up calls, reassuring the client to stay with this idea. It's not the presentation that's important – it's the follow-up."

Building rapport with clients is critical, but what really sets creative suits apart is the relationship they foster with agency creatives.

One of the most important achievements of Mullen, Fallon, and other business-siders who run creative shops is the culture they've created. "Great work is the product of a great culture and an environment," Mullen believes. "So creating and maintaining that environment is the single most important thing I can do."

The same is true at Fallon, where veteran CD Bob Barrie credits Pat Fallon with "being very selective in the types of clients the agency pursues, pitches, and retains. Pat has said 'no' to the opportunity to pitch lots of sizable new business simply because he didn't feel it would be a good fit for our agency."

Mullen says that, in the end, a good business-sider can influence about 80% of great advertising – creating the environment, aligning creatives and client on strategy, making sure communication doesn't break down along the way, presenting the finished creative product in the best way possible.

"The thing we don't do," Mullen says, "is come up with the unexpected, the big idea. That, we leave to the creatives."

JUICY CASES:

6.1: Off on the Wrong Foot*

You're the account supervisor with three account managers reporting to you. One of the clients you supervise just appointed a new promotion manager for one of its divisions. No one at the agency knows this person or his background. Therefore, neither you nor the account manager is aware that this new division promotion manager had a bad experience with another agency.

As a result, he is extremely distrustful of your agency and is not at all happy that he has no say in the matter of what agency he works with or how your agency is paid for its services. The account manager is now bringing you up to speed on a situation that has gotten very nasty.

In an attempt to limit agency costs, this DPM is attempting to over-manage the agency. Recently, the agency presented five print ad concepts. Four were judged off-base and one was accepted as workable. The project assignment called for three concepts not five.

Now the DPM is challenging the billing, saying that the agency should eat at least 50% of the billing.

What agency mistakes led to this mess?

Which two of the "Eight Traits" would help in handling this situation?

*Inspired by a case in *How to Get the Best Work from Your Agency* by Nancy Salz.

6.2: Lesser of Two Evils

You are the account manager, and yesterday you approved a rough layout for an ad that is already behind schedule. The art director was going to tighten up the layout and have it ready for you to present today. When the art director delivers the layout, the ad bears little resemblance to the one you approved yesterday.

When asked why, the art director informs you that the creative director changed the direction of the ad last night. What's more, you have major issues with the ad and its apparent deviation from the brief.

What do you do? Present the ad as is or beg the client for even more time?

And what steps do you take internally relative to this situation?

AD-ROBIC EXERCISES:

6.1: Being a Proactive Communicator

In Chapter 4 there's a case called "Radio Heartburn." Here's the answer:

The account manager and the agency media department need to take immediate action.

The account manager needs to deliver a written memo to the media department immediately, outline the time of the unacceptable adjacency. The media department, not the account manager, should contact the station.

The media department should let the station sales rep know that there is a crisis at hand and the following actions are immediately required:

1. The station rep must check the station log to see if the two spots are paired again for a future airing. If so, change the log.

2. The station rep needs to check all past station logs since the start of the restaurant schedule to see how many other times this unacceptable pairing might have occurred.

3. The agency strongly believes it is appropriate for the station to offer a make-good spot for every occurrence. The agency has also asked for a few free spots – just in case the client is really ticked.

4. The station should have all the answers within 24 hours, so the agency can tell the client exactly how the whole situation is going to be happily resolved.

It is now 9:15 in the morning.

You call your client to inform him about this situation. He has not yet arrived at his office, so you leave him a short message telling him that an issue came up this morning on the radio schedule and that you have left him an e-mail explaining the whole thing.

Now write the e-mail to your client.

6.2: Evaluate a Creative Concept

Pick an ad from a national magazine.

The best subject for this exercise is a one- or two-page ad for a national brand with at least 20 words of copy that make an attempt to persuade. Avoid retail ads and automotive ads that simply list product features.

Evaluate the ad as if it were in concept stage and being presented to you, the account manager, for reaction. Use the D'Arcy/Ogilvy/Bernbach model to accomplish your assessment and then write a memo to the creative team summarizing your opinion of the ad.

BURNING QUESTIONS:

6.1:

Clients rely on their account mangers to have an opinion on issues, to have a point of view. How do account managers best reconcile this client expectation with the need for the agency to speak with a united voice?

6.2:

Give an example of when and how an account manager effectively wears the following hats:

a. Facilitator
b. Psychic
c. Performer
d. Reporter
e. Critic

6.3:

In the context of account management, what is the difference between ambassador and cheerleader?

7.0 THE BUSINESS OF NEW BUSINESS

GROWING EXISTING CLIENTS AND LANDING NEW CLIENTS is the lifeblood of an agency. Account managers who are good at this are destined for stardom in the agency business.

This chapter provides another perspective on the agency-client working relationship and explains the key function of business development.

- **"Evolution of the Agency-Client Relationship"** exposes the gritty side of the agency-client relationship, how to tell if its good, and what to do if it is not.

- **"In Search of the Ideal Client"** describes the characteristics that agencies like to see in new accounts. It also describes what account managers are responsible for developing in their existing accounts.

- **"In the Hunt: New Business 101"** illustrates how agencies get new business (and why they don't).

7.1 Evolution of the Agency-Client Working Relationship

Advertising is a fun, energy-charged business. But, without being fatalistic, it is important to know the realities of the business. Accounts come and, unfortunately, accounts go. The average tenure of high-visibility national accounts is now 5–7 years, although there are many agency-client relationships that have been in place for decades.

The purpose of this section is to illustrate the evolution of the agency-client relationship, with special emphasis on managing and perpetuating the relationship after the honeymoon is over.

The 70/30 Rule (also the 80/20 Rule).

There's an unwritten understanding in the business. Some call it the 70/30 rule (or the 80/20 rule). A new client may hire an agency with 70 percent of that decision based on the agency's perceived creative strength.

The decision to keep an agency, however, is a different story.

Up to 70% depends on the working relationship and the total service package delivered by the agency, while the importance of the creative can be as low as 30%.

Obviously the agency-client working relationship will have huge impact on how long an agency keeps the business.

This fact speaks volumes about the importance of the account manager and their responsibility for maintaining a healthy and positive day-to-day relationship with the client.

The operative phrase here is *day-to-day*. Taking care of the little stuff along with the big, good communications, follow-up, pushing for what you believe in, showing you care by paying attention to the scores of things in this book.

These are the things that make good work look even better and will prove to the client that they are lucky to have you and your shop on their team.

"Allison here has an interesting concept we're going to try for new business... do great work for our current clients."

I know times when my agency's creative work was OK – not great, just OK. My clients knew it, too. They stayed with the agency through the creatively lean times because of the great relationship and because they knew that, *in total*, they were still much better off because of the agency.

This need to demonstrate value on all fronts was a good thing. It made me look at everything the agency did and everything I did personally for the client from the standpoint of accountability and added value.

This way of thinking became my standard way of operating.

It made me a much better account manager.

The total package received from the agency is what clients ultimately evaluate. The work, the results, the relationship... the total package.

It is said that an agency starts losing an account the day it's landed. That's kind of pessimistic, but there's at least some truth in this statement for at least some agencies.

A valuable rule I learned early is this: The best way to avoid having to a do a lot of new business pitches is to keep your current clients happy. And the way to do that is never take them for granted. Instead, every client should be treated like a new business prospect.

Easier said than done, but a very good philosophy!

Agency-Client Relationship Life Stages.

Every agency-client relationship goes through stages.

From my point of view, there are five stages:

- Courtship
- Honeymoon
- High productivity
- Deterioration
- Break-up

Courtship.

The "courtship" stage is prior to a formal working relationship, where there are behind-the-scenes discussions about what the client is looking for in an agency and how a specific agency is an "excellent fit."

Courting sometimes includes small projects that the client gives to an agency just to see how they work. This is true business courtship.

Courtship can include a formal agency presentation. In most cases, the account manager most involved in developing the pitch is the one who would handle the business if the agency is hired.

Honeymoon.

The "honeymoon" stage is right after an agency is hired.

Everyone is excited to see what the new shop comes up with.

This is the time a lot more learning takes place and the account manager spends a lot of time with the client, learning more about their products, customers and the culture of the client's organization.

This is also the time the agency is likely to be given the most creative freedom. The result, if successful, can be glorious. If there are problems due to high-risk creative, well, the honeymoon can sometimes be over quite quickly.

High Productivity.

"High productivity" pretty much says it. Everything is clicking.

The account manager has found the formula for the agency team and the client team to work as one well-oiled machine. Neither client nor agency rules the relationship.

Both make their rightful contributions. Things are wonderful. The role of the account manager is to use all their intellect, energy, and skills in this book to extend the highly productive phase indefinitely.

Many agency-client relationships are happily stuck in this high productivity stage, due to the fine work of the account manager.

Deterioration.

Unfortunately, account attrition is a fact of life in the agency business. The relationship can deteriorate for a variety of reasons. The average client stay at an agency is two to three years. Most agency reviews and terminations are triggered by a change in client marketing management, and, as marketing turnover has become more volatile, so has account turnover.

This is just one of the vagaries of the business.

Break-up.

Break-ups happen for a variety of reasons, but most often they can be traced to a loss of respect, where one party losses the respect of the other or a mutual loss of respect spirals the relationship downward quickly. Much of the blame assigned to agencies will include the client complaint that the agency is "not listening."

Sometimes, agencies resign business. It can be a "difference in philosophy," which means the client was an SOB to work with.

Or it could mean the agency wanted to do edgier creative work than the client was willing to risk. Or it could mean the agency wanted to save face and pre-empt the inevitable.

Later in this chapter is a list of reasons (most of them avoidable) that lead to a break-up and the signs that there is trouble ahead in the relationship. Pay special attention to these when you become an account manager. They can save you from a good amount of grief that will befall you if you don't.

Whatever the reason for the break-up, it is important to maintain high professional standards and behavior. Never bad-mouth an account as they are becoming an ex-client.

Just because they are walking out the door right now, you never know when an ex-client might become your next new business opportunity. It's a strange business that way.

The good personal relationships you had with clients should not end just because you may not be working with them anymore. Stay in touch with those people.

The next "courtship" could be just around the corner.

Eleven Deadly Sins in Agency-Client Relationships.

Perpetuating the "high productivity" stage of the relationship is the responsibility of the account manager. While trying to do everything right, here are a few sins you definitely do not want your agency (or yourself) to commit.

The original "Eleven Deadly Sins" was created by Edward DeMingo and appeared in the "Perspective" column of *Advertising Age*.

#1. The Sin of Silence.

Not listening. Poor communications. Not managing expectations. Not demonstrating value.

The importance of good communications cannot be overemphasized. It is at the core of so many things that impact the relationship, from efficiency to trust.

#2. The Sin of Craziness.

Creativity for creativity's sake. Offensive concepts. Off-target proposals. Weird behavior. Unpresentable people.

While clients hire agencies for creative work, the agency needs to know the boundaries. It may seem cool to show how "out there" the creative people can be. What it shows the client is how willing you are to waste their time and money.

#3. The Sin of Arrogance.

An air of superiority. Disrespect. An attitude that the agency is the only source of good ideas. Unwillingness to cooperate with the client's team.

It's supposed to be a partnership, this agency-client relationship. Neither can think that they are better individually or collectively better than the other. Agency people may be better educated or better paid, but no one is a better person. If winning awards is making the agency cocky, watch out. Glory is fleeting. The fallout of arrogance lasts a lot longer.

Surprising as it may seem, sometimes agency top management looks down their nose at the ad manager with whom the account manager works every day. Very short-sighted and very bad PR.

#4. The Sin of Broken Promises.
Missing deadlines and not delivering on other commitments.

The account manager is supposed to guarantee that the agency is something the client does not have to worry about. Be seamless, dependable, and careful never to overcommit.

#5. The Sin of Sloth.
Sloppy work. Poor budget management. Inadequate attention to detail.

The need for creativity and innovative thought should never blur the need for absolute professionalism in the way the whole service package is delivered.

#6. The Sin of Overselling.
Promising greater results than your ad program can deliver. Proposing advertising the client doesn't need.

Many accounts have a bad experience with their first agency.

They usually blame the agency for promising greater results than they deliver and recommending programs or projects of questionable value.

The only profitable agency-client relationships are long ones.

The relationship doesn't last long when you oversell.

#7. The Sin of Complacency.
Neglect. Poor personal service. Inadequate staffing.

Clients need attention. They need assistance. Agency complacency is harmful to a client's business because it denies them expertise and leadership. It is much better for an agency to resign an account than hurt a client's business through neglect.

#8. The Sin of Neutrality.
Lack of direction. No opinion. No passion. No added value.

You may be able to get by for a while just going through the motions and taking directions from the client. Sooner or later the issue of agency leadership and contribution will be raised. It always is.

#9. The Sin of Appeasement.

Being a "yes man" and living in fear of the client. Not pushing for what you believe in.

Account managers who are simply mouthpieces for the client don't do the client or the agency any favors. Appeasement robs both sides.

#10. The Sin of Disobedience.

Not heeding the advice and direction of senior agency management. Not following good agency business practices and procedures.

While account managers are entrepreneurial and relatively independent operators, there are right ways and wrong ways to do things. Procedures are in place for a reason, and senior management didn't get where it is by being dummies.

#11. The Sin of Blindness.

Not recognizing the "early warning signs."

It's too bad, but this is a paranoid business. Be ever vigilant for signs of things that need to be diverted or corrected.

Note: See the "Buzz" article at the end of this chapter titled "Just Asking for Trouble" for 10 more sins to avoid.

22 Early Warning Signs!

Even when the account manager is doing the best possible job on an account, things can happen. Vulnerability can raise its ugly head.

In addition to avoiding the Eleven Deadly Sins of account service, here are some pretty common warning signs that trouble could be around the corner. At last count, there were twenty-two of them.

#1. Change in client's head marketing position, change in client contact person, increase in client MarCom staff.

Most agency reviews occur after a change in client marketing management. Suddenly getting a new client contact person is not fun. If MarCom staff is increasing, some or all of the account may be heading in-house.

#2. New brand manager for an important brand or new manager for a large division.

Even though brand managers and division directors do not normally select agencies, the more important ones have clout and can potentially exert a lot of influence over the MarCom manager.

#3. Major disagreements on strategic direction.

If the agency and client can't agree on major marketing and creative strategies, it makes little sense to have the agency make ads.

Such a problem is often symptomatic of large philosophical differences, lack of client trust, and the inability of the agency to sell its point of view.

#4. A lot of grumbling from important constituencies.

Clients have clients, internal and external. If the client starts to hear a lot of grumbling and criticism from dealers, licensees, venture partners, and others, it can be as damaging as if the client CEO starts to criticize the agency.

#5. A lot more strange input.

Clients are not always known for clear and insightful input. One of the reasons they hire agencies is to bring clarity.

If, however, there seems to be an increase in mixed signals, contradictory input, and changes in direction, the agency work and the relationship could ultimately suffer.

#6. Sudden change in working relationship where agency is less involved and less respected.

Involvement is a key to success. If the client decides the agency does not need to be as involved as in the past, beware. The partnership attitude could be taking a backseat to another agenda.

Being ignored, dissed, or even ridiculed, when for years the agency has enjoyed a place of respect, is a sure sign something is wrong.

#7. Downturn in client sales.

Sometimes sales managers like to blame the agency for slumping sales. Forcing an agency review gives them time to figure out what to do with flagging sales and may end up giving them more say in the advertising decisions. Not good news.

#8. Reorganization, downsizing, or reduced budget.

The account is obviously experiencing some difficulties. Hopefully the agency is regarded as one of the resources that can help a client through a transition.

#9. New, unrealistic demands.

The client starts demanding levels of service that the agency could deliver on an emergency basis, but not all the time. And these new demands do not accompany any new compensation for the agency.

#10. Major, unexpected changes in corporate direction, marketing strategy, or promotional mix.

When the client suddenly makes a major change in its corporate direction or simply abandons its priority of building brands on television and wants to go to direct mail, someone is dictating a major change in marketing strategy. Unfortunately, the agency was not involved.

#11. Repeated references to "accountability" and "value maximization."

Phrases like this might indicate that someone is putting the heat on your client to justify the ad program and its budget.

#12. New competitive threat in the marketplace.

If your agency is historically a bit slow to respond and someone at the client is championing another agency, a new competitive threat can be a great justification to try a new agency "to get a second look."

One of the jobs of the account manager is to know the client's industry, be aware of rumors, and talk to the client about contingency plans for competitive developments.

#13. Another agency that works on a small part of the account is suddenly recognized for doing better work for less money. Gulp.

There are a lot of good agencies out there. Some small new "hot shops" may have less overhead. Or more luck. Furthermore, many agencies will put their very best effort and very best people on a small project for a big client – hoping to get a bigger piece of the pie.

If any of these things happen when you're sitting with the larger part of the client's business and the lesser part of the client's successful advertising, you've got a problem.

#14. No recognition of agency contribution to client success.
If the client ceases to give the agency recognition, or even worse, starts taking credit for agency work, beware.

#15. No new projects.
Account managers are supposed to be ever vigilant for new projects and new ways to provide more service to the client.

New projects are going somewhere. If you're not getting them, who is?

#16. Client becomes unresponsive.
If you keep bringing proposals to the client that they asked for and you get no feedback (good or bad), something is weird. There is a reason the client is not communicating and not making any decisions.

#17. Slow pay.
Slow pay on bills indicates three things, none good: (1) the client is having money problems; (2) the agency has just become less important; or (3) the client contact is having problems with the agency billing and therefore is "sitting on them" rather than approving them for payment.

#18. Frequent criticisms and billing complaints.
Insecure client contacts can take their frustrations out on the agency. If the amount of unreasonable and unfounded criticisms increases, the client contact is probably getting a lot of heat from somewhere. Subjective creative work, the level of service, and agency costs are the most frequent areas chosen for criticism.

The compensation arrangement itself can also be a source of irritation, especially if the client contact is new and essentially "inherited" the agency relationship.

#19. Restricted access.
If a client, who used to be available and generous with his time, stops returning phone calls, there is a problem. It probably will become very difficult to arrange and keep a meeting with them.

#20. Change in key agency personnel.

Not all threats to the relationship come from the client side. Sometimes agencies are their own worst enemy. When key people on the account either leave or get moved on to other business, the agency is vulnerable.

This is especially true when a much-loved account manager gets moved to another account without adequate agency attention being paid to the transition.

Upper agency management contact with the client during times of transition is extremely important to the "shamelessness" of agency service and how important the client feels he is to the agency.

#21. Sudden change in size of agency or account.

There is an element of fit that has to do with the size of the agency and the size of the account. If the agency lands a new account that significantly increases the size of the agency, smaller accounts can feel less important.

Similarly, if an account is already one of the agency's largest and then the account doubles in size, the client may think the account is now too big for the agency.

#22. Conflicts of interest.

If the client acquires a company in another industry and an agency account competes with that new acquisition, it could be a problem. And, if your agency's involved in a merger, conflicts can arise.

Similarly, the agency can land a new account that has another company or division that competes with an existing account.

These are issues that need to be worked out by agency top management and client top management, with the agency initiating the discussion.

Early Warning Signs, Part 2: What to Do.

Many of the early warning signs are the results of things happening inside the client organization. What you can't prevent from outside, you'll have to react to.

How you deal successfully with the root causes of any of the 22 early warning signs depends on many variables. Sometimes you're just going to lose the account. But here are some broad guidelines anyway:

1. **Know these early warning signs** and be on the lookout for them. Look for concrete evidence when your gut tells you something could be wrong.

2. **Know what is going on inside your client organization.** This is best done when your client contact considers you an ally with whom they should share family secrets.

3. **Avoid as many problems as possible** by staying ahead of the client, especially on those issues where you could be criticized for not being proactive. Try to bring up problems – and their solutions – before the client does.

4. **Depending on the relationship, be proactive** in discussing your perception and/or concerns with your client... always from a "benefit to them" perspective.

5. **Keep your superiors involved** in the account enough so they can be brought into potential problem situations without it looking like they are "fighting a fire." Most of these problems are not of your causing, and agency management does not expect you to solve them alone.

Coping with Clients.

In his book *Advertising Realities*, Wes Perrin does a masterfully entertaining job of describing six different client types and how they could be dealt with. Any attempt on my part to cover this subject would fall short by comparison. So, with permission, an excerpt of *Advertising Realities* Chapter 2, titled "Coping with Clients," is found in the "Buzz" section at the end of this chapter.

Not only will you enjoy reading it, you'll learn a lot. (Thanks, Wes.)

7.2 In Search of the Ideal Client

Ad legend Leo Burnett once said, *"You can't have good advertising without a good client."* Account managers need to know their agency's definition of a good or even "ideal" client. Once the account is landed, the account manager is expected to evolve the client into that ideal.

Making a client a "better" client is a lot easier said than done. Not only do you have to manage the agency work, you have to sometimes change a person's or a whole organization's attitude and perspective on advertising.

While the agency review process is client driven and designed to facilitate agency selection, it is not all a one-way street for the advertiser. The agency is sizing up the client to see how well it matches the agency's profile of the "ideal" client.

On many occasions, agencies on the short list will decide that, based on what they now know about the potential new client, there is no way it can ever be a good client. Yes, agencies do actually have the guts and sense to make such a decision. Not very often, but it does happen. In those cases the agency will withdraw from the competition.

Here are the signs that indicate an account has potential to become a great client.

You'll notice there is no mention of product or market in this list. We assume the client is desirable on those points. Here we're concerned with the mindset, the personality, and the culture of the client organization as they impact the agency working relationship.

Once the account is landed, the account manager's job is to work around the client's "shortcomings" and manage the evolution of the account toward the agency's ideal.

Some clients are totally resistant to even the best account manager's efforts to make them better. When you get an immovable client, the best thing you can do is identify those weaknesses that adversely affect the relationship and the agency the most, and try to work around them.

Note to Clients:

If you're not totally happy with your agency relationship, maybe it's not all the agency's fault. See how you stack up relative to this assessment tool. Better yet, ask your agency how you stack up.

Key Questions about the "Ideal" Client.

A yes answer in all cases would be nice, but it's practically impossible. Nonetheless, these are questions you need to keep asking.

Because part of your job is helping accounts become better clients and generating more and more "yes" answers to these questions.

Are they committed to high standards and the agency's "best work?"

In the same way the account manager does, clients should constructively challenge the agency to make sure agency ideas are stellar solutions. The client should say, "I want this campaign to be the best work you've ever done for us." Watch out for clients who constantly say, "Give me something quick, dirty, and yesterday."

Are they capable of giving clear, consistent direction and objective feedback?

Clients should assign problems and objectives, not solutions. They should be so clear on their original input that there is very little change in direction as the creative process moves forward.

The creative evaluation process is as difficult as it is important. Feedback should be objective, actionable, and set against some pre-established standards.

Can they make decisions quickly?

Sometimes clients delay any official reaction to creative proposals because they don't like the ideas and they just don't know how to tell the agency. Indecisiveness and drawn-out approval processes can drain the energy and enthusiasm out of projects.

Agencies don't expect to hit home runs every time. Well thought-out bad news is better than no news when it comes to client responses to creative proposals. If the client insists on concept and copy testing to help remove reservations about a campaign, it should be done quickly.

Are they open-minded, and do they value objective, constructive candor?

Smart clients know that their advertising agency is one of a small handful of business partners who can tell them (the client) the uncoated truth about, for example, their product or their customers. Other clients say they value candor, but aren't really ready for it.

Do they understand that good advertising takes time?

Enlightened accounts know that strategically driven creative work and effective campaign integration does not happen overnight. Discussion, reflection, and experimentation is part of the process, and the amount of time provided by the account will affect the quality of the end product.

Will the client be a champion for the agency's work inside their own organization?

Nothing takes the place of a strong client who can enthusiastically champion the agency's work within the client organization. This can include selling the agency work to top management if the agency is not allowed to do so.

There can be many people within the account who think they know more about advertising than they actually do. Often, a client must promote and defend agency work when the agency's not there.

Championing agency work does not prudently include the practice of showing the work around the office during its development.

MarCom managers who do this are normally looking for reasons to reject or modify the work. Given the thought and preparation that went into it, the agency is the best presenter of its work.

The client must also make sure the agency gets credit for its work. A client who takes all the credit is a dangerous person. Agencies are starved for recognition. The client who gives the agency public recognition for its fine work is making a very wise investment.

Will the client contact be a firewall?

Good client contacts are strong people who protect the agency from internal sniping. They'll do their darndest to keep the agency from being an easy target of blame for the internal ills of the company.

Do they regard the agency as a "valued partner" and part of their own organization?

In order to make the maximum contribution to a client's success, the agency can't be treated as just another vendor. The account manager and a senior agency executive should be in the client's inner circle. The agency should be involved in the client organization and privy to important sales and marketing data.

Do they respect agency expertise and judgment?

Letting go takes trust, and that trust must be earned. The ideal clients intellectually challenge on the big issues, don't nit-pick the small issues, and research-test only when absolutely needed.

Will they take reasonable risks in order to stand out?

Advertising must stand out to be outstanding. Clients need to realize that boring ads can be riskier than bold, surprising work. Agencies build trust by showing clients that safe can be risky and risky can be good business.

Do they expect to be surprised, pushed, and challenged by the agency?

Clients need to understand that it's the agency's job to push them and make them nervous with breakthrough, "big ideas." In order to stand out, advertising has to break some new ground. A client who expects to be surprised and a little uncomfortable (initially) is an agency's dream.

Creative people will kill to work on such an account.

Will they spend money to get results?

While it's the agency's job to find least-cost solutions, results still cost money. Big and small cost decisions alike impact effectiveness. The size of the media budget is one thing, but many other issues often make a big difference in the effectiveness of the final product.

We're talking anything from the value of good voice talent and superior printers to the selection of specialized photographers and the quality of film versus video.

If the potential client is looking at new agencies because they are anticipating a big increase in the ad budget, it is important to know how solid the budget is. Sometimes clients go shopping for a new agency and then the big budget never appears.

We call these "vapor clients."

Actually these client types are called a lot worse, since the competing agencies invested significant resources and no one got anything, not even the winner.

Do they value advertising, and do they still understand its limitations?

Some clients actually place little importance on advertising. They only do it because the competition does. Others expect advertising to make up for a list of marketing maladies of their own causing. Placing importance on advertising as a business tool and understanding its limitations is at the very foundation of a good agency-client relationship.

Do they have good business fundamentals?

Are they savvy businesspeople, or are they successful in spite of themselves? Good clients are smart businesspeople.

Will they use all the appropriate services offered by the agency and rely on the agency for integration?

Some clients don't like to give the agency "too much power." Some parts of the media mix may be done in-house, and the integration is done at the client level. This system can work, but it is especially challenging for the account manager because the relationship with the client is just not the same.

Will they delegate and really let the agency do its job?

It takes a tremendous amount of trust to hand over your future to another person and organization. But if clients want the success they need, they must let go and give the creative process time to happen. Then it's up to the account manager to make sure the agency delivers.

Do they believe the agency should make a profit on their account?

The value of an idea is hard to determine. Since the agency is in the idea business, it's hard to set a value on the total service the agency provides. Nonetheless, an agency that operates efficiently as it adds to the client's marketing success is due reasonable compensation for the professional services it provides.

Can the agency adapt to their work culture?

A key job of the account manager is to adapt the agency to the client culture. In so doing, you find out what kind of people you are really working with. The dot-com wave of the late nineties revealed a breed of client whose claim to fame was that they were arrogant and impossible to work with.

Are they involved and accessible?

It's a fine line between productive collaboration and too much client involvement. You only find that line through experience. Some clients love to co-create while others don't even have time to deal with the agency during normal business hours. Both are challenging.

And finally, some questions where the answers are self-explanatory:

Are they good people that the agency can honor and respect?

Do they pay their bills on a timely basis?

Do they like to have fun?

Do they want to be the best client the agency has?

In Chapter 2.1, we talked about "making a better client." The list you have just read is nirvana for an agency. No client, however, is going to be great on every point.

Like anything else, every client is a work in progress, providing the account manager with plenty of opportunities to make them better.

A Special Note to Clients.

At the risk of sounding redundant, let us state again that ad agencies are unique in the realm of professional service organizations. Further, the relationship between client and agency is as important as it is sometimes difficult.

Clients are often linear, pragmatic, and quantitative. They understand clout and market share. Ad agencies, on the other hand, are populated by people with a passion for inspired creative work.

It's one of the realities of the business that creative-minded people throughout the agency can be inspired or not, based on the client's behavior. It's called "share of heart."

A client with a boring product who is, by the above definition, great to work with, can get more inspired work from the agency than a big-budget, sexy-product client who is tough to work with.

The agency's most talented people don't necessarily want to work on the accounts with the biggest budgets.

Instead they would prefer to work with those clients who, by their behavior, demonstrate that they want the agency's best work and understand what it means to be a great client.

Given the importance of "share of heart," the account manager shouldn't be the only one who wants his account to be the best in the agency. Each client should realize the value of such a reputation.

7.3 In the Hunt: New Business 101

"New business" is extremely important to an agency.

Growing the billings from current accounts is normally not enough to replace the clients every agency loses over time.

Plus, an agency that is landing new accounts is perceived as being a "hot shop." Clients like to think that their agency is a hot shop. Accounts looking for new agencies are attracted to hot shops.

How advertising agencies get new clients is an intriguing and often secretive process which is usually the responsibility of a senior agency manager who came up through the account service ranks.

While the young account manager will probably have little involvement in the new business process, it's important to know how new business works. Being tapped for involvement in agency new business is generally a good sign that management thinks you have a future at the agency and they're comfortable in presenting you to prospective clients.

This section is designed to provide the young account manager with insights into this critical agency function. When the opportunity to get involved in new business finally presents itself, these insights can help you look at the agency pitch with a fresh and enlightened eye.

This section will help you make an important observation or key suggestion that makes the agency pitch more powerful. Developing a good feel for new business is serious job security and the quickest way to increase your compensation.

The New Business Process.

There are two basic ways that agencies get new accounts.

First, the "scoop," where due to relationships and timing, the account moves to an agency without a formal review.

Second, and more common, is the more formal agency review process. This is the one we'll focus on.

The Scoop.

Every once in a while, an account will simply switch from one agency to another. This normally doesn't happen on large national brand accounts, but smaller, less visible accounts will occasionally make this move.

The "scoop" (aka "lay down") is often the result of some very adroit courting by the new agency behind the scenes. Through private talks over weeks, months, or years, management of the new agency has convinced the prospective client that the current agency needs to go and no review is needed.

The scoop is often the result of a long acquaintance between the top management of the client and the courting agency.

It could be years of being members of the same golf club or service club, or even being neighbors. Agency management just keeps after the client until the old agency makes a big mistake or consistently does inferior work.

The courting agency takes advantage of the situation, and the client decides it's time for a change. "You know you need a new agency, and we are the right agency for you. Make it official, and let's get to work before your business suffers any more." This would be a typical call to action by the persistent courting agency.

The Agency Review.

The customary new business process in the advertising industry is the agency review. Agency reviews are triggered by client dissatisfaction. Client dissatisfaction is triggered by a feeling that they are not getting the respect they deserve from the agency.

The review can take a variety of forms, but the end objective is the same – building mutual respect. This is a competition of sorts which often includes the incumbent agency.

With some government accounts, a review might be mandatory when the contract is being renewed. But, in general, being an incumbent agency and having to go through a review with your own client can be a trying experience.

Step 1. Getting Invited.

For the other competing agencies, getting invited to participate in the review happens in one of three ways:

1. Behind-the-scenes courting which finally led to a formal review. (Not exactly what the courting agency wanted, but at least the account is now up for review.)

2. An excellent reputation and perhaps some experience in the client's industry. (More about this in the agency promotion part of this chapter.)

3. The agency new business team has its antennae out for rumors about accounts up for review and is successful in getting their agency added to the list.

In a growing number of instances, the invitation to participate in a review will come in the form of an RFP – request for proposal. The RFP is something the private sector has adopted from the way the public sector does agency selection.

The U.S. Army account, the Nebraska Tourism account, and the Springfield County Public Utility District all use RFPs. The RFP essentially describes what the client is looking for in terms of services and how the selection process will unfold. This may sound very cut and dried. It isn't.

There's still a lot of subjectivity in the RFP selection process and a lot of opportunity for creativity in presenting your agency work.

Step 2. The Credentials Presentation.

Once an agency has been invited to participate in the review, the next step is normally a "credentials" presentation. This is where each agency has an opportunity to present, in writing or in person, things that will hopefully get the agency onto the short list for the creative pitch.

The credentials presentation normally covers things like:

- **Client list.** Does the agency have respected clients that look like "good company" to keep? Are there conflicts? Do they work with clients who have similarly sized budgets?

- **Agency creative style.** This includes creative philosophy, problem finding/solving technique, their creative "point of view" and, of course, the work. Many creatively driven agencies have a strong style that results in much of their work having a certain look and feel.

- **Use of research.** How they turn information into intelligence to do things such as "seeing inside" a target audience.

- **Relevant work and expertise.** This covers such things as case histories focusing on creative work, target audiences, relevant media use, and results. Demonstrating how the work is relevant in this portion of the presentation is especially important when the agency does not have any direct experience in the client's product category.

- **Strategic thinking and a business sense.** Do they add value with nonadvertising ideas that expand brand equity?

- **Agency work style, how they work.** Do they demonstrate the ability to listen? Does the agency appear to be a well-run organization, built for speed?

- **Integration capabilities.** Ability to integrate a diverse promotional mix, especially the interactive component.

- **Digs and gigs.** Factors like the agency environment and culture can also have an impact.

In addition to taking all of this information in, the prospective client will often be looking at:

- Energy and chemistry of the account team.

- Role of the agency's top management in the agency-client relationship.

- Internal agency processes that ensure quality and speed.

- Agency organization and current size of agency staff. (Many prospective clients are concerned with the number of new employees the agency must hire in order to properly service the account. Doubling the agency staff overnight, for instance, is likely to wreak havoc in the agency infrastructure and have a negative impact on the early days of the new agency-client relationship.)

- Experience of the proposed account team. (Many account teams look good on paper when in fact they have never worked together before.)

- How the agency handles criticism of their work and service.

- The type and amount of work the agency hires out to freelancers and subcontractors.

- Insightfulness of questions asked by the agency.

- Brilliance of the agency responses to questions asked.

- The size of the agency egos and who the powerful people are within the agency.

- The billing fit. (Many savvy clients believe that if their account is less than 5% of agency income they will not get enough attention from the agency and if their account is more than 25% of agency income, the agency may be too afraid of losing the business to give objective counsel. This unwritten industry standard is known as the "5 and 25 test.")

- The importance of account service within the agency.

Some Common Agency Mistakes.

Agencies sometimes make stupid mistakes during the credentials stage, then wonder why they didn't make the short list.

- Submitting a flashy written credentials piece riddled with typos. (That really impresses people.)

- Showing past work not done by anyone in the room, or even worse, by the agency. This often happens when creative people (and their portfolios) move from agency to agency.

  If relevant or impressive, some agencies will show work done by new creative people even though it was done at another agency. Unless the agency is brand new, this can be a problem.

- Showing work that isn't relevant to the prospect or not drawing parallels to establish relevancy.

- Letting a senior agency person present just because they are senior rather than a skilled presenter.

- Showing work for a client who left.

- Not showing how agency processes result in breakthrough work.

- Not showing how the agency adds value, quality, and responsiveness

- Focusing on agency creative style rather than client brand personality.

- Showing edgy, off-color creative to public-sector clients.

- Using the entire time in the credentials presentation talking about the agency and not leaving any time for bilateral Q&A.

- Not getting to know the prospective client. The prospective client should always feel part of a two-way interview. They are interviewing agencies, and the good agencies will interview them about their needs, their advertising philosophy, the way they work, and their expectations.

- Disparaging the other agencies in the review in order to set themselves apart. If an agency can't positively sell itself, what's a prospective account supposed to think?

Some agencies try to short circuit the review process by doing such a fantastic job in the credentials presentation that the prospective client says, "OK, this is the agency we want. Why waste any more time on the review." Such a credentials presentation would have to hit home runs on almost every evaluation point listed above, while the other agencies would have to strike out a lot.

A presentation that pre-empted the review process would probably include some "spec" (speculative creative) or at least some strategic research and recommendations that were not requested.

Some highly creative shops are impatient with the methodical review process and are willing to take their best shot in the credentials stage.

It's risky, but then again, this is a risky business.

The Short List.

In an RFP that involves a single project and not a long-term relationship, the credentials portion and the creative pitch may be combined and submitted in writing. A short list of agencies will then be interviewed based on a specific project proposal.

Deciding not to participate.

The credentials portion of the new business/agency review should be a bilateral interview process. Not only should candidate agencies ask probing and insightful questions about the communications challenge at hand but they should also try to determine the quality of the client they are pursuing.

There are good reasons for a client to look for a new agency. The prospective client should be able to give a good reason why they are going through the time-consuming process of an agency review at this time. If they can't, it could signal some major dysfunction within the client organization. If nothing changes, the new agency could find themselves in an ugly review in a short while.

Step 3. The Creative Pitch.

So far so good! The credentials presentation was good enough to get the agency on the short list. Now the fun really begins.

The advertising agency new business pitch is one of the most exciting events in all of business. Rightly so.

You'll see more insights, creativity, boldness, and polish in an agency pitch than you will see almost anywhere else.

Preparing a pitch is about as wild as it gets, full of adrenaline, secret research, late-night take-out Chinese food, arguments about layouts and strategy, rehearsals. Everything you do on a regular account you do in a new business pitch and more, except you have less time, no budget, and little involvement from the client. What a way to work!

In a "creative shoot out," the prospective client gives all the agencies on the short list the same creative assignment. It could be as general as how to approach a new market segment or as specific as a new product rollout campaign.

Common Issues in Creative Pitches.

Creative pitches range from simple presentations of mounted layouts in the agency conference room to theatrical productions in unique venues. The client is going to try to cut through all this showmanship and look at issues such as:

- Did the agency ask insightful questions during the assignment stage? What kind of outside research did they conduct?

- How well did they use the materials provided?

- Are they good listeners?

- Do they know how to segment audiences and turn information into valuable customer insights?

- Do they have a problem finding/solving process that doesn't rely on luck? What is their road to "a-ha"?

- Did they present creative ideas that would meet evaluation standards?

- Is it "clean" creative work? (Simple, insightful, focused, clear... you know, "clean")

- Can they integrate across a broad media mix, including the Net?

- How well did they respond to questions asked on the Q&A?

- Do they act like they can accept constructive criticism?

- Who's on the account team? Who's the account manager? Has this team been at the agency for a while? Have they worked together before?

- Did the people who will do the work do the presenting or did one of the agency's "heavy breathers" do the pitch?

- Is there a high degree of mutual respect and balance between the account manager and the creative team?

- Is senior agency management directly involved?

- Did they attempt to stay within the meeting brief?

- Do we like these folks, and can we work with them?

- Did they mind the little things? (Were the introductions handled well? Did they have name tags? Did they have pastries and beverages? Was the agency tidy and businesslike?)

- Can they work with our internal communications department in a collaborative and positive manner?

- Are they fairly priced and affordable?

Two Kinds of "Spec" Work.

The word "spec" is short for speculative. It refers to creative work that competing agencies will do for free in the pursuit of a new client. Most spec work is in the form of ad concepts.

Some spec work is in the form of strategic thinking.

Strategic spec work can actually be a better measure of how an agency thinks than a single creative assignment. Any agency can get lucky once in a while and come up with a great idea for a spec ad.

The more important issue is the insights and strategy that led to the ad. The client isn't only buying ads, they're buying a process. It's important to demonstrate how the agency develops its creative strategy.

In other words, "what is the agency's road to a-ha?"

The Leave-Behind.

In a new business pitch, the agency wants to show how creative it can be in every way possible, from where the pitch is held and the type of presentation to the content of the presentation and the document that goes home with the client after the pitch.

This document is called a "leave-behind," and its purpose is to give the client the same chills they got during the pitch itself. Since the leave-behind contains all the details of the pitch, it is the last thing to be done and is a miracle in the making.

One way to get into the new business circle fast is to volunteer to work on the leave-behind. Expect some late hours and super stress if you volunteer for the leave-behind team. But it can be worth it.

The Dark Side of the New Business Process.

Senior agency management will decide which new business pitches the agency will pursue once invited. There are some aspects of the agency review process in which agency management may decide it does not want to participate.

Here are times when an astute agency principal may wish to say "thanks, but no thanks":

- **The "Cattle Call."** This is when the account invites half the agencies in the world to pitch the business. It often means the people running the review are more interested in making a full-time job out of the review than they are in finding a good agency. For every agency, win or lose, it will be hugely expensive.

- **The "Moving Target."** Here, the review process lacks structure. This allows the account to change the rules as it goes. Basically it means the account is not sure what it's looking for.

- **The "Wired Review."** The account has already picked the agency it wants, and the review process is just window dressing to make it look like their process was credible. *Not.*

- **"Idea Shopping."** During this review, the account is really just looking for new ad strategies and creative ideas.

  This often happens when an in-house account says it's looking for an agency. Then they take the pitched ideas, don't hire any of the participating agencies, and use those free ideas in-house. It's very unethical and, in some cases, illegal.

- **The "Consultant Squeeze."** Some accounts use a consultant to assist them with the agency review. As reported in a recent article in the *Journal of Advertising Research,* consultants did not seem to have much impact on the quality of the agency selection. The most effective use of the consultant was to negotiate lower service fees from the new agency without the client looking like the bad guy.

Creating a Better New Business Environment.
Here are some of the things you and your agency should be doing on a regular basis to create an environment that results in new business. And here are some things you should look for to make yourself an important part of that environment.

Young Account Managers and New Business.
Since new business is the lifeblood of the agency, it is left to the vets. So being included in a pitch is a good indication that management thinks you have potential.

What they look for is coolness under pressure and the ability to convincingly play a speaking role in a performance.

In fact, public speaking, debate club, school plays, and sales training courses are excellent training for agency new business.

Agency Promotion.
As good as agencies are at telling clients how they should promote, most agencies promote themselves in a way that would be embarrassing by comparison. In many cases, the agency is so busy serving clients that self-promotion is irregular and poorly managed.

Agency promotion serves three broad purposes:

1. First and foremost is new business development.

2. Then comes client retention. Existing clients like it when the agency showcases the work done for them.

3. Third, is talent recruitment. Talented creative people are attracted to shops that do cutting-edge work and smart businesspeople are attracted to agencies that are "on the grow."

Agency Reputation.

The first part of the new business process starts before the first phone call is placed or first presentation is made.

Agency reputation can be a big factor in how easy it is to "make the hunt." Highly visible work, awards, new client wins, and industry expertise all go into establishing a reputation as an "agency to consider."

These newsworthy items are often publicized through news releases to local newspapers and trade publications.

Newsletters.

Some agencies do their own newsletters, designed to showcase their work. The design and the writing are also intended to demonstrate agency creativity.

Newsletters are, however, very labor-intensive to produce. For a shop that's already busy, they can be a royal pain in the you-know-what.

Agencies often start a newsletter when they see a softening in their billings. A couple of issues get produced, then it dies because it's too much work and the person who started the newsletter gets distracted.

Too bad. Newsletters are a great way to showcase a wide variety of the agency's best work in a quick, creative, and informative way.

Web Sites.

It's relatively easy to throw some work up on an agency Web site. Print and television can be displayed with minimal explanation.

These sites are good for people who want to see an agency's current work and client list.

But Web sites cannot land on the desk of 100 target accounts the same way that a newsletter can.

Networking Target Accounts.

Good agency new-business people are consummate networkers and relationship builders. Most agencies have a short list of accounts with whom they would like to work. These accounts are normally headquartered nearby.

The CEOs and MarCom managers live in the same community and are accessible. Getting to know these decision makers is part of the new business process. Social, service, and athletic organizations are good ways to accomplish this.

Some agencies have a person in charge of coordinating the new business networking effort. Hopefully, it's a senior partner who has clout in the agency.

They'll try to coordinate contacts made by different account managers with the agency's list of target accounts, manage the creation of newsletters, supervise the Web site, and perform the most exciting job in all of advertising – maintain the agency mailing list.

Staying top-of-mind with prospective accounts also includes an occasional magazine or newspaper article sent by the agency to the person being courted. This relevant information shows the that the agency is thinking about them and is making an effort to learn their business even before they get hired.

The Account Manager and Agency Promotion.

As discussed in the "ambassador hat" section, every account manager is a new-business agent. As a young account manager, it is important to show senior management you understand this.

You never know when and where you might meet someone who becomes a valuable new business contact.

Be eager to meet people and find out what they do.

When you make a contact that might turn into something, make sure you get a business card.

The person in charge of new business at the agency likes to hear about contacts made by account people. It's a good idea to follow up with a note and a copy of the latest agency newsletter (if there is one) and also add this person to the agency mailing list.

Making new business contacts also includes staying in touch with people who used to be clients.

Whether they moved on or fired the agency, things and people change. If you are proud of the job you did for these people, stay in touch.

It may seem a bit gung-ho to say that account managers are new-business agents 24/7, always ready to be the agency ambassador. But once you understand how important new business is to an agency and how people who are good at new business get ahead, you'll understand the importance of this role.

So schmooze on!

7.4 A Short Course in New Business

The purpose of the new-business process is to show the prospective client that your agency can provide new customer insights, strategic thinking, and creative solutions that will help them grow their business and solve specific MarCom challenges. Because of its importance, the new business function in an agency is normally managed by a very senior person who is an accomplished strategist, project manager, and presenter.

In a new-business competition, you basically develop a comprehensive advertising plan without much client input.

The prospective client not only looks at the ideas you present, but the process you went through to come up with your recommendations.

So the method you use in the preparation of a new business pitch is important, not only for the ideas it can produce but also for its ability to show you have a good process for coming up with inspired thinking.

The purpose of this section is to provide a short but proven road map in organizing a new-business presentation.

How to Write a New-Business Brief and Develop a New-Business Pitch.

Here is a straightforward new-business method. A new-business brief is a distillation of steps 1 though 5.

Step 1. State the Challenge.

Sounds simple enough if there is a specific communications challenge, like a new product introduction. Or the communications challenge could be a vexing awareness issue, a fuzzy repositioning opportunity, or the need for some specific and immediate action from the marketplace. This challenge may not be what you end up with, but you need some place to start.

Step 2. Do a Streamlined Situation Analysis.

Many advertising textbooks call for situation analysis to be done at the beginning of any new-business effort. You can find an outline for a situation analysis in almost any advertising textbook. Most are very broad in scope, so you can streamline the activity by focusing on those things that are communications related.

Pay special attention to who the target audience is demographically and geographically, and their mindset psychographically and behavioristically. (See Chapter 3.3 on the creative brief for more details on audience profiling.)

Part of your new-business process should be to create a "brain food file." In the frenzy of energetic inquiry and analysis, ideas and valuable information should be flying. Ideas and inspiration are precious. You can't lose them. Ad reprints, benchmarking samples, and research that seem to have little relevance now may be the source of wisdom and breakthough ideas later. Create a repository for reference materials, and put someone in charge of keeping it in order.

Step 3. Do a Category Review.

Get advertising samples of all the client's competitors and post them on a wall at the same time. Look at strategy, content, and execution. See what can you learn from advertising being done by competitors.

Step 4. Do a SWOT Analysis.

Strengths, Weaknesses, Opportunities, and Threats

The SWOT analysis is the outgrowth of what you learn about the client and the marketplace as your examine it through the lens of the stated problem and the target audience.

In the SWOT analysis you boil down your situation analysis and the category review to a handful of key points:

Strengths: Here you explain the client's internal and external strengths as they impact the marketplace. This can be product superiority, marketshare leadership, image dominance, a unique selling point – those things that give the client its power.

Weaknesses: These are internal and external weaknesses that have to be dealt with in the MarCom environment. They could be weaknesses in distribution, poor dealership control, pricing disadvantages – essentially barriers that have to be overcome.

Opportunities: "O" also stands for "Open Ground." Here is where you look for a place that the client can "own" in the future. Review the state of mind of the target audience. Revisit what the category review is telling you about where the competition is going with its ads. Review the strengths and weaknesses. Review the communications problem given by the client.

Make this activity as visual as possible. Stick significant points on a big board or a wall and let it simmer. Let your subconscious work on it for a little while. This is an organic, intellectual process. The open ground is the ability to say something new or to say something old in a way that no one has done before.

Threats: These are threats imposed externally, mostly by competitors. But you also need to consider the threats of not taking specific actions – counteroffensive measures that might neutralize a competitor while you execute a new campaign or the price to be paid for not boldly seizing the open ground.

Step 5. Restate the Challenge.

Confirm in your own mind that the problem is what the client says it is. Often it is not. Steps 1–4 will often reveal a different problem along with a fresh strategy to address it.

There is obvious risk in restating the challenge. But a redefined problem can often lead to a whole new way of looking at the issue. (See the Bank of America example on the next page.)

Step 6. Write the Campaign and Creative Briefs.

Based on all the previous steps, here you outline the inspired communications strategies you have developed to address the challenge as you see it. How are you going to seize the open ground? What basic message are you going to deliver and to whom?

Focus on a creative strategy that will lead to strong, distinctive ads.

Step 7. Benchmark.

Before you start making ads, you need to revisit the mindset of target audience and the environment in which your ads will run. Examine the "best-in-class" for these categories:

- Who is doing the best job advertising to your target audience, regardless of product category? What can you learn from them?

- Who is doing the best job of overall promotion within the product category you are working with? What can we learn from them?

- Who is currently doing the best job of using the mediums you are going to use? What can we learn from them?

- Who has recently executed a terrific sales promotion campaign? What can we learn from it?

- Who has the best-in-class Web site and interactive strategy? What can we learn from them?

There may be other things relevant to your specific campaign that you want to benchmark in a similar way.

Step 8. Make Ads Like Crazy.

By this time, ideas for ads should be covering the walls and littering the table. It's a natural outgrowth of the whole process that creative minds develop possible ads as the new-business process unfolds.

Now is the time to bring out all those early ad ideas and let the creative juices really flow. Use the D'Arcy/Ogilvy/Bernbach model to evaluate early ad ideas as well as the new ones.

Pick the best three concepts that are noticeably different from one another but still on strategy. This will show the client how the overall strategy can be executed in a variety of ways.

Try to come up with a total of three ads under each concept. This shows that each concept has "legs."

Step 9: Wind Up and Pitch

Review Chapter 3.4 on how to write the creative rationale and how to present creative work. Also review Chapter 7.3 on other issues to keep in mind when you are pitching creative work.

An Example of a Winning New Business Strategy.

In the 2002 National Student Advertising Competition the client was Bank of America Investment Services Inc. (BAISI). The question was how to increase the number of people signing up for their $50,000 investment management account and what to call the investment services part of the bank during its rollout.

The immediate conclusion was to do ads on how wonderful this investment account is. But that's not the strategic solution that was needed. Through a streamlined situation analysis, some key characteristics for this affluent market were identified:

- Their decisions regarding investment-service providers were based on relationships that sometimes went back two generations.

- Investors would be more willing to invest new money with a new investment service provider and less likely to move existing investment initially.

- In order to even consider a new investment service provider, the affluent customer would test their capabilities in some way before making any big move.

- Affluent people found five categories of financial services valuable (this is key):

  - College savings plans
  - Cash management accounts
  - Growth portfolio management
  - Retirement accounts
  - Trusts and estate planning

  This package of services became the strategy that would allow the affluent to test BAISI's capabilities without making a big commitment. It provided a much broader opening to the affluent market than just trying to land $50,000 investment accounts.

  At least one of these five services could be provided on an à la carte basis to every affluent customer. This allowed BAISI to show its expertise in serving the affluent market and thereby expand investment services provided to each new customer.

- A category review showed that this package of services was unlike anything being presented in the industry from other banks, brokerages, insurance companies, or direct funds.

- Finally, in addition to being unique, this package was unbelievably simple to understand in a sea of investment service confusion.

In this example, the client asked for a name and an advertising solution to sell big ticket accounts. They got back three things:

1. Key insights into this challenging market segment

2. A way to distinguish themselves even though they were late entering the market

3. A strategy that provided a much broader appeal and access to the affluent market

That's an example of a winning pitch – the kind of practical yet insightful strategic thinking that clients hire agencies for.

Coping with Clients.

From *Advertising Realities* by Wes Perrin (McGraw-Hill, 1992)

Client Type 1: The Closet Creative Director.

This kind of client wants an agency just to refine and upgrade his or her "terrific" concepts. Ogilvy once said, "Why keep a dog and bark yourself?" This client wants to bark.

Creative giant Tom McElligott calls them "control freaks." He says, "They have to write the ad, to over-involve themselves to the point where they just destroy whatever enthusiasm a creative shop has."

Ways to Manage:

- Find ways to keep these clients busy on creative projects within their own organization. Let them vent their creativity on sales meetings, in-house newsletters, trade shows and other important areas outside the agency's sphere of interest.

- In presenting recommendations, make a point of referring to the client's earlier input, especially in front of his superiors. The best account managers can make a recommendation sound like a joint effort. So what if the client gets some credit he doesn't deserve. What matters is the approval to produce some very good work.

- Have a good answer ready if the clients huffs: "This isn't what I wanted! Weren't you listening to me?" You respond with something like: "Of course I was (we were). Let me explain how your input helped us reach this recommendation."

Author's Comments: It always helps to show a right-brain client how their "insightful input led the agency" to a creative solution.

Client Type 2: By-the-Numbers.

These clients live and die by so-called hard data and regard computer printouts as aphrodisiacs. They are totally and blindly left brain.

If something goes wrong, these people look slavishly at the numbers to find the answer. They always have a state-of-the-art pocket calculator or PDA – a Palm Pilot kind of thing.

They hyperventilate at the possibility of complex research projects and, given the chance, will pretest headlines syllable by syllable.

Ways to Manage:

- To work with this client you must be able to demonstrate that you know almost as much about the subject as they do. Stay up nights becoming super-knowledgeable about research methodology and trends.

- Include data from behavioral psychologists and other social scientists in your recommendations to add credibility.

- Look for precedent-setting examples of other creative approaches to show along with your recommendation.

- Delicately remind this client that research in not fail-safe.

Author's Comments: The By-the-Numbers type client is obviously risk-averse. To succeed here, the account manager must convincingly demonstrate that breakthrough advertising is not risky at all and that "safe," highly researched advertising is the riskiest of all.

Client Type 3: The Double Agent.

Basically, your age-old Mr./Ms. Two-Face. These clients adore everything you present when you are present. But it's a different story when it moves upstairs for final okay. Career advancement and job scrutiny are paramount, but they don't want to "hurt the agency's feelings."

This client can blind-side you handsomely because they never turn down a proposal when there are just two of you in the room. They are loathe to break any bad news personally.

So you leave the meeting thinking that everything is approved, and the next morning you receive a message that "a number of revisions are needed."

Ways to Manage:

- You simply cannot depend on this type to do justice to your recommendation. Somehow you must find a way to show the work directly to the final authority.

  Ideally, you can convince the "double agent" to do it with you.

  But if the presentation goes badly, you must be prepared to shoulder all the fire and brimstone. If this client as well as your recommendations are roundly criticized, he or she will be exceedingly reluctant to present again in tandem.

  Conversely, if the meeting goes well, be sure the client contact gets to bask in the applause. It's important that he or she believes this is a practice worth repeating. The better your client contact looks, the better the agency looks.

- If the client contact totally stonewalls you and does not permit you to "go upstairs," you are dealing with someone who sees the gatekeeper role as vital to job security.

  This is a tough situation for any account manager. Once or twice you may be able to bring in your boss (an agency big wig) and thus force the issue of a meeting with the client contact's higher-ups.

  Or, you can try to set up situations where it is necessary (because of client travel, illness, or vacation) that it become necessary for the you to deal directly with the final authorities.

  This, too, is a risky tactic.

Author's Comments: It's hard for account managers to understand how much of a threat advertising agencies can be for some client contacts. In the situation of a "Double Agent," it is important to realize that you are again probably dealing with a very insecure person.

The best way to deal with such a client is to demonstrate that your personal reason for being is to make them look good. If you can pull this off, over time the agency will become a big ally rather than a threat.

This is one of the most demanding political manipulations performed by account managers as they reconcile the client needs and the agency needs. But this is one of the proofs of truly skilled account managers.

The ability to get the creative team to "work with" this type of client is difficult. After a couple of times being burned, creatives can get cynical about such clients and wonder why account managers even bother trying.

Client Type 4: The Obsessive Bean Counter.

There is a fine line here. A strong ad manager patrols his or her budget relentlessly, properly monitoring agency estimates and bills. But there is a certain kind of client who feels duty-bound to question every item on a monthly bill, including number of photocopies and why a delivery was made by cab instead of messenger.

It's a sad fact that this individual fundamentally does not trust the agency and is certain that with enough digging he or she will find scallawaggery. Account managers and media and production departments must spend inordinate amounts of time justifying each monthly billing, eroding the profitability of such accounts.

Ironically, this client type is frequently slow to pay.

Ways to Manage:

- Document everything as each project progresses. Leave nothing to memory. If conditions change during a project – for example three photographs are needed instead of two as originally planned – submit a revised estimate.

  Coax this kind of client to sign it. ("Wait a minute," you protest. "Are you saying that this persnickety client won't sign a routine estimate?" I am indeed. That's precisely what the Bean Counter conveniently buries on a crowded desk.)

- Learn to anticipate this client's questions and prepare a defusing response. Call out areas that might be disputed and explain your position in detail. Never just send a bill and hope for the best.

Author's Comments: Take the initiative on this client. Show them that in everything your agency does, you are minding their money like your own.

As recommended elsewhere in this book, hand deliver the agency monthly bill and walk the client through anything you think they will question. Make sure the bill is prepared in a way that will streamline approval within the client organization.

Client Type 5: The Ghost.

Now you see 'em. Now you don't. These clients love to travel. Given even the slightest reason, they're on the road again. When you need a decision, they're in a meeting two time zones away.

These clients will call you from airports but can't approve anything because they don't have the stuff with them or the airline has just made its last boarding call.

When you do hear from them, it's usually because they changed their mind on something they approved the day before and since it is after hours, everyone else in the agency has already gone home.

You begin to wonder if these people are real. Since they are constantly in motion, numerous hard decisions are ducked and virtually everything is last-minute. Ghosts are also reluctant to delegate any authority to subordinates left at home.

Ways to Manage:

- Forget about conducting business during normal hours. Outfox them by arranging to conduct business at airports and by phone with them at night in their hotel rooms.

  Learn to make presentations in air terminals, while driving them to the airport and in restaurants early in the morning or in the evening (they have to eat).

- If the Ghost won't allow subordinates to make some approvals, seek ways to show the work to higher-ups in their absence.

  Make sure you don't give the appearance of making an "end run" on this client. Persuade the Ghost that doing this is
     (1) in their best interest as a manager and
     (2) necessary to keep projects on schedule.

- For an extremely important project, you may have to get on a plane and chase the client down. It may mean catching a red-eye for early coffee in Chicago – and then hot-footing it back before close of day.

  But what's a 28-hour day when you can sell outstanding work?

Author's comments: Telecommunications technology and the trend toward less travel makes the Ghost easier to deal with, but their basic nature of avoidance may just manifest itself in other ways. You'll need to be very nimble, assertive, and flexible to work with this one.

Client Type 6: The Shopper.

These clients are always looking for a better cost alternative, particularly on the creative end. They like to assign projects to freelancers and other agencies "just to keep my shop on its toes." (*AdWeek* once described this type as "like the little kid on the block who pulls wings off flies.")

They rarely have much taste and lack patience with anything subtle.

They like to point out to superiors that they have ways to get advertising work done "a lot cheaper than our big-time agency does it."

Ways to Manage:

- It's virtually impossible. Once in a great while, through patient education and meticulous service, you can modify such behavior.

  But in most instances it is hopeless because all that matters to this type is how much something costs. (They really belong in the purchasing department.)

Pray that a transfer is forthcoming for this client. Use your agency top management's pull with the client's top management to keep him busy on assignments that are less important to the agency. [See Type 1: The Closet Creative Director.]

- One of my former mentors once advised me to take one of these types out to the parking garage and deliver a hard punch to the kidneys. (At the time I laughed. Now I'm not so sure he was kidding.) There will be times with this type that you have to exercise extreme restraint not to heed his advice.

Author's Comments: This client type is a nasty combination of some of the others. They have no appreciation for the value of ideas and the contribution the agency makes to the strength of their brand.

They also farm out projects because they don't want the agency to handle too much of the coordination and integration. (They have major control issues as well.)

If you're going to make any progress with The Shopper, it will be on the basis of value rather than price.

[Editor's Note: Though now out of print, you can still find a copy of Wes Perrin's excellent Advertising Realities: A Practical Guide to Agency Management by going online. Last time we looked, a number of used book sites had it available.]

Just Asking for Trouble.

by Bill Sinnott, Promo, *February 2002*

Ten phrases that will have clients thinking about RFPs.

The account is going great when, all of a sudden, your client contact asks you to stay back after a routine meeting. He tells you either that it's completely over, or that he'll be having a "shootout" and you'll have a chance to keep "your" business.

You huddle back at the agency, expressing shock and confusion. You "can't understand" what happened. After the denial period wears off, you experience an awakening. You remember the "little things" that cropped up which, at the time, didn't seem like much. In retrospect, they take on greater magnitude.

What happened? If you remember uttering any of these 10 phrases during the relationship, you know.

"Same Song, Second Verse."

Agencies exist to develop business-building ideas that efficiently give clients a competitive edge. Period.

Everything else contributes to developing, implementing, and evaluating these ideas, which are perishable over time.

There's no competitive edge if everybody is doing them. Agencies sometimes get comfortable and keep doing variations of the same concept. But the safe choice can make you sorry later on.

"Don't Clutter My Mind with Anything New."

You win the business. You have the mind-numbing "briefing day." You start developing concepts, and you're off.

Project lists fill up. You're in "doing it" mode, running at 150 percent. Unfortunately, that "briefing day" becomes history.

And what you know about the client and its competitors becomes dated. Pretty soon, you're "fighting today's war with yesterday's strategies."

"We Don't Do That."

Integrated marketing gives your clients more possible places to get a competitive advantage.

Most agencies should, at a minimum, offer the following services: sales promotion, merchandising, direct/CRM, co-marketing/account-specific, multicultural marketing, interactive, event marketing, experiential/urban marketing.

Within this portfolio should be a strategy, or a combination of strategies, that help your client win.

"Your Logo Goes Here."

A client once challenged me before a presentation: "I don't want to see ideas where I could put my competitor's logo on the board without a change."

The idea has to build and specifically reinforce the brand essence. So you must have an in-depth understanding of what makes the brand special.

"It's About What I Expected."

This may be a good comment if you run a fast-food chain, but it can spell disaster for an agency.

You must stretch the client's horizons with innovative thinking. We usually present three concepts: one we think they'll probably do, one we think they might do, and one we think they'll never do.

You guessed it. The "never-do" alternative (or at least part of it) more often than not gets selected. Don't assume the client is always looking for comfortable solutions.

"Where Do You Sell This Stuff?"

Any successful promotion must take the sales channels into account. Otherwise, the most creative idea falls flat, as merchandising support evaporates and the sales force screams for trade deals to make their numbers.

Check stores, go on a few headquarters calls, read some trade journals. Understand the channels, and make the client happier.

"We Don't Have an Agency Bill of Rights."

This is the client's right to the Right Idea at the Right Time in the Right Place at the Right Cost. Right Now! Usually, this is laid out in the initial contract and agreement.

Sounds simple and obvious, right?

But it sets up expectation and simple evaluation criteria.

If the agency isn't delivering on any of these, it needs to understand why and fix it. Maybe the client isn't getting the right idea, for instance, because she hasn't set the right objectives.

"That Will Cost You Extra."

Last-minute changes are the rule, not the exception. Business situations change. Competitors do unexpected things.

The agency must be prepared with systems in place to accommodate them. It drives clients crazy to see a lot of added charges for changes that shouldn't be a crisis or over-time situation. So be sure that you're ready for the "last minute."

"Hey, It's Only Money."

This can really get you in trouble. Great ideas? Yes. But not at the expense of profitability. The best statement about being budget-conscious came from a client of mine. "Throw around nickels like they're manhole covers."

This means detail-oriented budget monitoring and tracking systems. Quick information flow is also critical. There should be no surprises when a client gets the final invoice.

"They'll Work It Out."

This is a people business. At crunch time, client and agency may spend more time with each other than with their spouses. Without mutual respect and a desire to work together, the relationship can unravel pretty quickly.

Be sure the right people are on the business. Understand personality types and avoid obvious inconsistencies. That's it. Avoid using these phrases and you just might avoid that dreaded meeting, too.

7.1: She Did What?

You are the account supervisor at an agency that has a reputation for being account driven but is trying to become more bold creatively.

You've just received a very upsetting phone call from a very upset client. Here's the background: A week ago the client met with your account manager and the creative team to review client comments on the creative work they had presented for an upcoming campaign.

At that meeting the client and agency team discussed the changes the client felt were needed. The client felt that everyone left the meeting satisfied with the adjustments discussed. The agency was going to rework the creative and re-present it in five days.

This morning the client called the account manager, just to check on the progress of the revised creative work. The account manager informed him that the agency had changed its mind about the revisions and they think the original creative should be presented at the client's quarterly marketing meeting next week.

Or... the agency would be happy to back to the drawing board and present some additional creative work in two weeks.

You, the account supervisor, were caught totally unaware of this situation.

The account manager obviously made some critical mistakes that have put the agency in a very bad position.

What were the mistakes made by the account manager?

In this case, what "Deadly Sins" were committed by the agency and the account manager?

7.2: The Jealous New Client*

You're an account manager for a new client who has also just hired a new advertising manager. While it looks like you're going to be able to work with this person, there is one issue coloring the relationship.

The new client contact is jealous of advertising agency people. He thinks the agency business is glamorous and resents the big salaries he thinks are made by agency people.

What to do?

* Inspired by a case found in *How to Get the Best Work from Your Agency* by Nancy Salz.

AD-ROBIC EXERCISES:

7.1 Evaluating Agency Performance.

Using input in Chapters 4.1 and 7.3, develop an agency performance evaluation system using up to 12 performance criteria that seem most important and relevant to you, if you were the cleint.

7.2: Not by Bread Alone.

Take a look at the bread exercise in Chapter 5. Now pick another fairly high-traffic item – either a common grocery store item or a restaurant chain. Do some organized observation.

And, if you can do it without upsetting the manager, try to interview a few customers.

Follow that up by seeing if any of your relatives or acquaintances have purchased that item or eaten at that restaurant chain.

Or, at least, get their opinion of the brand. You'll find that after you get a dozen or so observations and/or responses, you'll start to see what's important.

7.3: Briefing for New Business.

Select a business in your town that is of interest to you. This can be a retail business with competition in the market. Or it can be a product manufacturer or service company with statewide or national marketing.

Using the outline in Chapter 7.4, do a new business brief on this business.

BURNING QUESTIONS:

7.1:

What is the connection between "seamlessness" and the 70/30 rule?

7.2:

In Chapter 2.1, we noted that one of the functions of an account manager is to make a better client.

What five characteristics do you think are hallmarks of a great client?

8.0 MANAGING YOUR CAREER

IF, AFTER READING THIS BOOK, you still think account management sounds like a fascinating, challenging, and rewarding career, *Great!* You are right, and you already know more than most account managers learn in their first five years on the job.

The First Five Years.

While this book can be helpful to account managers at any stage of experience, this chapter is specifically designed to help you navigate the first five years of your career.

Among the many textbooks on advertising, the best one for advice on career planning is *Advertising & the Business of Brands* (The Copy Workshop, 2000). The chapter dealing with early years in the business is informative but relatively general.

This chapter is specifically for young aspiring account managers trying to get their career started on the right track.

"Remember that Junior Promo Manager we used to diss all the time? Guess who's my new MarCom Director!"

Having a successful career in advertising is a lot like any other competitive endeavor. You'll need preparation, a game plan, determination, and a little luck. This chapter is broken into four parts:

- Educational prep, including internships and mentorships
- Getting the first job
- Getting the next job
- Some final pearls

8.1 Educational Preparation: Internships, Mentorships

Like most future professional service providers, your preparation will start in college. There's much to do before you graduate. In fact, the first five years of your career start at least a year before you graduate.

Most account managers have degrees from schools of business, journalism, or communications. The biggest complaint agency managers have about entry-level account people is that the ones who come out of journalism and communications don't know much about business.

Account managers have big responsibilities which require an understanding of how advertising relates to other aspects of the client's business, like production, distribution, and finance.

If you're studying advertising in a journalism or mass comm program, make sure to take all the business courses you can. Courses that best prepare you for account management are:

- **Basic business**
- **Marketing**
- **Media planning** (Even if you do not plan to go into media, take this course so you can appreciate what media people do and how difficult their job is.)
- **Creative strategy** (As with media, even if you do not plan to be a creative, take this course so you can appreciate what creative people do and how difficult their job is.)

- **Campaigns.** A class where you study, in depth, the development and execution of a national multimedia campaign from research to the creative and media planning. Two of the best formal campaigns type classes offered at many universities are:
  - **National Student Advertising Competition (NSAC)**
  - **General Motors Marketing Internship (GMMI)**
- **Consumer behavior**
- **Marketing research**
- **Economics**
- **Basic accounting**
- **Public speaking**
- **Business statistics**
- **Psychology**
- **Business writing**
- **Agency internship**

The Agency Internship.

No question, an internship will be the most valuable thing you do in college. On a résumé, it sets you apart. Even if your internship is not with an agency, if it's in the advertising business (client side or media) it will still give you credibility.

It will also give you a tremendously valuable experience.

There's a lot of variation on the quality and content of an internship. In an effort to achieve some uniformity in internships, Portland State University and the Portland Ad Federation worked together to develop an internship template.

This template shows the student and the host agency what an agency internship should look like if it is going to receive university credit. When shared with a host agency manager, it helps the agency, student, and faculty advisor to understand what they're going to try to accomplish together.

Advertising Agency Internship.

To Students, Host Agencies, and Faculty Advisors:

Even though internships have been a part of the higher education scene for a long time, there is still confusion, inconsistency, and lack of understanding of what an internship should be.

The following information attempts to provide a standardized template for an internship with an advertising agency.

This template was developed in a cooperative effort between the Portland Ad Federation and the Portland State School of Business.

The goal, over time, is for everyone to accept these templates as the industry standard, thereby ensuring a consistently high-quality educational experience throughout the advertising industry.

There is already national interest in these standards.

Students are urged to take this template to their host company as a way of communicating student and university expectations. Host companies are urged to review this template to make sure they're willing to invest the time to deliver the experience as outlined. Faculty advisors are encouraged to use the template for management and evaluation purposes.

The internship described on the next pages is expected to be a 10–11 week experience earning the student a graded three (3) or four (4) credit hours and requiring 12–16 hours per week spent with the host company. In reality, up to 30 hours a week may be optimal.

Agency work happens fast. Important, learning-rich projects can come and go in an afternoon. You need to be there in order to get the assignments that will teach you what the business is really like.

Otherwise, the internship is likely to consist of lower-level tasks that are not as mission-critical.

Overview.

This internship is an educational experience, intended to provide the student with an overview of how an advertising agency operates, plus practical experience in an area of interest. To be consistent with Department of Labor guidelines, the internship should be broad in scope and not designed to replace or provide additional agency staffing.

During the term of the internship, there should be one executive at the host company who acts as internship supervisor.

This executive should have the responsibility and authority to ensure that the internship provides the opportunity for the following list of learning objectives and activities to be accomplished.

Learning Objectives.

- To gain a complete overview understanding of what functions are performed in an advertising agency.

- To understand the working relationship between the various functions in an agency.

- To understand the working relationship that the agency has with its clients.

- To understand the working relationship the agency has with the advertising media and suppliers.

- To perform specific tasks in at least one area of interest that will significantly enhance the understanding of that function.

Activities.
With Senior Management

- Interview agency CEO on issues such as agency history, philosophy, vision, areas of expertise, approach to new business, etc.

With Account Service

- Observe and participate in an internal research meeting, a start-work meeting, and a strategy/planning session.

- Observe a client work meeting and presentation of creative work to a client.

- Draft functional documents (such as a conference report or campaign brief) for an account executive.

With the Media Department

- Interview the media director to obtain an overview of what the media department does.

- Observe a meeting between media staff and account manager.

- Observe a meeting between media staff and a media rep.

- Prepare a media estimate using media reference materials and services such as Nielsen, Arbitron, and SRDS.

- Prepare an insertion order from an approved estimate.

- Reconcile media invoice with agency insertion order.

- Tour a major radio or TV station, including the sales and promotion departments.

With Account Planning

- Discuss the account planning process with a planner.

- Attend a meeting where the account planner and account manager discuss the brief with the creative team.

- Review the qualitative research and the creative brief that flowed from the research.

- Review a recent creative brief and the creative work that was produced from it.

With the Creative Department

- Interview the creative director to get on overview of what the creative department does and the guiding creative philosophy.

- Observe and participate in a creative team concepting meeting.

- Observe an internal presentation meeting where initial creative concepts are shown to the account executive.

- Discuss with a senior art director and a senior copywriter the important aspects of art direction and copy.

- Visit a photo shoot or commercial shoot.

With Production and Traffic

- Track a real print job from approval of creative to delivery.

- Visit a printer during a press check.

- Visit the production facility of a major radio station, television station, or independent studio during the recording or editing of a commercial.

- Track a real broadcast project from approval of creative to delivery of spot to stations.

- Observe and discuss the estimating process.

With Interactive

- Observe development of a Web site and Web advertising strategy.

With Public Relations

- Interview the PR director to obtain a management-level view of the relationship between advertising and PR.

- Observe and participate in PR department activities to understand application of various PR tools and services.

With Billing

- Interview the director of accounting to better understand various agency compensation practices.

- Walk through the billing process and an actual billing with the account manager of a major client.

Student Deliverables

- Maintain a diary of daily activities. This diary is for reference purposes when preparing the final report and may be requested by the faculty advisor.

- Check in via e-mail with faculty advisor once a week or more to report new experiences and progress, or lack thereof, in accomplishing the above list of activities and objectives.

- Arrange (at faculty advisor's request) a tour of host company and meeting with the general manager.

- Submit a final report summarizing the highlights of the internship relative to learning objectives and list of prescribed activities. This report should not exceed five pages and should be reviewed with faculty advisor as part of the final evaluation.

Agency Deliverable

- Host agency internship supervisor should complete a short evaluation form to submit to the faculty advisor.

A Note on Compensation for Internships.

There are some pretty strict Department of Labor rules about internships. These rules have to do with the granting of academic credit and the quality of the experience as defined by the variety of things a student does during the internship.

Some internships involve compensation – which is not to be confused with minimum wage.

Other internships will provide an honorarium at the end, which may vary slightly depending on how well the student did.

While money is important, it would be much better to have an academically accredited internship with great experiences and no pay, as opposed to a paid internship consisting of boring and repetitive tasks. It is up to the student to make sure the internship delivers to its potential.

Faculty Advisor Deliverable

- Assuming the internship proceeds consistently with this template, the only obligation for the faculty advisor is to attend the agency site visit and to grade the students final report. If, through the weekly e-mail updates, it becomes obvious that the internship is not meeting expectations, the faculty advisor may have to intervene and try to remedy the situation.

The Agency Mentorship.

Some agencies, ad clubs, and universities have mentorship programs. They take different shapes, but basically they are like a mini-internship.

The following information is a template for an agency mentorship program for students interested in pursuing a career in the agency side of the advertising business.

Ideally, this mentorship would be coordinated through an academic office, a local ad club, or both. When the student does not have an existing program available, he or she is urged to show this description to a possible host agency as a way of communicating the desired experience, and how the agency can make it happen without committing excessive amounts of its resources.

Here's how it works…

Overview.

This program is designed for host agencies who are not able to commit to a 12-week internship but still want to play a useful role preparing students for a career in advertising.

An Agency Mentorship Program can provide students with something similar to a "Day in the Life of an Advertising Agency."

A designated executive at the host agency should supervise the student and ensure that the mentorship program delivers on its promised activities.

The agency mentorship should have three basic components:

1. Three half-day agency visitations

2. Being the guest of the agency at one industry event such as the luncheon meeting of the local ad club

3. Post-visitation availability by phone or e-mail

Agency Visitations.

Three half-day visitations have been found to be best in order to ensure the agency executive can spend quality time with the student and still cater to the day-to-day demands of the position.

During the three half-day visitations, the student activities would be geared toward the following objectives:

- To gain an overview of the agency-client company relationship
- To gain an overview of the agency-media relationship
- To understand the basics of a working relationship between various functions in an agency
- To attend (as an observer) as many meetings and activities as possible that help accomplish the above focus

Suggested Agency Activities.

- Interview senior agency executive regarding company history, philosophy, areas of expertise, etc.
- Observe a client-agency meeting involving the presentation or review of creative work.
- Interview the media director to obtain an overview of what his or her department does. Observe a media rep call if possible.
- Observe an internal agency status meeting.
- Observe an internal strategy meeting between creative and account manager.
- Visit a photo shoot, commercial shoot, TV station, radio station, press check, or similar outside activity.
- Have lunch with an account manager and client.

Guest at Event.

Many local advertising clubs have monthly luncheon or breakfast meetings with guest speakers. These are excellent ways for the student to hear a speaker and see what a local industry gathering looks like.

Occasionally there are creative award programs or workshops that are wonderful experiences, especially as a guest of a host agency.

Post-visitation Access.

Mentorships are real eye-openers. They often create more questions in the student's mind than they answer.

On a limited basis, the host agency executive who coordinated the mentorship should be available by phone or e-mail to answer an occasional question.

Student and Host Agency Deliverables.
Although mentorships do not normally qualify for college credit, there should be some documentation about the program upon its completion.

Ideally, the student submits a short report or diary that summarizes the highlights of the three half-day sessions and event. Formally organized mentorship programs will also have an evaluation form for both the student and the host agency to fill out.

Ideally, the student can also ask the host firm for a letter which states that the student participated in a mentorship and did so with great interest, knowledge, professionalism, and maturity.

8.2 Landing Your First Job

12 Months and Counting.
It's probably not necessary to say this but, what the heck: "Advertising is a highly competitive business." If you wait until you graduate to start looking for a job, you will be at least a year behind your more aggressive competitors.

Early on, build a list of agencies for whom you think you'd like to work. Start doing informational interviews with as many agencies as possible.

Informational Interviews.
An informational interview is one where you are not applying for a job. You are just asking them for a few minutes of their time to help you better understand the advertising business and the account manager position.

Call for an appointment. Don't just drop in. Ask for a senior account manager or the manager of account service.

If you catch them at the right time and sound like you won't waste much of their time, they may give you a tour, talk briefly about their job, and tell you about their agency.

Advertising people love to talk about how they got started in the business. You should use this to your advantage.

The key to successful informational interviewing is to present yourself as someone who is interested in what they do because you are thinking about a similar career. In an informational interview, you are *not* looking for a job.

Try to get as high up the account management chain of command as possible. In a year you will be looking for a job, and you want the right people to remember you.

Always, always send a note or card thanking them for their valuable time. No e-mails, please.

Looking for a Job Is a Full-Time Job.

If you think you can send out a few unimaginative résumés, do the Monster.com thing, and get a job, think again. That may work in some high demand fields like information systems. EEEEEEEK! This is advertising. Advertising is not high tech, it's high touch. Personal contacts and networking are all key to getting interviews and getting jobs.

The "Eight Traits" in Chapter 6.2 describe the personality traits that are the best predictors of success as an agency account manager. No one can be perfect in all areas, but this list gives everyone something to shoot for.

As if the Eight Traits aren't demanding enough, there are three other traits employers look for in an entry-level person:

1. Sense of direction.

2. Ability to sell yourself.

3. Hunger and willingness to pay your dues. (Persistence and patience in finding a job is part of this important mindset.)

Developing a Sense of Direction.

Since you are this far in a book about a specialized discipline, the chances are good you are considering a career as an account manager or (depending on your bent for research) an account planner.

So the "sense of direction" is not so much about the position as it is the specific shop or type of agency where you would ultimately like to work (maybe even own).

All agency work is stimulating and high-energy, and every agency has its own personality. You may think the "ideal" job is in a large office of a mega-agency, with the prestige of national brand accounts. Or your research may tell you the 20-person shop in your hometown allows you to do many more things in service to the client.

You may relish the accountability of the business-to-business and direct-response agencies, or you may like the promotional energy of a retail and packaged-goods agency.

Maintaining flexibility on this issue is a good idea, since your opinion is likely to change as you learn the business from the inside.

The important thing to recognize is that agency human resource people are not impressed with applicants who "think they want to be in advertising," and directors of account service want people who know where they want to go.

When you go for an interview, the company considering you is interested in your career goals – if they're compatible with the company's goals. They're looking for a "fit."

You need to demonstrate your understanding of the variables... the size of agency, the type of agency, the philosophy/orientation of the agency, the agency's industry specialties, and the type of accounts on which you would like to work.

Interview as much as you can. It's good training, and you'll learn a lot about the personality of the agencies.

A Word about Advanced Degrees.

The advertising business tends to reward experience over additional academic training, although a growing number of clients like to have MBAs working on their accounts because the MarCom managers are MBAs with increasing frequency.

For the first job, my impression is that other issues covered in this chapter, like being hungry, are more important than graduate school.

The Battle Plan.

Graduation is approaching, and you've decided to skip the three-month trip to Europe so you can look for a job in advertising. Good move. Europe will always be there. The perfect first job may not.

Your arsenal the first time out is:

- Your intro package
- Your cover letter
- Your résumé (or flyer)
- Your book (portfolio)
- Business cards, stationery, and mailing label
- Box of thank-you cards
- Your plan
- Your determination
- Your appearance

Let's take them one by one.

Your Intro Package.

This is advertising, remember? You are a one-of-a-kind brand – and your goal is to stand out. Remember, presentation skills and the ability to sell yourself carry a strong message to employers that you will be skilled at presenting and selling agency work.

If you choose the conventional résumé route, your intro package becomes even more important. Is there anything about you that can be leveraged into something attention-getting and memorable? Do you live in an unusual place?

Is your name hard to spell? Do you have the entire collection of Absolut Vodka ads? Write a headline and put it on the outside of your envelope. Try to use whatever you can to maximize the look of your package as it arrives on the HR desk.

The Cover Letter.

Though it is not asked for, write a short cover letter consistent with your theme. Since the ability to write well is a key job skill, the cover letter is your first opportunity to show you have it.

It's OK if it's a little creative and lets your personality show through. Project the feeling that you'd be a great hire.

In general, they'll appreciate your being proactive and, unless it's too off the mark, your attempt to be different.

There are books of business letters available in libraries, bookstores, and online. Proofread and have an experienced business person read your letter. If you have a working acquaintance with an agency executive, ask that person to look over your letter. Emphasize that you're not hitting them up for a job. You just need someone to look at your three-paragraph letter and shoot holes in it.

The Résumé.

Different people in the business have different opinions about the most effective structure for a résumé. You can buy entire books about résumés. My advice is this... *don't do one.*

Say What!?!?

Well... don't do a traditional résumé. Sure, you can cover the needed items in a standard $8\frac{1}{2}$ x 11" boring format, but the goal is to stand out. Remember? With graphics programs and color printers so accessible, you would be well-served to consider a different format.

You can learn the programs and print out your résumé at Kinkos or, if you don't have the time, you can concentrate on content and hire a graphic design student to do the layout. Don't be limited to $8\frac{1}{2}$ x 11".

You can put more on $8\frac{1}{2}$ x 14" folded twice, and it will definitely be different. With a scanner and digital camera, it is easy to incorporate a picture or two of yourself, giving a talk or working with a committee. Get creative. Sell yourself like you were a premium product.

Most agency HR people and those who hire entry level account people agree on the importance of the following:

- Immediate career objective
- Long-term career objective
- Relevant work experience
- Internship (agency, media, client)
- Student advertising competitions
  - National Student Advertising Competition plans book
  - General Motors Marketing Internship final report

- School projects with advertising components
- Advertising/marketing student association involvement (it's important to participate in industry-related organizations early in your career, while you are still in school.)
- Community projects with advertising components
- Outside interests, publications read, creative hobbies, passions beyond advertising
- Degree

And last but not least…

- References

If you're confronted by an agency that wants a résumé by e-mail, then send them two attachments:

- a cover letter; and
- a jpeg or pdf file of your printed flyer.

In general, I'd recommend that you don't send electronic résumés and brochures unless asked to do so.

It's presumptuous to expect that a busy ad executive is going to take the time to look at or print out such files unless you've built interest in some other way through personal contact.

If you go the traditional résumé route, make sure you "art direct" both your résumé and your cover letter.

Do everything you can graphically to make your written materials stand out and read easily. Bullets, underlining, colors, italics, different type sizes and faces are all graphic tools you can use. Avoid all caps. They're hard to read.

- Other than an internship with a hot agency, the National Student Advertising Competition is as close to the real ad biz as you can get while still in school.

  See section 8.5 in this chapter for more information on AAF/NSAC.

- The General Motors Marketing Internship is a one-term or one-semester class project, normally an on-campus event or a promotion for a youth-oriented GM product in conjunction with a local GM dealer.

Like the NSAC, GMMI is very "hands-on." Again, see section 8.5 in this chapter for more information.

To a great extent, NSAC and GMMI complement each other rather than duplicate each other. GMMI tends to focus on local promotional strategies which are basically void from the national scope of NSAC. Therefore, I recommend students do both.

Your Personal Manifesto.

A new twist in advertising résumés, one that has become standard in Portland, is the personal manifesto.

The manifesto started as an agency creative exercise at Wieden+Kennedy to enliven the expression of brand personality more than a positioning statement could.

Since advertising is a business of differentiation, personality, and fit, the concept of the brand manifesto has some interesting possibilities in the area of landing an advertising job.

When done correctly, a growing number of prospective employers and applicants find a personal manifesto can add a dimension of personality that may not be possible with a résumé or cover letter. Most agencies will appreciate the fact that you understand the importance of personal differentiation and the effort that went into your manifesto.

Since your résumé should be no more than a page-and-one-half in length, there should be plenty of space for your manifesto on the bottom half of the second page.

Here in Portland, manifestos are pretty popular, due to the leadership of Weiden+Kennedy, its acceptance by other agencies, and our own advertising management program.

Keep in mind, however, that not everyone may know about or appreciate the personal manifesto for what it is intended to do.

Even if you do not choose to put your manifesto on the back of your résumé, I still heartily encourage you to write one that can be used in those situations where you know the interviewer will "get it." In our account management course at PSU we've also discovered an additional benefit – people realize and discover things about themselves that they never had articulated before – and a résumé won't do that.

Here is a personal manifesto written by a woman who was applying for an account planning position at a major agency. While the content of this manifesto would be different than one written by an account management applicant, it should give you a good idea of what a personal manifesto looks like.

Let Me Tell You a Few Things about Myself.

I like goosebumps, and I like to cry. I thrive in the space between what is and what could be. I breathe life into "what ifs" and "why nots."

I am a chameleon. People tell me secrets, willingly. It's a gift. I feel subtleties of everyday life. I crave fun. I am completely alive when I am on the threshold of contrast – like the shore – or where thunder and lightening are made. I always have an opinion, but don't always have to be right. I see things sideways. That's a gift too. I am addicted to smart people. I love to solve problems. I am not afraid of much. I'm a pleasure pig. I hate rules. I have Texas, London, and Canada in my soul. I believe mediocrity is death. I play well with others, but I run with scissors. Brands and advertising are my passions, and I am driven to do something beautiful and important. I was born to do planning and believe I'm good at it because I love it.

Obviously, the personal manifesto is a very personal statement and could contain any number of interesting things about yourself, including:

- How you spend your free time
- What you spend your money on
- The things you are passionate about
- Exactly what about advertising attracts you to it
- What excites you
- What gives you joy
- What makes you mad or sad
- The brands you relate to and why

- What your logo would look like

- What makes you, you

Two final recommendations on your résumé:

- First, when you use someone as a reference, make sure they are aware you are doing so and are OK with it.

- Second, hand-deliver résumés whenever possible. Even if you don't get to see the person for whom the résumé is intended, the fact that you hand-delivered it and tried to see them will make a good impression.

Building Your Book.

Students aspiring to a job on the creative side are trained in the art of building a portfolio (or book) of work that will help them get a job. Account managers should be no different. Your book will show how you think and how you sell (in this case, yourself).

The portfolio for a recently graduated account management applicant could contain:

- Examples of work done or campaigns worked on during an internship. Include a short written explanation of the role you played.

- NSAC plans book or GMMI final report.

- Ad projects worked on during school or as volunteer in community service.

- A writing sample, preferably a proposal or a report.

- Letters of recommendation specific to advertising or marketing skills.

- Sample ads from up to three recent ad campaigns you really like. One paragraph explanation about why you like the campaigns. Be insightful. Think underlying strategy, key insights, and integration.

- Articles about you or ad projects on which you worked.

- Up to three recent trade journal articles you found especially interesting. Highlight the key sections. If the articles are about account-service issues and your interviewer hasn't read them, they may ask you for photocopies. How cool is that?

- Your transcript.

- Something to put it all in. The local art supply store will have portfolios. Invest in a good one that helps you do a good job of displaying the contents.

The Interview.

It's show time! Your intro package (thematic envelope, cover letter, and nonrésumé-looking résumé) helped separate you from the many others competing for a position. Then what?

You'll probably get an interview. Maybe three or four with the same firm. Be up and be patient. The following information should help you make a good showing while interviewing at a big agency in a major market as well as smaller agencies anywhere.

At least part of this interview will be predictable. You'll want to have memorable responses to the predictable questions and have a set of questions that shows how sharp you are.

Some Typical Questions.

Here are some typical questions that agencies may ask entry-level account people. You should have some good answers:

Why do you want to be in advertising?

There must be a reason you are attracted to the advertising industry. What is it? Think about this. Be concise. What is the source of your passion for the business? Is it the concept of brands? Is it the ability to emotionally connect with mass communications? Whatever you do, don't say "because I'm a people person" or "because I like photography."

What is your favorite ad campaign?

If you really like advertising, you study advertising and you have favorite campaigns. They're in your book, right? Be concise about why you think the campaigns are good. Customer insights, the prose-like copy, the creative big idea, unique media choice, and multimedia coordination are some of the good reasons for liking a campaign – but not the only ones.

It's OK if, on one campaign, you just "really like the art direction."

What do you know about account service?
The best answer here is that you know it's "demanding work." Your interviewer should acknowledge with a confirming nod of the head. Be ready to expand on your answer with examples of why the job is so demanding.

What are your strongest attributes you think will help you succeed in this business?
Hint: think "Eight Traits" plus those mentioned at the beginning of this chapter. Pick three that seem to be the best for the moment.

Please, don't say, "I'm a people person."

Tell us about the one experience you've had so far that relates most directly to account management.
Hopefully you have an example of how you brought order out of chaos or helped a group achieve success.

What would you do in this situation?
Gulp! They might pose to you a short "case problem" not unlike the cases in this book.

Why are you interested in this agency?
This assumes you know something about the agency. What a novel concept. Ahead of time, get their client list and study the work they've done for some of those clients. Visit their Web site and do a news search on them. They'll be impressed that you did your homework and flattered that you really like a campaign they created for one of their clients.

What do you do in your spare time?
Agencies are looking for interesting people with unusual interests. Take up an unusual, creatively oriented hobby. You'll need it later to keep your sanity.

Is there something you are really passionate about?
Advertising people often march to a different drum, and passion is a common characteristic. Do you have a passion? And how might it relate to advertising?

Who were the following people, and what did they contribute to the practice of advertising?

- Alex Osborn
- Leo Burnett
- David Ogilvy
- Bill Bernbach
- Fairfax Cone
- Dan Wieden
- Don Belding
- Mary Wells
- Pat Fallon
- Donny Deutsch
- Jay Chiat

Where do you see yourself five years from now?

This question relates back to your sense of direction.

What are your impressions of a client-side vs. agency career?

While this book does not specifically describe the job of a MarCom director, you should have a good idea of how work on the client side differs from account management.

Possible Questions to Ask.

When interviewing agencies, clients take note of the kind of questions the agencies ask. The same is true for the job interviewing process.

Good questions will improve your chances of standing out.

Without being pretentious or arrogant, your posture should always be that the interview is a mutual thing; that you're also interviewing them. A softer attitude is that interviews are like dating. You want to get the other person to talk about themselves.

It's always a good idea to take notes during interviews, so include a note pad and pen in with your book. Here are some questions that can help you in the interview.

- How would they describe their agency to a new business contact? What's their "10-second elevator speech?" (This will tell you how management sees the agency.)

- What are they looking for in a person to fill this position?

- How many account managers do they have on staff?

- How many people on the staff have been with the agency for more than five years? How do they decide when entry-level people are ready for their own accounts?

- What kind of training program do they have?

- Who owns the company, and what are their positions?

- Who are they currently pitching? (This may be confidential, so qualify the question as you ask it.)

- Accounts won and lost in the last two years?

- Does the agency have a newsletter (or recent mailers), and could you get a couple of recent editions?

- Who are their advertising heroes? Whose work in the industry, past and present, do they respect?

- Could you see a sample of some of their "B2B" work. (Business-to-business advertising is often a harder creative challenge. So it's a good demonstration of creative strength.)

- If there's no open position right now or if someone else gets the job for which you are interviewing, is it OK if you stay in touch with them? Would they prefer voice mail or an occasional e-mail?

- (Don't ask this one, but try to find out how long they keep accounts. Some shops are great at winning accounts and very good at losing them within a couple of years.)

Additional Interview Tips.

Headhunters and job-placement experts offer these additional tips, which aren't specific to the advertising business but still good advice:

- First impressions are very important. Even if the company granting the interview has a reputation for informality, it's a good idea to dress a little on the conservative side, be polite, and take it real easy on perfumes or colognes.

- Know who will be interviewing you and know how to pronounce their name. It's best to call them by Mr. or Ms. through at least the second interview.

- Bring extra résumés with your portfolio and notepad.

- Always send a follow-up note or thank-you card after the interview. Many applicants are still not thoughtful enough to do this. It's especially effective for male job applicants to do this. It is so unexpected.

- Be persistent. Whether it's trying to get an interview or being a finalist for a job, keep calling, keep adding to your case, until they tell you to stop.

The Importance of Flexibility.

While an account management position is your goal, your route may not be direct or nonstop.

You may encounter a situation where an agency has no account management position but there's an opening in media, production, research, account planning, or traffic. Take it.

You'll learn a lot about the job of the account manager from some other vantage points and be the first one to know about an account service opening before the rest of the world.

Your Second Thank-You Letter.

It is strongly recommended that you send a thank-you card or short letter after each interview. But that's not all. Keep a list of people with whom you interviewed, the date, and when you sent them a thank-you. On this list, keep track of which companies or people you still might like to work for some time in the future.

When you do finally land your first job, send a second letter to all those people with whom you want to stay in touch. In this letter, thank them again for the time they spent with you. Let them know that you accepted a position and generally what you will be doing.

The people who granted you interviews in your first job search can be valuable resources later on. If they liked you but did not have a position for you then, just remember, things change.

In this second thank-you letter you should sound cordial, appreciative, and eager to learn what your new job has to offer. You will be remembered for your thoughtfulness and superior networking skills.

8.3 Landing Your Next Job

The first five years in the business seem to be the true test for most people. After five years, perhaps sooner, you'll know if you're cut out for the business, and you'll have figured out a lot of things.

In those first five years, there will be new accounts that come to the agency and account managers who leave. This fluid, everchanging landscape will provide opportunities for you to be assigned new account responsibilities.

It's quite appropriate that young account service people make their desire to work on a specific account known.

Astute career management can be enhanced by a mentor who can shorten and flatten your learning curve. This is someone inside the agency who you've come to respect as a real pro and a nice person.

Without becoming a nuisance, try to get close to these people and learn as much as possible from them, even if they are not your direct report. The way that I worked with mentors was not to ask their advice on how to solve a problem. Rather, I asked them if they had any experience with a certain kind of problem and how they handled it.

Few people spend their entire career at the same agency.

Advertising can be a transient business; you may have to move on to move up. While you work your heart out for your clients and your agency, always remember, only you are going to manage your career.

Managing your career should always be in the back of your mind. Think about where you want to go and if you think you're getting there in terms of experience, compensation, job satisfaction, and enjoyment.

Stay focused on doing the best possible job for your agency and your clients, but always be ready to consider an opportunity to move on and move up.

Risk Management for Account Management.
Any move has risks, but when and if the time comes to move on, you need to look at five things.

When looking at a new agency, consider these:

1. Quality of the work the agency is doing

2. Level of importance the agency places on account service

3. Clients/accounts you will work on

4. Supervisors you will work under

5. People you will work with in other departments

Building Your Credentials: The Annual Activity Report.

For the most part, academia adopts operating philosophies and practices of the private sector.

There's one practice, however, that business would be well-served to adopt from academia. In the meantime, ambitious account managers should do it on their own.

This practice is called the "annual activity report." The annual activity report, prepared for review by deans and review committees, summarizes activities undertaken by the professors in the area of research, community service, teaching, curriculum development, etc.

The parallel in the ad business would include the following:

- Major highlights of work done on each client, with emphasis on the personal contribution made to the quality of work in any category of service provided by the agency. It's nice to have associates in the agency recognize your contributions, but don't be bashful about including accomplishments of which you're rightfully proud.

- New business activities (pitches in which you were involved in some way)

- Agency promotion projects

- Agency management (committees, projects)

- Agency representation activities (in the industry, community)

- Media coverage (coverage of your work, quotes, published articles)

- Training undertaken

- Accomplishments toward personal goals set last year
- Personal goals for this coming year

Even when things seem to be going well and your career with your current agency looks good, it's important to do this report.

Use your hiring anniversary date to do the annual activity report. The personal discipline of the report has three benefits:

1. It will force you to keep track of the good things you do.

2. It will force you to do more things that look good on the report and your professional profile.

3. It will help management appreciate the great talent they have in you.

Start a File.

Keep a file folder on things you want to include in the annual report so, when it comes time to do it, the job can be done and your professional profile can be updated in the least amount of time.

The Brand Stewardship Report described in Chapter 3.6 and the client binders described in Chapter 3.1 should also provide a good source of material for your annual activity report.

If you're still wondering what you do with your report, here are some suggestions:

- Give it to your supervisor and suggest it be the outline for an annual performance and compensation review.
- Send a copy to the HR manager and ask that it be placed in your file after they've reviewed it and sent you any comments. Place a copy in your own personal file.

Leader Brands vs. Challenger Brands.

Especially early in your career, every position you take should be viewed as a major learning opportunity. When you are in the enviable position of being able to pick from two job offers, evaluate those offers on the basis of their learning potential. While being assigned to a market leader account may be prestigious and seductive, you may learn more by working on a "challenger brand." They often provide more opportunities to do breakthrough work, take more risks, and learn how to be more resourceful. Good lessons, don't you think?

Your Professional Profile.

As you move on in your career, a "professional profile" can take the place of the résumé. It's a simple presentation of your experience and accomplishments during your career:

- Job experience

- Client experience

- Industry experience

- Education

- Professional honors and awards

- Board memberships

- Community service

- Publishings

These are the things of which professional profiles are made.

And Someone Who Needs No Introduction...

If you plan to do any amount of public speaking, the people who introduce you will want a professional profile.

So it's good to update that profile each time you write your annual activity report.

Final Words on Self-Promotion and Interviewing.

Network. Stay visible. The agency business can be volatile. One day it's wonderful. Then two major accounts leave, and staff gets trimmed.

It could be you. Think... if you weren't where you were, where would you want to be? Maybe you should try to get to know those folks.

If and when it comes time to do some interviews for the next job, the tips provided in the earlier part of this chapter will serve you well for subsequent job searches and opportunities.

There are, however, two primary differences between interviewing for your first and second job:

1. The reason you are leaving

2. Salary

In dealing with the first issue, it's good policy to explain why you left in a way that does not reflect badly on your previous employer or yourself. Be honest but be positive.

Agency human resource people understand that the agency business is a volatile, fluid business, and they also understand the need for talented young people to grow.

In dealing with compensation, experts say that salary should be one of the last things discussed. Be flexible and have a range you can live with. Remember, the first couple of jobs are to get experience and credentials.

Agency Training Programs.

Once, agency training programs were common, and there was no textbook. Now we have this book, but only a few large U.S. agencies have training programs. Hopefully, this book will help agencies of all sizes do a better job of structuring their training programs.

In the meantime, here is the collective center of agency training:

- Bozell Worldwide Academy
- DDB Worldwide University
- Foote Cone & Belding
- J. Walter Thompson's Specialized Communications Training
- Leo Burnett's Lab
- Young & Rubicam's Buzz U

It's most unfortunate that just when account managers need more training to meet the needs of the changing position, agency cost pressures have taken training in the other direction.

If you feel the need for training in a certain area, talk to the person in charge of account service. There may be a seminar available. Or if there's a consensus among account managers for the need of specific training, there may be a local consultant available.

For instance, the 4As (American Association of Advertising Agencies) Institute for Advanced Advertising Studies (IAAS) is delivered on a local basis by local practitioners.

If your agency is a 4As member, ask your account supervisor or VP of account service if they would investigate the possibility of an IAAS in your town.

Show Me the Money and the Benefits.

Discussion of starting salaries has been avoided on purpose.

First, starting salaries are so low in some areas that it's embarrassing to talk about it.

Second, any discussion of starting salaries is going to be obsolete in a few months.

Let's just close with these two thoughts:

Compared to the client side, the advertising agency business has low starting salaries at entry level. But the good news is that agencies tend to offer quick advancement for the stars because they pay for talent and performance.

Depending on the agency, there can also be an opportunity to become a partner in ten years or so.

Second, because of the low starting salaries, you need to distinguish yourself and add to your perceived value in every way possible.

Compensation is on a salary basis. Paying account managers on a commission basis would be contradictory to the objective, consultant, partnership posture that is so important to the client relationship. Bonuses are paid by some agencies when times are good or an employee has been instrumental in landing or growing an account.

Benefits typically include health and dental insurance and disability and life insurance. Two weeks paid vacation after one or two years and profit sharing are pretty standard.

However, the post–September 11 recession really set the industry back. So there may have been some ground lost on the benefits and salary fronts which won't be regained until competition for staff and talent heats up again.

Gender Bias.

The percentage of account managers who are women is quite high.

Those who chose to talk about this phenomenon attribute it to the belief that women are inherently better listeners, better at building relationships, and better at detail.

All of these are important for account managers. For entry-level jobs, there may actually be a bias in favor of women.

While I'm not sure such a sweeping generality can be made, it's a possible prejudice you should keep in mind. Then again, this cuts both ways. I've heard some agencies pay special attention to résumés from promising young men – since, in many cases, so few apply.

One good generality should be mentioned. All agencies are more interested in attaining diversity and balance in their hiring practices.

Historically, a business that marketed to women has had its share of women in key positions. This has been true since the early days of JWT, where Stanley Resor ran account management and Helen Resor ran the creative department. Or, in more recent times, when, for a while, the highest-paid person in advertising was Mary Wells.

Today, there also seems to be an opposite gender skew on the creative side. While entry-level jobs may seem fairly evenly distributed, the higher you go on the creative side, the more it seems to become a bit of a men's club – some say a boy's club.

The good news here is that this has always been an industry where you're valued for your talent. So though there may be some long-term career concerns that are gender-related, they probably won't be critical during your first five years.

Alternative Career Paths.

The career path inferred in this chapter is the progression up the standard account service pecking order: account coordinator, account manager, account supervisor, etc.

There are, however, some alternatives.

Copy/Contact. There still are some small shops that do copy/contact work, which means the account manager also does creative work. If you like to write copy, in addition to handling the account service side, then you might look for a copy/contact shop.

New Business. Specializing in new business is another alternative path. This comes later in life when it is clear you have what it takes to spend full time on new business. This "Rainmaker" position is most often found in larger agencies and is very stressful.

Market Research. You may find the research part of the business is much more to your liking than the day-to-day responsibility for the myriad details. So you may want to shift to account planning. If your background, education, training, and personality all fit, this can be a viable move.

Marketing Specialties. You may find you especially like one of the specialty services such as sales promotion, event marketing, public relations, interactive, or trade relations. While some additional training will be required to become a specialist, this too is a viable move for account managers.

Client Marketing Department. Lastly, you could become a... client. Actually many account managers do move over to the client side.

When the MarCom manager moves up or out, the agency account manager is often the perfect candidate, because he or she knows the client's business and industry as well as being an advertising expert.

They know the communications business, and they know the client's business. It's very interesting at the agency when an account manager all of a sudden becomes a client, *very* interesting indeed.

The Other Ways.

In some instances, the MarCom manager on the client side will take a stab at agency account management. This normally does not work for some pretty simple reasons.

When you're a client, you have power. When you're an account manager the only power you have is your skills, your smarts, and your energy.

When you're a client, you're used to having people be respectfully nice to you. When you're an account manager, you must earn respect.

Every so often you'll find a media rep who's a good fit for agency work.

They know how to work with the media department, may know quite a bit about the creative strategy for a specific agency account, and have a long relationship directly with the client.

So media can be a potential way into the agency business.

There is a basic difference, however, between media sales and account work. Media people are paid to sell, agency people are paid to advise. Some media reps have a hard time with that shift in paradigm, in addition to the other challenges of account work.

8.4 Some Final Pearls

I've tried to include everything in its rightful place with appropriate emphasis and economy. But there are a few things that bear intentional repeating.

For this, I asked a dozen client types and agency principals for their suggestions as to "what's important." Here's what they told me:

The Importance of Staying "Hungry."
Competition is the driving force behind advertising. Everything that is done in advertising is done against a competitive backdrop. Being creative is good. Being smart is good. But there is no substitute for being truly hungry to achieve success for your clients, your agency, and yourself. Work ethic ultimately rules. Commit yourself to constant improvement. Persist, persist, persist.

The Importance of Leading and Pushing.
Taking risks is not something that clients like to do. They need to be led and pushed to achieve success.

The Importance of Trust.
Account managers can't lead, push, and do the rest of their job unless the client has total trust in them. Everything an account person does should be done with one eye firmly fixed on trust. This is true for the account manager's relationship with everyone else, too, but especially the client.

The Importance of Passion.

People die of boredom, not overwork. There's no substitute for loving the business, believing in what you do, and truly caring about the people for whom you do it. Whatever you end up doing for a living, make sure you enjoy it and that it is worthy of your time.

The Importance of Integrity and Honesty.

This is a relationship business. Keeping your word and honoring commitments is imperative. So is doing the right thing.

If you don't know what the right thing is, find out. Be honest. Admit your mistakes quickly. Learn from them. Take the consequences and move on. The industry is surprisingly small, and reputations travel quickly.

The Importance of Being Involved in the Client's Business.

There's no substitute for detailed knowledge about the marketplace, competitors, and the internal operations of the client's business. Want a place in the client's inner circle? This is the cost of entry.

The Importance of Staying Out of Client's Politics.

Being deeply involved in a client's business in order to provide expert advice is different than getting involved in their internal politics. Whatever you do, make sure you do not lose your personal reputation or your agency's reputation for objectivity and candor.

The Importance of Knowing Your Client's Customers.

It sounds surprising, but clients are so busy worrying about so much other stuff that the agency can easily know more about the client's customers than the client does. Knowledge is power.

The Importance of Top Management Relationships.

You can do the greatest job of servicing an account that anyone could do, and things can still go wrong. A senior agency person absolutely needs to have a close relationship with the CEO or top marketing executive in the client organization.

The Importance of Ideas.

Advertising is an idea business. Account managers are just as responsible for ideas as copywriters. In the new era of integrated marketing communications, the account manager is charged with thinking about issues that no one else is responsible for. Creative thinking on all fronts is crucial!

The Importance of Knowledge.

You never know enough in this business. To stay ahead of clients and associates, always "look for the learning." Stay flexible and open to new ideas. Never let a day go by where you don't get smarter than you were yesterday.

The Importance of Being "Seamless."

In order to deliver everything it can for the client, the whole agency team must operate like a well-oiled machine.

The account manager is guarantor of "seamlessness." No hitches, no glitches, no gaps, no flaps.

The Importance of Managing Up.

Manage the expectations of superiors through proactive communications. Avoid information voids and information overload. Keep your supervisors in the loop. Clearly and concisely let them know what support you need from them and why.

The Importance of Teamwork.

The best account manager in the world can't be great if he or she is not getting the best work out of everyone else on the team.

The Importance of Speaking for the Agency.

Always remember that the client is hiring the collective wisdom and expertise of the agency – not just you. Your opinion, of course, should be represented in the work.

The Importance of Proofreading.

Mistakes make you look stupid.

Don't let small, overlooked errors and typos detract from the credibility and impact of the work you present.

Names, titles, phone numbers, addresses, Web sites, and mathematical calculations need to be double-checked along with the normal grammar, spelling, and punctuation. Proofread twice.

And while you're at it, make sure you can pronounce everyone's name.

The Importance of Having Fun.

This is a crazy business. It helps if you are a little crazy, too. You either love the energy, the stress, the "thrill of the new," the late nights, the highs and the lows or… you don't. If you don't, you'll be happier doing something else.

This is no dress rehearsal. Life is too short. Enjoy it as you live it.

Dickinson's Axioms of Account Management.

There are a few natural laws and facts of life I've discovered along the way. For your reading pleasure and application, here they are:

- Most input is incomplete. Keep digging.

- The walls have ears. Be careful what you say "off the record."

- As soon as you leave for more than 48 hours, there will probably be a crisis.

- The client's view of the world is your reality.

- Be nice to everyone. You never know who will be your client or your boss tomorrow.

- Under-promise and over-deliver. That's a lot better than the other way around.

- Remember, you're in the business of creating change, not ads.

- The two craziest weeks of the year in the agency business are the first week of the new year and the week after Labor Day. Don't ask me why. Just be ready.

- You should fight about the work with colleagues and fight for it with clients. (From *Brain Surgery for Suits* by Robert Solomon.)

- Phony deadlines will come back to haunt you.

- Anyone who says business travel isn't hard hasn't done much of it.

- The things in life you will regret the most are the things you could have done but didn't.

- It's always better to proofread other people's work with a colored pencil. Don't use black or blue, it could be missed. And don't use red. While it's the most visible, some people find it harsh. Green or purple work well.

- An employee with average intelligence and a passion for good work is much more preferable than a lazy genius.

- Never let or ask a client to fight your internal battles.

- Probing questions are the best way to expose weak ideas.

- If you really want to show accounts that you value their business, go to their trade shows.

- If you want to someday be an owner of the agency, you need to start acting like an owner.

Dickinson's Seven C's of Vulnerability.

Computers (including printers and e-mail), Copiers, Cell phones, Children, Cars, Clients, and Coworkers can develop big problems when you can least afford it. Have contingencies.

8.5 Other Resources

Books and Publications.

When I decided to offer a course in account management, the best I could do for a text was to liberally reference two books.

First was Wes Perrin's *Advertising Realities: A Practical Guide to Agency Management,* available at the time from McGraw-Hill Higher Education (1992). It's an informative and entertaining book written in anecdotal style by an old friend and one of the cofounders of the well-known and respected Portland agency Borders, Perrin & Norrander.

The second book, and the one that provided the most inspiration and material for discussion and assignments, was by Nancy Salz: *How to Get the Best Work from Your Agency,* 4th edition, from McGraw-Hill Higher Education.

This book is a classic for young and otherwise inexperienced MarCom managers who could use a few tips on managing one of the most valuable resources their organization can have: their advertising agency.

Why, you may ask, would anyone use a book written for client-side managers to instruct students on the fine art of managing accounts on the agency side? Well, just like in any relationship, when you understand the other person's expectations and points of reference you are much more able to make the relationship work.

Reading Salz from the perspective of the account manager gives a good glimpse of the client's view of the world and some of the ways they define good agency account service. Thanks to Wes and Nancy for giving me a good place to start.

There are a ton of other books written about advertising, but few about account management. There is one other book that is worth reading if you can find it: *Brain Surgery for Suits: 56 Things Every Account Person Should Know* by Robert Solomon, Strategy Press (2000).

Other Books That I'd Recommend:
Bendinger, Bruce. *The Copy Workshop Workbook*. The Copy Workshop, 2002. This is the book that started this little publishing company, and it's become successful for good reason. It won't teach you how to be brilliant – that's your job – but it does a great job of communicating the nuts and bolts of good advertising thinking.

Cone, Fairfax. *With All Its Faults*. Little, Brown and Company, 1969. You may have to go to a used book site for this one, but I think it's packed with great good sense.

Fortini-Campbell, Lisa. *Hitting the Sweet Spot*. The Copy Workshop, 1992. This was the first American book on the account planning approach, and I think it's particularly useful if there's no account planner around. It's a smart way to get to know your consumer.

Levitt, Theodore. *The Marketing Imagination*. Free Press, 1986. A classic that communicates the real creativity that's in marketing.

Ogilvy, David. *Confessions of an Advertising Man*. Atheneum, 1987. Read it and watch an advertising man promote his agency.

Ogilvy, David. *Ogilvy on Advertising*. Crown Publishers, 1983. Some overlap with *Confessions*, but a solid well-organized overview of our business.

Poppe, Fred. *50 Rules to Keep Clients Happy*. Harper & Row, 1987.

Steel, Jon. *Truth, Lies and Advertising*. Wiley & Sons, 1998. The account planner who helped develop "Got Milk?" tells you how and where he found useful insights.

Twitchell, James. *Adcult.* Columbia University, 1997. A pretty interesting book about "The Triumph of Advertising in American Society." You might also want to pick up Twitchell's *20 Ads That Shook the World.*

Publications.

There are eight publications I think every account manager should read on a regular basis:

1. *Wall Street Journal* – daily "Marketing and Media" column

2. *New York Times* – advertising column

3. *Advertising Age*

4. *AdWeek* – here you'll also find regional news. And be sure to connect with their online service.

5. *Promo*

6. *American Demographics*

7. *Communication Arts* Advertising Annual. Be sure to check out the sections on design and interactivity as well.

8. *The One Show Annual* – you'll work a lot better with creatives if you're familiar with what the industry regards as the best work. You may not agree with some of the award-givers' decisions, but it will improve your credibility and give you solid common ground in one of your key tasks – working with creatives.

Organizations and Education Programs.

For the most part, from the beginnings of account management as an agency discipline, account managers have learned on the job by trial and error, observation and osmosis.

Yes, there are a few other forward-thinking universities who are doing a credible job of teaching account management. University of Texas at Austin, Ball State, Marquette University, Virginia Commonwealth, University of Oregon, Oklahoma University, University of Nevada–Reno, University of Florida, Northern Arizona University, and, of course, Portland State University come to mind.

Academic Practicums: NSAC and GMMI.

Other than an internship with an agency, the National Student Advertising Competition (NSAC) is as close to the real ad biz as you can get while still in school.

Sponsored by the American Advertising Federation (AAF), this annual program provides a national brand client, background information, objectives, and a budget.

After receiving the case information in the early fall, the AAF chapters in colleges and universities around the country form advertising agencies and develop a new business pitch.

The presentations are made at regional competitions around the country in the spring. The presentations are made in front of five industry judges and hundreds of enthusiastic onlookers.

Then, in June, winners from each region compete for national honors at the AAF's national convention. It's a great program.

If there's not one at your school, ask your advertising instructor about starting an AAF chapter and competing in NSAC. Your team plans book alone will loom large in making your own book stand out. The AAF/NSAC Web site address is www.aaf.org/college/nsac/html.

The General Motors Marketing Internship (GMMI) is a one-term or semester class project normally centering around a promotion for a local GM auto dealer. The class gets an assignment, some communications objectives, and a small budget.

Like NSAC, GMMI is very "hands-on," and while much shorter and narrower in scope, the GMMI final report booklet can be another excellent book component.

In our 2002 EdVenture Partners classes, we did a project for Citibank. The client liked the student's work so much that they adopted the campaign theme, the interactive promotion, and recorded our radio scripts with professional voices for use around the country. Way cool.

GMMI is administered nationwide by EdVenture Partners of Berkeley, California. EdVenture Partners also has a growing list of nonautomotive clients ready for student projects. Faculty are encouraged to visit the EdVenture Partners Web site at www.edventurepartners.com.

To a great extent, NSAC and GMMI complement each other rather than duplicate each other. GMMI tends to focus on local promotional strategies, which are basically void from the national scope of NSAC. Therefore, I recommend students do both.

Agency Training.

Before the latest economic downturn there were a few large agencies with formal training programs, among them DDB Worldwide, Young & Rubicam, J. Walter Thompson, Foote Cone & Belding, Leo Burnett, and Bozell Worldwide.

There may be others not mentioned, and with the ad slump of 2000-02, some training programs were mothballed, and their resurrection is uncertain.

Clubs and Associations.

Many local professional ad club chapters of the AAF have some form of training program which may or may not include account management.

Some larger ad clubs such as Boston and Chicago offer more formal continuing education programs from time to time.

The AAF Educational Services can be contacted in their Washington, D.C., office at (802) 898-0089 or look under "College Connection" at www.aaf.org.

The American Association of Advertising Agencies (the 4As) is the national trade association of the advertising agency industry and is a very good resource for aspiring account managers. While your agency has to be a 4As member to access some of their services, many are available to employees of nonmember agencies.

The 4As professional development services include:

- National conferences
- Local seminars
- Booklets, bulletins, white papers, and other publications on advertising and agency management
- Internships
- Scholarships

- Online e-learning programs

In some cities, local 4As councils conduct the AAAA Institute of Advanced Advertising Studies for young professionals who want to learn more about the business than their job allows.

To find out more about what the 4As does and what they offer in terms of professional development opportunities, visit their Web site: www.aaaa.org.

BUZZ...

Plan on It.
The Most Important Account You'll Ever Manage? Your Career.
by Jim Kessler, AdWeek, September 4, 2000

In my 20 years in account management on the agency side and 15 years as an executive recruiter, I've been reminded almost daily how poorly people manage their careers. I am not just talking about junior people. In fact, the longer folks are in this business, the less they seem to know about how to promote themselves and manage their careers.

Some dismiss career development and self-promotion as office politics or a distraction from the client's business. But let me tell you: If you don't make it a priority to manage your career, to promote and merchandise your own accomplishments, it won't get done. The person down the hall isn't going to help. He or she is your competitor. You have to do it yourself.

You may have already learned that hard work – and expecting work to speak for itself – will not get you where you want to go. As a former creative director used to tell me, "If you don't know where you're going, any road will get you there."

That's why you need to plan your career.

The good news is, your work in agency account service and marketing makes you uniquely qualified to solve this problem.

Simply use the tools you already have.

Do for yourself what you do for your clients daily.

Develop a Plan.

The first step is an in-depth situation analysis. Because you are the ultimate expert on yourself, it should be easy and lots of fun. Your plan doesn't need to be a perfect document. There are no right and wrong answers. Just take an honest look at your career and your life. Ask yourself: "Which way is north?"

To get started, I recommend that you keep three legal pads – one on your desk, one in your car, and one on your night stand.

Write things down whenever they come to you.

Figure this input stage will take at least three to four weeks.

Your plan should include, but not be limited to, things like: What am I good/bad at? What do I like/dislike? What's good about my current job? What would I change if I could? Do I make enough money?

How do I feel about my coworkers? Is my career dependent on difficult people? Do I feel burned out, underappreciated, overmanaged, or undermanaged? Is my job affecting my health? Am I good in front of groups? Do I really like advertising? Who am I doing this for? Where do I want to be?

It's also a good idea to get outside help – ask a few friends for their input. Read a career guidance book.

At some point in the process, the light will come on. If you've taken your task seriously, your objectives and strategies will practically write themselves. It will be clear what you need to do.

As with all effective plans, you need to budget the most valuable commodity there is – time. If you do not allocate a specific amount of quality time on a daily basis, you will fail. Make a commitment of 30 minutes a day and hold on to it, even if it's just reading what you have already written down.

Advertising is a wonderful, rewarding business, filled with exciting and interesting people. But no matter how thrilling – if you don't run your career, it will run you.

You know what to do. Now go out and do it.

Jim Kessler is the founder of JFK Search, a Minneapolis-based recruitment firm.

401

JUICY CASES:

8.1: In Title Only.

You're a new account manager, just promoted from account coordinator. You are taking on an account where the account manager is moving up to an account supervisor position.

Only one problem – nothing has changed.

The client still deals with your account supervisor, who shows little interest in letting go of the account.

What to do?

8.2: New Business Overload.

You're an account manager for an agency you have been with a year. Your account load has grown to five. You're "maxed-out" in terms of capacity, and you are just now starting to feel that your relationship with each of your clients is anywhere close to where it should be.

All of a sudden, the agency has been invited to pitch a piece of business, and you're the only account manager with any expertise in that industry.

Knowing your valuable expertise and the quality of your work, management expects that you will be taking the lead role in this pitch.

What are your concerns, and what should you do?

AD-ROBIC EXERCISES:

8.1: Write a Résumé.

Write or revise your résumé, based on the guidelines provided in this chapter. Make it as nontraditional as you can.

8.2: Write a "Personal Manifesto."

Using the example provided in this chapter, write a 100 word (or so) personal manifesto to include with or in your résumé.

8.3: Plan Your Book.

Using the example provided in this chapter, outline what you would actually put in your "book."

BURNING QUESTIONS:

8.1:

From the standpoint of the agency, the client, and the account manager, it is important to have agency top management involved with each account. Why?

8.2:

What is the connection between a Brand Stewardship Report and an annual activity report?

9.0 HOUSEKEEPING

9.1 Bibliography

Over the years, in subconscious preparation for this book, I collected countless articles on the state and future of account management. Those articles helped frame my thinking or helped me make a point. Here is a list of those significant articles:

"Agencies Teach Skill Building."
Advertising Age. 5/1/00.

"Attracting Best and Brightest…"
Advertising Age. 12/4/00.

"The Bad Review."
AdWeek. 5/27/02.

"The Beatles vs. Planning."
APG Group Web site, www. apgus.org.

"Becoming Strategic Partners in the 1990s."
Advertising Age. 6/8/98.

"The Brand Inside: Agencies Can Profit from a New Way of Thinking."
AdWeek. 7/15/01.

"Brand Relationships Key to Agency of the Future."
Advertising Age. 11/18/99.

"Continuing Education Courses."
Ad Club of Greater Boston. 1998.

"Courses and Seminars for 2000."
San Francisco Ad Club. 2000.

"Disappearing Act: What Ever Happened to Account Planning?"
AdWeek. 5/8/02.

"The Ethicist."
AdWeek. 7/15/02.

"Exploring the Use of Advertising Agency Review Consultants."
Journal of Advertising Research. 2/02.

"Finders Keepers: Ten Rules for Choosing an Agency in the Next Century."
AdWeek. 12/13/99.

"Follow the Money."
Advertising Age. 6/17/02.

"Forging a Strategic Chain."
Advertising Age. 9/4/00.

"Fostering Client-Agency Relationships: A Business Buying Behavior Perspective."
Journal of Business Research. 9/00.

"Fresh Milk: Whose to Blame for Creative Impotence? The Beloved Client."
AdWeek. 8/7/00.

"The Future Is Now."
Promo. 6/02.

"How US Clients View Account Planning."
APG Group Web site, www. apgus.org.

"How to Implement Account Planning."
APG Group Web site, www. apgus.org.

"How to Survive an Agency Review."
Promo. 1/01.

"Innovation + Integration = Success."
Promo. 7/00.

"The Jacks of All Trades."
Advertising Age. 11/7/96.

"Make a Commitment to College's Brightest."
Advertising Age. 7/24/00.

"Marketers Look at New Ideas, and PR Becomes the 'Closer.'"
Advertising Age. 7/29/02.

"Monster Mash: Media Agencies Don't Fade Away, They Just Get Bigger."
AdWeek. 7/30/01.

"Moving Pictures: Account Planner Scramble to Capture New Consumer Mindset."
AdWeek. 11/15/01.

"The Oracle Workers."
Advertising Age. 6/12/00.

"Planning and Its Relationship to Account Management."
APG Group Web site, www. apgus.org.

"Playing Well with Others."
Wall Street Journal. 9/9/02.

Principles of Management.
by David Ogilvy.

"An Rx for What Ails Agencies."
Advertising Age. 11/8/98.

"Seven Deadly Sins: The Do's and Don'ts of Making a Pitch."
AdWeek. 2/28/00.

"Small Shops Beg to Differ."
Advertising Age. 6/10/02.

"Striving for Synergy at OgilvyOne."
Advertising Age. 9/24/01.

"Think Differently: In the Quest for New Business; Tips from a Pro."
AdWeek. 4/3/00.

"Trading Places."
AdWeek. 9/16/02.

"Twenty Key Principles of Account Management."
Ogilvy & Mather. 1975.

"What Every Account Executive Should Know About Account Management."
4As. 1997.

"What Every Account Executive Should Know About Account Planning."
4As. 1998.

"What Is the Client Relationship to Account Planning?"
APG Group Web site, www. apgus.org.

"What It Takes."
Promo. 9/1/99.

"Wild Pitch."
AdWeek. 5/6/02.

"The Whole Truth."
AdWeek. 6/24/02.

9.2 Index

M

MarCom: 13, 14, 16, 18, 43, 48, 71, 73, 80, 83, 99, 136, 175, 180, 208, 248, 282, 315, 323, 342, 371, 380, 390

MarCom matrix: 69, 72

McCabe, Ed: 224

McCann-Erickson: 47, 54, 88

McDonald's: 27, 57, 260

McElligott, Tom: 302, 346

McGrath, Pat: 161–64

McQueen, Grace: 162

media buying: 15, 16, 21, 24, 32–34, 197

media mix: 71, 80, 96, 233, 237

media planners: 10, 34, 197–203, 360

mentorship: 360, 367–69

Michelet, John: 6

Moffat-Rosenthal: 2

Moorman, Rob: 162

Morris, Bourne: 6

MRI: 30, 198, 204

Mullen, Jim; Mullen, Inc.: 87, 301, 304

multimedia and programming (MM&P): 45

N

Nelson, Tom: 260

new business: 11, 67, 80, 217, 243, 247, 327–46, 390

newsletters: 338, 340

niche marketing: 44

Nielsen, A.C.: 30, 198, 268, 364

Nordstrom: 292

Novartis OTC: 163

NSAC (see AAF/NSAC)

O

Odishoo, Dan: 259

Ogilvy, David; Ogilvy & Mather (O&M): 6, 53, 54, 123, 380, 396

O'Hearn, Denny: 162

O'Leary, Noreen: 52, 87,

OMD: 32

Omnicom: 53

One Show: 80, 195, 397

operational chart: 50

Osborn, Alex: 380

Owens, Ron: 220

P

Proctor and Gamble (P&G): 161, 188

Paetro, Maxine: 225

Papdellis, Randy: 162

Pasqualucci, Angela: 161

Peiros, Larry: 260

Penner, Tim: 161

Perrin, Wes: 4, 196, 320, 346, 352, 395

personal media network:

pitch: 80, 334–335

point-of-sale (POS): 46–47, 70, 81, 87, 137, 138, 232, 234, 240, 246

Poppe, Fred: 396

Portland Ad Federation:

Promo: 7, 258, 278, 353, 397

promotional mix: 70, 74, 81, 116, 174, 267

psychographics: 117, 212, 341

public relations (PR): 14, 15, 18, 25, 44–45, 60, 72, 138–39, 365

9.3 About the Author

Don Dickinson is a true veteran of the advertising business, with media, client, and predominantly agency experience. His client experience includes food products; automotive; higher education; federal, state, and regional government agencies; professional services; hotel and travel; restaurants; retail; insurance; health care; industrial equipment; packaged goods; utilities; and high tech.

His media experience includes all national media types plus local media, direct response, interactive, sales promotion, and PR. The wide variety of products, media, projects, and campaigns he supervised during his professional career now provides a wonderful knowledge base to share with aspiring account managers.

He has an MBA, and comes from 30 years in the business, most of which were spent as senior vice president and partner at Gerber Advertising Agency (now Gard & Gerber) in Portland, Oregon.

As the Director of Advertising Management at the Portland State University School of Business, he is known as a dynamic educator who is passionate about his field.

Dickinson undertook the writing of this book because the role of the advertising account manager has increased in importance as the advertising industry has changed. He is passionate in his belief that account management is much too important a job to go any longer without a comprehensive (and entertaining) book dedicated exclusively to it.

Notes:

412

Notes:

About The Copy Workshop:

Our Mission.

"To help young men and women prepare for an industry undergoing revolutionary change." We hope this book helps you do that.

This Book.

The New Account Manager is the result of one of the truly innovative programs in the U.S. advertising industry, where an important urban university (Portland State) and a cutting-edge advertising market (Portland, OR) teamed up to create a course that would provide the right kind of background for one of the most demanding jobs in American business. We think Prof. Dickinson has done a superb job on a difficult task, and are proud to publish this book.

About Our Other Books...

We try to install "best practices" into a reader-friendly format with some of the leading practitioners in advertising and ad education. The result is some truly exceptional books – readable and useful. *If you'd like to know more (and save 20%) just visit our Web site:* www.adbuzz.com